■ Risk Management in Turbulent Times

Risk Management in Turbulent Times

Gilles Bénéplanc

Jean-Charles Rochet

OXFORD
UNIVERSITY PRESS

Oxford University Press, Inc., publishes works that further Oxford University's
objective of excellence in research, scholarship, and education.

Oxford New York
Auckland Cape Town Dar es Salaam Hong Kong Karachi
Kuala Lumpur Madrid Melbourne Mexico City Nairobi
New Delhi Shanghai Taipei Toronto

With offices in
Argentina Austria Brazil Chile Czech Republic France Greece
Guatemala Hungary Italy Japan Poland Portugal Singapore
South Korea Switzerland Thailand Turkey Ukraine Vietnam

Published by Oxford University Press, Inc.
198 Madison Avenue, New York, New York 10016
http://www.oup.com

Library of Congress Cataloging-in-Publication Data
Beneplanc, Gilles.
  Risk management in turbulent times / Gilles Bénéplanc, Jean-Charles Rochet.
    p.   cm.
  Includes index.
  ISBN 978-0-19-977408-1 (cloth : alk. paper)   1. Risk management.
  2. Risk management–Methodology.   I. Rochet, Jean-Charles.   II. Title.
  HD61.B46 2011
  658.15′5–dc22
  2010043430

9 8 7 6 5 4 3 2 1

Printed in the United States of America
on acid-free paper

■ *This book participates in the Paul Woolley Research Initiative on Market Dysfunctionalities at IDEI, Toulouse. Its financial support is gratefully acknowledged.*

■ CONTENTS

■ Risk Management in Turbulent Times

■ INTRODUCTION

The risk management methods and concepts used by most corporations have been designed for "normal times." Typically they rely on simple statistical risk measures and assume that financial markets behave smoothly and efficiently. The problem is that we are living in more and more "turbulent times": large risks materialize much more often than predicted by simple models, and financial markets periodically go through bubbles and crashes.

The Subprime Crisis, which started in August 2007, is a good case in point. It must be viewed as an historical event of major importance, with worldwide and durable consequences on the economic life and on the organization of financial and banking activities in many countries over the world. It has completely shattered public confidence in the risk management methods that were used by banks and financial intermediaries. These **risk management methods must be adapted to "turbulent times."** The main objective of this book is to dissect these methods, to explain why they have failed, and to propose amendments for the future.

Doing this, we are careful not to throw the baby with the bath water. Unlike some commentators, who basically claim that sophisticated financial methods are nothing but uninformed speculative bets and that risk professionals are essentially incompetent crooks, we take the more reasonable view that these methods are potentially useful but have to be used with a lot of caution. Recent crises have shown the dangers of the "exuberant optimism" that was often expressed by many risk professionals and that is well-illustrated by the following statement by former Federal Reserve Chairman Alan Greenspan in 2004: "Not only have individual financial institutions become less vulnerable to shocks from underlying risk factors, but also the financial system as a whole has become more resilient."[1] This optimistic statement was soon to be severely contradicted by the facts.

The view we put forward in this book is more of an "informed skepticism": by dissecting the main risk modeling methods and the (sometimes hidden) assumptions that they rely upon, we are able to clarify the conditions of their validity. We will insist on four fundamental recommendations that were often forgotten by the risk managers of well-established financial institutions (which, as a result, have incurred massive losses during the Subprime Crisis):

- **Always get a complete picture of your risks:** Forgetting just one risk can be fatal, even if all your other risks are precisely modeled. Even if some risks are difficult to assess, they have to be incorporated in some way in the global risk mapping of the corporation, which risk managers should be able to provide to their top management.
- **Adopt an "informed skepticism" approach to risk modeling:** It is fundamental not only to understand your risk models but also to be aware that they can sometimes be plain wrong. This is the case in particular for all

the models that assume normal distributions and constant correlations between risks. These models are easy to use and they behave well during "tranquil times." But they are totally wrong during "turbulent times," where large losses become more likely and correlations between risks increase.

- **Never fully trust financial markets:** Financial markets are usually efficient because they are usually characterized by absence of arbitrage opportunities. However, there is always a possibility that they go wild: prices can be unreasonably high (bubbles), plummet brutally (crashes), or just stop working, as was the case of interbank markets in the aftermath of the Lehman bankruptcy on September 15, 2008.
- **Don't forget incentives:** Financial crises are not natural catastrophes like hurricanes or earthquakes. They result from the behavior of human beings, who are driven sometimes by their emotions, but mostly by their interests. Financial risks are not purely exogenous but depend on the remuneration schemes of traders, fund managers, bankers, CEOs, and the like.

■ THE AUTHORS

Gilles Bénéplanc

Gilles Bénéplanc is the head of EMEA region of Mercer. He joined the firm in 2000, having previously worked for AXA in the area of corporate and international risks.

Gilles has a degree in civil engineering from Ecole des Mines de Paris and a Ph.D. in economics from University of Toulouse. He is a Ph.D. Member of the French Institute of Actuaries. In addition, he served as an associate professor at the University of Toulouse and as a visiting professor at the University of Paris Dauphine.

Jean-Charles Rochet

Jean-Charles Rochet is a professor at University of Zürich (Swiss Banking Institute and Swiss Financial Institute) and University of Toulouse (Toulouse School of Economics). He has written more than 60 articles in international scientific journals and 5 textbooks. His research interests include corporate finance, theory of contracts, banking crises, and solvency regulations for financial institutions.

Jean-Charles is a former student of Ecole Normale Supérieure (Paris) and holds a Ph.D. in Mathematical Economics from University of Paris Dauphine. He has taught in Paris (Dauphine University, ENSAE and Ecole Polytechnique) and London (London School of Economics). He is a senior member of the Institut Universitaire de France and has been a Fellow of the Econometric Society since 1995.

■ FOR WHOM IS THE BOOK WRITTEN?

We have repeatedly taught this book in the Masters in Finance programs at Toulouse and Zürich. It is thus calibrated for masters students but contains mathematical appendices that can be taught to Finance Ph.D. students. We have also used it for executive teaching in AXA College and the Bank of Japan.

The targeted audience is quite wide: it ranges from risk professionals (like the first author), to academic researchers (like the second author), and to finance students. Our objective was to provide a consistent approach to risk management in turbulent times, subject to the requirements that our recommendations be (at the same time) rigorously founded and relevant in practice.

■ CONTENT OF THE BOOK

The first part of the book (**Risk Management: What Must be Changed**) illustrates the recent failures of classical risk management methods and shows the dangers of using these models without precaution. It also presents the necessary ingredients for a proper methodology of risk management.

The second part of the book (**What is Behind Risk Modeling**) systematically dissects the statistical models that have been designed by academics and risk professionals for measuring risks and shows their dangers.

The third part of the book (**The Perfect Markets Hypothesis and Its Dangers**) shows that the two most popular tools used by economists for assessing financial risks (risk neutral valuation and the Capital Asset Pricing Model) can also be very dangerous. It is true that they give raise to simple methods for pricing risks and managing them, but they rely on assumptions that are particularly unrealistic during turbulent times—namely, that markets are perfect (complete and frictionless) and that asset returns follow normal distributions.

The fourth part of the book (**Financial Frictions and Shareholder Value**) shows how financial frictions can be taken into Account and how they modify the traditional methods for assessing shareholder value. It explains the core of our methodology: the mechanics of the shareholder value function.

Finally, the fifth part of the book (**What To Do in Practice?**) explains how the shareholder value function can be calibrated in practice and how it can be used to derive a precise set of recommendations for risk management. We illustrate our methodology on the fictitious (but realistic) case study of a pharmaceutical company.

■ PREREQUISITES

Some familiarity with financial modeling may be useful, but the book is self contained. It is accessible to anyone with a college education in math. All mathematical tools (risk measures, pricing formulas, shareholder value functions) are explained in an elementary fashion (e.g., two-state models). For the advanced reader, appendices explain the sophisticated version of these tools, which requires elementary knowledge of stochastic calculus.

■ COMPLEMENTARY READINGS

Our book fills an important gap in the flourishing literature on risk management. However, the interested reader will benefit a lot (like we did) from books that cover other important aspects that are not developed here:

- The applications of contract theory to corporate finance are superbly explained in Tirole (2006). For more classical presentations of corporate finance, *see* Brealey and Myers (2000) or Grinblatt and Titman (2002).
- The applications of stochastic calculus to financial modeling are very clearly presented in Duffie (1992), Musiela and Rutkowsky (2000), Bjork (2004), or Malevergne and Sornette (2005).
- The methodology of Integrated Risk Management in financial institutions is remarkably presented in Shimpi (2001).
- For state-of-the-art references on the statistical methods of Risk Management, *see* McNeil, Frey, and Embrechts (2005) and Embrechts, Klüppelberg, and Mikosch (1997).
- Finally, for the economic and financial perspective, there are several textbooks on Risk Management that constitute useful complements to this book, such as Crouhy, Galai, and Mark (2001), Stulz (2003), or Doherty (2000).

■ REFERENCES

Bjork, T. (2004), *Arbitrage Theory in Continuous Time*, 2nd edition, Oxford, UK: Oxford University Press.

Brealey R., and S. Myers (2000), *Principles of Corporate Finance*, 6th edition, New York: McGraw-Hill.

Crouhy, M., D. Galai, and R. Mark (2001), *Risk Management*, New York: McGraw-Hill.

Doherty, N. (2000), *Integrated Risk Management*, New York: McGraw-Hill.

Duffie, D. (1992), *Dynamic Asset Pricing Theory*, Princeton, NJ: Princeton University Press.

Embrechts, P., C. Klüppelberg, and T. Mikosch (1997), *Modelling Extremal Events for Insurance and Finance*, Berlin: Springer.

Grinblatt, M. and S. Titman (2002), *Financial Markets and Corporate Strategy*, 2nd edition, New York: McGraw-Hill-Irwin.

Malevergne, Y. and D. Sornette (2005), *Extreme Financial Risks: From Dependence to Risk Management*, Berlin: Springer Verlag.

McNeil, A.J., R. Frey, and P. Embrechts (2005), *Quantitative Risk Management*, Princeton, NJ: Princeton University Press.

Musiela, M. and M. Rutkowski (2000), *Martingale Methods in Financial Modelling*, Berlin: Springer.

Shimpi, P. (2001), *Integrating Corporate Risk Management*, New York: Texere.

Stulz, R. (2003), *Risk Management and Derivatives*, Mason, Ohio: South-Western.

Tirole, J. (2006), *The Theory of Corporate Finance*, Princeton, NJ: Princeton University Press.

■ ACKNOWLEDGMENTS

We acknowledge the invaluable assistance of Marie-Pierre Boé, as well as very useful comments and suggestions by Michel Dacorogna, Thomas-Olivier Léautier, Sébastien Pouget, and Paul Seabright. We also benefitted from the feedback from our students at Toulouse, Zürich, the Bank of Japan, and AXA College.

PART ONE

Risk Management: What must be Changed

Taking risks and managing them have always been a fundamental part of any human activity, from hunting or fighting for conquering new lands to the development of modern corporations. In fact, the concept of risk encompasses two different and antagonistic notions: the occurrence of undesired events (e.g., fires, floods, or earthquakes) that destroy or disrupt lives and properties, but also the upside risks that are associated with entrepreneurship. Indeed, taking risks is the essence of entrepreneurial attitude and a condition for reward and success.

Accepting risks is not new in business and economic activity; for example, at the end of the fifteenth century, Venice merchants were already financing chartered boat expeditions that brought back precious goods that they sold for profit. These investments were especially risky because of pirates, tempests, and possible sailor corruption. Today's financial analysts would probably have considered these activities as highly volatile and speculative.

Although the management of risky activities has a very long history, the last decades have witnessed a fantastic revolution in Risk Management, with the development of new, very sophisticated methods. Yet recent crises have revealed major flaws in these new methods. The first part of this book analyzes these major flaws and explains what must be changed. Chapter 1 explains the objectives of risk management and presents some of the failures revealed by these recent crises. Chapter 2 illustrates the consequences of living in turbulent times. Finally, Chapter 3 explain how a proper methodology of modern risk management must be implemented.

1 Lessons From Recent Financial Crises

1.1 THE BASIC GOALS OF RISK MANAGEMENT

The fundamental role of the risk management division of a modern corporation is essentially to assist the top management in making the following decisions:

- Decision 1: How much risk to take
- Decision 2: How much of this risk to retain and how much to insure or transfer to financial and insurance markets
- Decision 3: How much capital to keep as a buffer against losses because of this retained risk
- Decision 4: How much liquid reserves to maintain

Decision 1 refers to the size or volume of the different risky activities that the firm undertakes. Decision 2 refers to the fraction of the associated risks that will be transferred to insurers (through insurance contracts) or financial markets (through hedging or securitization), the remaining risks being retained (or self-financed) by the firm. Decision 3 refers to the maximum amount of net (i.e., after the transfers arranged by Decision 2) losses that the shareholders of the firm are ready to bear themselves: This amount corresponds to the own funds or equity capital[1] of the firm. Finally, Decision 4 refers to the level of liquid reserves that the firm keeps for being able to satisfy its future payment needs. If these reserves turn out to be insufficient, then the firm becomes illiquid.[2] The managers then have to finance these liquidity needs either by borrowing from a bank, issuing more equity or debt on the market, or selling some of the firm's assets.

Note that the core of risk management is fundamentally Decision 2 (how much risk to retain and how much to insure or transfer to financial markets). However, this book will show that investment policy (Decision 1), financing policy (Decision 3) and cash management policy (Decision 4) cannot really be separated from risk management policy (Decision 2).

1.2 WHEN RISK MANAGEMENT FAILS

In the last decades, large companies (notably banks and insurers) have elaborated very sophisticated quantitative methods for answering the above questions. These methods have generally proved very successful, but recent crises have also revealed that they can sometimes fail spectacularly. As illustrated by the AIG quasi-failure (*see* Box 1.1 below) and by other examples described later in this book, it is now commonly viewed that the majority of banks and other financial institutions that participated in the subprime markets (and the securities and derivative markets that were developed in connection with these subprime markets) had it all wrong.[3]

BOX 1.1 ■ AIG: The Fall of a Champion

AIG traces its roots back 90 years, when an American entrepreneur named C.V. Starr founded an insurance company (AIG's earliest predecessor) in Shanghai. What began as a small insurance business grew to become the world's largest insurer. By early 2007, AIG had assets of $1 trillion, $110 billion in revenues, 74 million customers, and 116,000 employees in 130 countries and jurisdictions. Yet just 18 months later, AIG found itself on the brink of failure and in need for emergency government assistance.

This quasi-failure of AIG, which had been for several decades the most successful and the most respected player of the insurance industry, is probably the most significant event in this industry in the first decade of twenty-first century. Many articles had celebrated AIG's "robust" business model pointing at the ingredients of "success": strong management, ability to use the reinsurance cycles, international orientation, wide range of products (Property & Casualty, Life, Financial Products). The irony is that AIG 's management was known for its "control-oriented culture."

Unlike most of its competitors, AIG quickly expanded into a range of financial services businesses. One of these, created in 1987, was AIG Financial Products (AIGFP). Among other activities, AIGFP sold credit default swaps[4] to other financial institutions to protect them against the default of certain securities. If AIGFP activity remained small compared to the insurance activity, it incurred huge losses, mainly because of the strong deterioration of the U.S. mortgage market. AIG only survived because of the intervention of the U.S. government. To stabilize AIG and prevent potential systemic effects that would have occurred in case AIG had been declared bankrupt, the U.S. government extended a 2-year emergency loan of $85 billion on September 16, 2008. In fact, AIG was almost nationalized: the U.S. government got hold of 79.9% of the shares of the company and forced AIG to select a new chairman and a new chief executive officer. As the financial industry continued to falter in October and early November 2008, it became clear that the original plan would not be sufficient to save AIG. On November 10, 2008, the initial government loan was restructured to include a $40 billion injection by the U.S. Treasury through the Troubled Asset Relief Program (TARP). Moreover, a 5-year credit facility was granted to AIG by the Federal Reserve Bank of New York with a borrowing limit of up to $60 billion.

More specifically:

- banks have taken too much risk (Decision 1);
- banks have retained too much risk (Decision 2);
- banks have kept too little capital (Decision 3);
- banks have kept too little liquidity (Decision 4).

1.3 WHAT SHOULD BE DONE?

Without going into all the details of the circumstances that led AIG to virtual bankruptcy, it is important to understand how all this has been possible and what

BOX 1.2 ■ Some of the Biggest Corporate Bankrupcies in the United States.[5]

Lehman Brothers (2008): $639 billion
WorldCom (2002): $104 billion
Enron (2001): $64 billion
Managerial Incentives (Stock Options)
$300 million (1998–2001) for Jeff Skilling, CEO of Enron
$250 million (2004–2007) for Richard Fuld, CEO of Lehman Brothers

lessons can be drawn from this catastrophe. Even if, at the time of writing of this book, we do not have all the elements needed to answer these questions fully, it is already possible to offer some explanations that illustrate well the main messages of this book:

- **Corporate governance should be closely monitored:** The structure of the top management's packages of AIG (and many other financial institutions that were hit by the crisis) encouraged excessive risk-taking behavior. The distorted incentives of top management and traders prevented the implementation of efficient risk control. The board did not impose consistent risk appetite across operating companies (especially, of course, in the financial products division). Finally, reporting on risks and exposures was not adequate.

- **Tail-dependence should be properly estimated:** Most risk measures and solvency models are based on normality assumptions that imply a constant correlation between different lines of business such as securities lending and real-estate investments. During tranquil times, these lines of business are weakly correlated, but during crisis times they all become strongly correlated. In the jargon of risk professionals, tail-dependence is very high. In the case of AIG, one event (the deterioration of the U.S. mortgage markets) impacted AIG in several of its activities: severe valuation losses on AIGFP's credit default swap portfolio and heavy losses in its securities lending operation (which invested mostly in high-grade residential mortgage-backed securities); at the same time, other AIG real estate–related investments also suffered sharp losses.

- **Systemic institutions should be closely supervised:** The main reason for the intervention of the U.S. government was to avoid a domino effect. AIG was deemed "systemic" because it was the counterparty to many banks and financial institutions. AIG was providing more than $400 billion of credit protection to banks and other clients around the world through its credit default swap business. Such systemic institutions should be supervised more closely than other financial institutions, especially because they are often very large and complex organizations. Their risk management policies are often too opaque and not enough grounded in the reality of day-to-day business operations. Regular review and audit of risk management policies should be undertaken by different stakeholders (e.g., the company board, the supervisors, and possibly some independent agencies).

- **Liquidity risk should not be underestimated:** As also illustrated by several earlier examples (like MetalGesellschaft or LTCM),[6] even a good business model can be jeopardized by a temporary deterioration in the conditions on global financial markets. Liquidity is mostly needed when financial markets do not function well: risk models that rely on the assumption of perfect financial markets cannot capture this risk.
- **Finally, managing large crises requires the cooperation between the public and private sectors:** A large crisis is precisely characterized by the incapacity of banks and financial markets to exert their normal functions of absorbing losses and providing liquidity to non-financial businesses. Some form of government intervention is therefore needed during such crises. However, if this intervention is massive and unprepared, it may well plant the seeds for a next crisis by letting shareholders and managers believe they will be rescued if they fail again in the future (the Too-Big-To-Fail Syndrome).

The main objective of this book is to understand why the sophisticated risk models used by large banks and financial institutions, which are usually very accurate, can also fail miserably in some circumstances. To do so, the second part of this book will analyze in detail the mathematical methods that are behind these models and explain why using them can sometimes be dangerous. Before that, the next two chapters provide some evidence on the difficulties of RM in turbulent times and will delineate the proper methodology.

2   Living in Turbulent Times

This chapter clarifies the main reasons why risk management methods have to be changed to account for the specificities of "turbulent times":

- risks are larger and some of them are new (2.1);
- managers' accountability increases more and more (2.2);
- risks are more and more global and have to be managed as such (2.3).

2.1 NEW AND LARGER RISKS

Risk management needs of large corporations have changed dramatically in the last decades. There are several reasons behind this. The most important of these reasons is probably the general perception in the business community that human activities are exposed to new and larger risks and that corporations—particularly large ones—are at the forefront for carrying and financing these new and larger risks. The tragic example of the terrorist attacks of September 11, 2001 illustrates the occurrence of risks that can be new by their nature but also by their magnitude. These terrorist attacks were indeed the most devastating loss of life and property suffered by the United States in peacetime since the Pearl Harbor attack in 1941. Their consequences were also unexpected; one of the main sources of loss was that the New York Stock Exchange (NYSE) was closed for 5 days (after which the Dow Jones Index fell by 7.1%); another consequence was the drop in activity that subsequently affected tourism and air transportation industries for several months after the event.

The September 11th events have also deeply undermined some basic principles of insurance and risk management. Indeed, insurance is traditionally based on the mutuality principle. It is commonly accepted that if one excepts peculiar risks like earthquakes, floods, and other natural catastrophes, most types of risks are sufficiently independent to allow insurers to diversify their portfolio across different lines of business. This tragic event has demonstrated the possibility of a correlation between risks that were considered before as independent: airplane crashes, collapse of two towers, and business interruption at the NYSE.

Another source of change for risk management affects more traditional risks like environmental hazards or natural catastrophes. Because of their growing importance, these risks have an increasing impact on the way to conduct business. Public perception of risks is sometimes more important than the risks themselves. In 1995, for example (*see* Box 2.1), Shell suffered from a boycott of its gas stations in Germany, organized by environmental associations following—false—information that the dismantling of one of Shell's offshore platforms in the North Sea was likely to cause environmental damage.

Natural catastrophes (*see* Boxes 2.2, 2.3 and 2.4), such as hurricanes, floods, and earthquakes, are another example of traditional risks that have a growing impact on our societies.

BOX 2.1 ■ Shell vs. Greenpeace

Brent Spar was an oil platform in the North Sea operated by Shell Group. In early 1995, this platform had to be dismantled, and Shell experts thought that the best solution was to sink the platform in an abyssal gap at a depth of 2000 m. At this time, based on the opinion of its own experts, Greenpeace considered that is was better to dismantle Brent Spar on land. Consequently, Greenpeace decided to start an intensive media campaign in the Netherlands and Germany asking for the boycott of Shell gas stations.

Very quickly, public opinion supported Greenpeace's positions. A Gallup poll revealed that 74% of the German population was favorable to the boycott. Within weeks, the 1,700 gas stations in Germany saw their revenue drop by 20%.

Consequently, Shell management declared that they would follow Greenpeace recommendations and dismantle the platform on land.

On September 6, 1995, Greenpeace admitted, in a very laconic press release, that their experts were wrong and that the solution proposed by Shell was more adequate from an environmental perspective.

BOX 2.2 ■ Hurricane Katrina

Hurricane Katrina devastated the southern United States in August 2005. After severely damaging Florida, it caused the flooding of 80% of the city of New Orleans and its complete evacuation (for the first time in its history). Katrina caused extensive wind-related property damage but also huge flood-related damages and pollution in New Orleans, as well as oil rig and refinery damages in the Gulf of Mexico and the coastal areas. Casualties are estimated at more than 1200 and insured losses at more than $66 billion. As a matter of comparison, the Gross State Product of Louisiana (the equivalent of GNP for a state) was $153 billion in 2004.

BOX 2.3 ■ The Five Biggest Catastrophes in Terms of Victims, 1990–2010 (Victims)[1]

- Earthquake (magnitude 9) and Tsunami in India Ocean (Indonesia, Thailand,..., 2004): 220,000 victims
- Earthquake (magnitude 7.0) in Haiti in 2010: more than 200,000 victims
- Tropical cyclone Gorky (Bangladesh, 1991): 138,000 victims
- Earthquake (magnitude 7.6), aftershocks, landslides (Pakistan, India, Afghanistan, 2005): 73,300 victims
- Earthquake (magnitude 7.7), landslides (Iran, 1990): 40,000 victims

BOX 2.4 ■ The Three Most Costly Insurance Losses 1970–2007
(in U.S.$, Indexed 2007).[1]

- Hurricane Katrina (United States, Bahamas, 2005): $68 billion insured losses
- Hurricane Andrew (United States, Bahamas, 1992): $24 billion insured losses
- Terrorist attack on World Trade Center and Pentagon (United States, 2001): $22 billion insured losses

Experts predict that a big earthquake is very likely to occur in California in the near future (the "Big One") with an estimated cost exceeding $500 billion.

However, big as those risks are, note that total market capitalization on world equity markets is above 50 trillion (as of May, 2010) and that day-to-day fluctuations are, on average, around $350 billion.

2.2 INCREASED MANAGEMENT ACCOUNTABILITY

We have thus illustrated the growing awareness that many corporations in most industries are facing new and larger risks. Confronted with this situation, regulators, analysts, and shareholders tend to exert more pressure on top managers to implement active risk management policies, even if these policies are costly and may ultimately reduce shareholder value. These internal and external pressures even induce large corporations to implement risk management strategies that protect not only the firm itself but also other stakeholders like governments or third parties.

New regulations also imply that managers can now be personally held responsible after the occurrence of a risk: they can suffer from financial losses, their reputation can be greatly altered by a media campaign, and they can even been prosecuted in front of a penal court. For example, managers of large corporations are now more and more likely to be sued following accidents that cause bodily injuries to some of their workers. Risk management is also an important part of the effort to improve the corporate governance of companies. The Sarbanes & Oxley Act (passed by the U.S. Congress to restore confidence after several financial scandals) gives another illustration of this increased management accountability. It requires that all financial statements be signed personally by the CEO and the CFO of the company, who may be held responsible in case of mistakes or errors. The Sarbanes & Oxley Act can be analyzed as a prescriptive set of risk management policies that are imposed on the management of large corporations; in this circumstance, the regulator is acting on behalf of the shareholders.

Managers are also more and more concerned by their risk management strategy because of increased competition. Should an unexpected and unwanted event occur (like a fire in a factory or the departure of a key expert), the pressure of competitors can be such that the firm may not be able to cope with a small financial loss or even the loss of time needed to replace the key expert. This has been illustrated by recent cases in the information technology or luxury goods industries.

BOX 2.5 ■ WorldCom

In July 2002, WorldCom, a large U.S. telecommunications company, suddenly collapsed, leading to the then (before Lehmann Brothers failure in 2008) largest bankruptcy in U.S. history and causing hundreds of millions of dollars in losses to investors. Some of these investors, led by the New York State Common Retirement Fund, sued WorldCom former directors for failing in their duties of protecting shareholders' interests. In January 2005, these plaintiffs obtained $54 million damages in a settlement with the former directors and the companies that insured WorldCom's directors and officers. Ten of the former directors of WorldCom paid $18 million of their own money. A similar outcome had occurred before, when former directors of Enron agreed to pay $1.5 million out of their own pockets to company workers who lost money in their retirement accounts (from the New York Times, January 6, 2005).

A well-known example is what happened to Gucci, the luxury goods company. In the 1990s Gucci was very successful under the leadership of two men: the CEO Domenico de Sole and the fashion stylist Tom Ford. Gucci became one of the premier global luxury brands. After a tough battle against LVMH, Gucci was acquired by PPR, a diversified group who had the ambition to build a luxury goods activity based on the Gucci successes and on the famous duo de Sole-Ford. Unfortunately for PPR, soon after the acquisition, Domenico de Sole and Tom Ford decided to leave Gucci, considering that they could not work with the new owners. The departure of these two key people led to a destruction of value for shareholders. Subsequently, financial markets reacted negatively, considering that the acquisition of Gucci had been a mistake for the parent company PPR.

2.3 NEED FOR A GLOBAL APPROACH

Until recently, the responsibility of the risk management system was kept at a local level—subsidiary, country, division—without consolidation at the corporation level. At the same time, risks were handled with a so-called "silo" approach: property/casualty risks managed by the insurance and risks department, personnel-related risks by the Human Resources department, and financial risks by the treasurer and the CFO with very little communication between them. The collapses of Lehman Brothers, Enron, and WorldCom clearly demonstrate that an efficient risk management system absolutely needs to be organized on a global basis and to adopt a holistic approach of risks.

First of all, the supply chain and the units of production are now more and more organized on a global basis with a greater use of outsourcing, cooperations between companies in *ad hoc* structures, or joint ventures. Thus, an unwanted event hurting one of the elements of the value chain can have very large consequences. Also, the interconnection of businesses increases their vulnerability to events often out of the control of the management of corporations. A well-known example is given by the automobile industry. To reduce inventories, some spare parts (like the seats of the cars) are made just in time (i.e., only when the making of car starts); it is clear that a fire in the supplier's factory could create huge difficulties to the car makers.

Another element in favor of a global approach to risk management is that the risk management tools used in insurance, banking, and finance are now organized globally. Financial markets provide the tools to manage a large part of the risks faced by corporations and their globalization is obviously one of the major trends of the last decades. Even if the evolution has been slower for the insurance and reinsurance markets, this industry is also moving toward a global market, dominated by a handful of international players.

To be efficient, the risk management strategy has to be holistic, which means that it must encompass the full spectrum and the variety of the risks that can hurt the corporation. The three main reasons for developing such a strategy are:

- to be as close as possible to a complete identification of risks and exposures;
- to be able to build the models needed to analyze the correlations between various risks;
- to facilitate the assessment of the firm by external experts and thus to reduce the costs of transferring some of the risks to insurers and financial markets.

The next chapter presents the main aspects of the methodology used by large corporations for attaining these objectives.

3 The Need for a Proper Methodology

3.1 THE NECESSARY INGREDIENTS

Risk management has a long history. Various techniques have been developed for many years in all areas of human activities. Classical examples are the construction of dams that protect against floods and the organization of fire brigades to fight against fires. It is only recently that a common methodology has emerged. Recent crises have shown that several ingredients of this methodology are crucial: mishandling one of them can be sufficient to provoke the failure of an established company. This section presents a summary of this methodology.

The necessary ingredients of risk management are listed below.

The **Identification** step consists of identifying the entire spectrum of possible risks that can hurt the firm.

The **Quantification & Modeling** step consists of estimating the frequency and severity of each risk and also, very importantly, the correlations between them. Ideally, one should be able to build a quantitative model giving the cumulative distribution function of losses (or gains) conditionally on external and internal variables.

The **Loss Prevention & Protection** step consists of the reduction of the frequency (prevention) and consequences (protection) of the risks. Taking the example of property risks, good maintenance of electricity systems improves loss prevention, whereas maintaining a sufficient water pressure on-site improves loss protection.

Finally, **the Risks Financing & Transfer** step consists of deciding which risks have to be financed directly (when the corporation decides to keep them) and which have to be financed indirectly (when the risk is transferred to financial markets or an insurance company).[1]

For many years this traditional approach has been applied to each specific family of risks, the oldest examples being property and marine risks. The occurrence of new and larger risks, together with their growing complexity and multiple interdependencies, required some improvements in the risk management methodology and instruments. We now study these improvements by following each step of the risk management approach: risk mapping for the identification and quantitative steps, loss prevention in new areas like fraud or liability, and, finally, the impressive array of new financial tools that have been created in recent years to transfer and finance risks.

BOX 3.1 ■ The Necessary Steps of Risk Management

Identification
↓
Quantification & Modeling
↓
Loss Prevention & Protection
↓
Risks Financing & Transfer

BOX 3.2 ■ Identifying the Relevant Risk

In the 1990s, the beverage company Perrier, which was at the time very successful in the North American market, was accused of having left traces of benzene in some of its bottles.

Perrier recalled quickly the bottles tampered with benzene, and no bodily injury or claims were reported, as the concentration of benzene was very small and completely harmless (and tasteless).

However, since this accident, Perrier never recovered its markets share in the United States and was ultimately purchased by Nestlé.

The lesson to be drawn from this anecdote is simple: In terms of risks, Perrier was more exposed to the loss of its image of manufacturing a healthy and pure product than to the risks of poisoning customers. No need to say that at the time of this accident, Perrier management had not identified, managed, or transferred this risk to insurance markets.

3.2 RISK MAPPING

Risk mapping is the modern, integrated way of implementing the necessary ingredients of risk management. It aims at giving a quantified representation of all the risks faced by a corporation. It is generally organized in four steps: identification and classification, quantification of the impact and occurrence, analysis of correlations and scenarios, and, finally, modeling the aggregate impact on the corporation. We now examine these four steps in succession.

3.2.1 Taxonomy

Taxonomy is a key step. Risks may be classified in different ways, for example:

- **Exogenous Risks:**
  - losses on property (fire, flood, explosion...)
  - natural catastrophes
  - liability suits

- **Economic and Financial Risks:**

  - recession (or boom)[2]
  - credit crunch
  - stock exchange crash
  - interest rate risk
  - currency risk
  - fluctuation of input or output prices

- **Operational Risks:**

  - loss of key employee
  - fraud or theft
  - quality deterioration of systems or processes

- **Strategic Risks:**

  - change in customer preferences
  - change in competitive environment (entry or exit of a close competitor)
  - strike of employees
  - change in regulations

In the financial industry, risks are also classified by the way they affect the balance sheet of the company. For example, the Box 3.3 shows such a classification of risks for an insurance company.

The last column of Box 3.3 shows the specifications of distribution functions usually adopted by risk managers according to the type of risk they want to model. More information on this topic is provided in Chapter 4.

The standard representation, often organized in two concentric circles and four quadrants, is sometimes called the *risks radar*. Figure 3.1 gives an example of such a risks radar. Another example will be found in Chapter 14.

3.2.2 Quantification

The next step is to quantify the risks in terms of their possible impact on the key financial parameters of the firm (earnings per share, cash position, market capitalization, market share) and also of their probability of occurrence.

At this stage, a first vision of the corporation risk profile is obtained by a map where each identified risk is located along two axes giving the severity and the frequency of the risks. One key question relates to the degree of precision of the estimation for the measurement of risks' severity and frequency; the users of such a map must be informed of the quality of the underlying data to keep a good consistency to the analysis.

An example of such a risk map is given below: for each individual risk, Figure 3.2 gives its potential cost (severity) and its estimated frequency of occurrence. In Chapter 4, we will explain how this risk map can be used to determine the histogram of risks.

BOX 3.3 ■ Classification of the Risks Confronted by an Insurance Company

Category	Risk Type	Key Exposures	Distribution Type
Asset	Credit	• Reinsurance ceded • Corporate bonds • Derivatives coutnerparty • Other receivables	Skewed (low frequency, high severity)
	Market	• Equities • Interest rates • Derivatives securities • Foreign exchange	Normally distributed returns, lognormal asset prices
Liability	Catastrophe	• Earthquakes • Hurricanes • Floods • Other natural disasters	Highly skewed
	Non Catastrophe	• Potential claims reported or paid at random times for random amounts	Varies, but generally close to lognormal
Asset-Liability Mismatch		• Shifts and flexes in the yield curve	
Operational	Business	• Changes in volume • Changes in margin	Normal
	Event	• Fraud • Unintentional errors • Systems interruption	Poisson events, exponentially distributed severity.

The notation used in Figure 3.2 corresponds to the classification of risks proposed in Figure 3.1:

Exogenous risks: E1 Fire, E2 Flood, E3 Liability Suit, E4 Earthquake, E5 Fraud
Economic and financial risks: F1 Recession, F2 Devaluation, F3 Stock Exchange Crash
Strategic risk: S1 Merger, S2 Increased Competition, S3 Change in Regulation
Operational risks: O1 Input Chain, O2 Audit, O3 Security Problem

The final step of risk mapping is a difficult and important one. It consists in an analysis of the correlations between the different risks and the identification of the scenarios with the largest impacts on the corporation. Each corporation has to choose the degree of complexity of the risks model that they want to use. This degree of complexity depends on the corporation's ambition but also on the time and the budget available. Building a risk mapping model is typically a multiyear project; refinements and improvements of the model can only be introduced progressively.

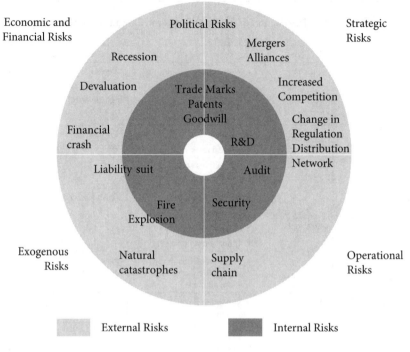

Economic and
Financial Risks

Political Risks

Strategic
Risks

Recession

Mergers
Alliances

Devaluation

Increased
Competition

Trade Marks
Patents
Goodwill

Change in
Regulation

Financial
crash

R&D

Distribution
Network

Liability suit

Audit

Fire
Explosion

Security

Exogenous
Risks

Natural
catastrophes

Supply
chain

Operational
Risks

External Risks   Internal Risks

Figure 3.1 An Example of a Risks Radar

BOX 3.4 ■ How New Risks Emerge and New Instruments Are Developed

After a long period of stability (the "Bretton-Woods era" between 1945 and 1974), interest rates started to fluctuate a lot around 1975. These fluctuations revealed the structural fragility of banks and life insurers, as the difference in the maturities of their assets and liabilities created an exposure to interest rate risk. Many banks and savings institutions were forced to close down for failing to identify and manage these risks before it was too late.

As a response to this risk, banks and insurance companies developed a wide range of techniques to manage jointly and consistently the assets and liabilities parts of their balance sheet. We will present these techniques, called Asset Liability Management (ALM) techniques, in Section 6.4.

The simplest way to proceed is to study in detail the specific scenarios that could have a sizable impact on the corporation. These scenarios are identified by the corporation on the basis of its (or its competitors') past experience. They typically combine different risks with high severity, or risks that are managed in separate departments of the firm. At this stage, it is a mix of "art" (for finding the scenarios to analyse) and "science" (for the measurement of the financial consequences, which requires a good level of precision).

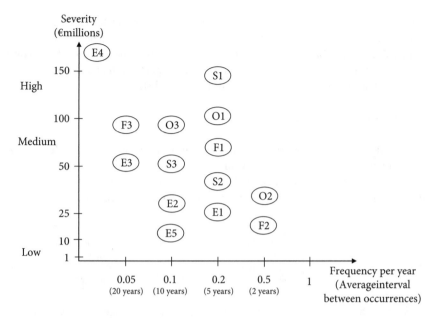

Figure 3.2 An Example of a Risk Map

A more sophisticated way to proceed is to have a complete stochastic approach and to build a model that:

- assesses to each risk its distribution function;[3]
- models statistical dependence between these risks either by a variance–covariance matrix[3] or by a copula.[3]
- incorporates external parameters (e.g. macro-economic data, interest rates) describing the environment of the firm.

Then it is possible to apply a Monte Carlo method (i.e., implementing a large number of computer simulations) and to detect scenarios with the greatest impact using some quantitative measure, like Value at Risk.[4] This methodology may be fruitful and provide a lot of information on the risk profile and the exposure of the corporation. It may also be too complicated if applied to the full spectrum of the risks and external environment parameters. An intermediate methodology is to develop a stochastic approach to a limited number of risks that are identified *a priori*.

Let us take the example of an airline company. Some of the key risk factors would be: oil price, economic situation, terrorist attacks, and the price level on the aviation insurance market. The September 11 events show that these risks can be correlated. An accurate risks mapping and the analysis of various correlations would be of great help for the managers of the airline and would also provide some interesting information to shareholders and financial analysts.

Risk mapping is proven to be a powerful tool for the corporation that aims at building a robust risk management system, as it provides a good framework for organizing the work of the different divisions and communication about this type of project. Like for other kinds of models, it is important to test their robustness and to maintain a good balance between the sophistication of the methods, the quality of data, and the know-how of the different fields experts in the risks management team, such as the treasurer or the loss control specialist.

3.3 LOSS CONTROL

Loss control is essentially twofold: on one hand, it consists in the reduction of the frequency of occurrence of unwanted events (prevention), and on the other hand, loss control deals with the reduction of the consequences of a risk after it has occurred (protection). Let us illustrate these concepts with some examples:

Risks	Action on frequency	Action on consequences
Fire	Prohibition of smoking in the factory	Firemen on site
Car accident	Speed limits	Safety belt
Product liability	Safe product design	Products recall campaign
Flood	Prohibition to build in certain areas	Emergency plan

Some actions can impact both frequency and consequences. For example, for the risks of theft of cash in transit, setting a limit on the sums that can be transferred in an armored car reduces the consequences as well as the probability of a theft as thieves' motivations increase with the quantity of money in the car.

All risk management policies have an impact on the two dimensions of loss control. The first priority is to reduce as much as possible the probability of occurrence of a risk. However, as it is virtually impossible to avoid all risks, risk management policies should also include some measures aimed at reducing the cost of unwanted events.

Historically, a lot of efforts have been deployed by the manufacturing industry and risks carriers in the management of fire risks:

- Many industries have developed a set of norms in relation to fire for building techniques and processes;
- Risks carriers and risks specialists propose to their clients the service of well-trained loss-control specialists who can visit and audit the surety and safety measures on site.

Loss control is a key element of the risk management methodology as it allows decreasing the frequency of the risks or reducing their unwanted consequences; its importance is even greater now as the environment is becoming more and more uncertain and new risks appear constantly.

We have also seen that the risks spectrum is characterized by very high correlations and interdependencies. It is therefore crucial to reduce the frequency of risks to the minimum to avoid a chain reaction effect with negative consequences. For example, a small leak of chemical products in a river can generate an environmentalist campaign and sometimes a massive boycott of the firm product.

Today loss control has to be part of senior managers' core philosophy and must encompass new areas like computer fraud and virus attacks, employees' loyalty, quality of products, and probability of a recall campaign.

BOX 3.5 ■ Failures of Loss Control: Some Striking Examples

Firm	Loss-control failure	Event	Consequences
Crédit Lyonnais (1988–1993)	Lack of shareholders control	Unsustainable external growth policy	$25 billion losses for French taxpayers
Barings Bank (1995)	Internal control of derivatives transactions	Nick Leeson	Bankruptcy and acquisition of Barings
Mercedes (November 28, 2005)	Quality control (tyres)	Crash during the presentation of a new compact car to journalists	Drop in sales of compact cars— Degradation of Mercedes' image
Société Générale (2008)	Internal control of derivatives transactions	One trader exceeds his authority	$6.5 billion loss for Société Générale shareholders

One of the lessons of the numerous examples of improper loss control policy is that the unwanted consequences of a risk are far more important than the cost of loss-control measures.

3.4 RISK ALLOCATION

The last necessary step of the risk management methodology is to decide how to allocate the risks faced by the corporation, either internally or by transferring them to other firms or investors. We now describe the basic principles of risks allocation and illustrate some of the techniques that have developed recently.

Once a risk has been reduced through the loss prevention, a corporation has to decide on the most appropriate treatment. The basic question is to keep it or to transfer it.

If the corporation decides to keep some risk, there are several ways to handle it:

- Self-insure (retention)—that is, not doing anything. The risk is paid (if possible and when it occurs) out of the corporation's own funds.
- Create a special purpose vehicle (SPV) to finance it *a priori*, like a dedicated fund or contingency reserves. In this case, if the risk occurs, its cost will be covered (at least partially) by the SPV.

The other possibility is to transfer the entire risk or part of it to another economic agent. Typology of transfers could be divided into three broad categories, which depend on how many agents ultimately bear the risk:

- *A single bearer:* The risk is borne by a single economic agent (e.g., a bank or a supplier); the contract specifies how the risk will be shared between the firm and its counterparty.
- *A finite number of agents:* This is the case for insurance and reinsurance, where the risks are transferred to a mutuality of agents. Other examples are securitization or derivatives, where the firm sells the risks to a group of investors.
- *An undefined number of agents:* Some risks, because of their characteristics or magnitude, have to be borne (at least in part) by society as a whole, typically through government intervention; classical examples are natural catastrophes or wars.

This is summarized by the following figure:

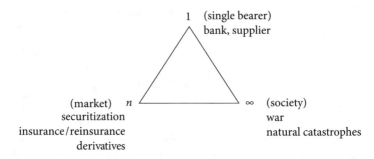

Figure 3.3 Risk transfer triangle

For some specific risks, the transfer must be allocated to several types of counter-parties, and the risks may finally be covered jointly by the State and private agents. Examples are the systems that several countries have developed against natural catastrophes. Such systems provide a cover against property damages caused by natural catastrophes like a flood or earthquake; in this case, the cover is typically split among the insured (who holds a deductible), the insurance and reinsurance market, and the State who gives its financial guarantee via a reinsurance cover. A similar system is used in the United States for terrorist attacks. It is a good example of the sophistication of hybrid systems, mixing market capacity and government support for the protection of the general public. Such hybrid systems are likely to develop in the future.

In the recent years, two major evolutions in the risks transfer techniques have been the rise of retention by large corporations and the use of financial markets to cover a larger fraction of the risks.

The increase in the retention of risks has been influenced by several factors:

- the increasing financial capacity of large corporations;
- the need to adopt a global approach of the whole spectrum of risks;
- the high transaction costs in insurance markets.

As a consequence, large corporations typically do not insure a lot of small risks and often finance them by using a captive. A *captive* is defined as a reinsurance or insurance vehicle, owned by a corporation that will use it for the management of its own risks; it is normally not active in the insurance or reinsurance professional market. Today nearly all large corporations own one or several captives, and there are approximately 4000 captives around the world. More details can be found in Chapter 13.

The second evolution is a development of new types of instruments, the most popular being finites and securitization.

A finite risk insurance (finite,[5] in short) is a contract between a corporation (or an insurer who wants to transfer some of its risks) and an insurer (or a reinsurer) that bundles risk transfer and risk financing. The main characteristics of this type of instrument are:

- it is a multiyear contract term;
- the insurers (or reinsurers) assume a limited part of the risk;
- the investment income is taken into account in the pricing of the contract;
- the profits generated by the finite contract are shared with the insurer.

The extraordinary development of financial markets has provided opportunities to offer new hedging instruments. Traditional insurance markets were not able to develop them at the same speed because of lack of capacity or insufficient competition. The idea behind these instruments is simple and consists of the corporation financing itself by a loan or bonds whose promised repayment is reduced if an unwanted event occurs. For example, if a storm occurs, then the corporation will not have to reimburse the principal of the loan and will only have to pay the interest to the creditors. The preferred area of development has been the one of natural catastrophes, where demand for capacity exceeds supply. A well-known example are catastrophe bonds, like the ones put in place for the financing of the Disney Park in Tokyo. In case of an earthquake of a certain magnitude in the Tokyo area, the owner of the Park does not have to reimburse the principal of the loan—only the interests.

PART TWO

What is Behind Risk Modeling

"All models are wrong, but some are useful." (old saying in Statistics)

Risk management cannot be envisaged without some form of risk modeling. However, one of the main lessons that can be drawn from recent financial crises is that models cannot always be trusted. The traders who have lost billions of dollars on financial markets were often confusing their models with the real world. At best, a model is a good approximation of the real world with a limited validity both in time and scope. All industries, and especially financial markets, are subject to regime changes: a model that has worked well for a long period suddenly ceases to be a good approximation of reality. Risk managers have to be ready to such regime changes. The second part of this book ("What is Behind Risk Modeling") is dedicated to a lucid presentation of the main tools of risk modeling. These tools have been elaborated by statisticians, actuaries, financiers, and economists. Each of these tools can potentially be useful but also has its limits. The purpose of the following chapters is to specify the assumptions that are behind each of these tools, so as to clarify under which circumstances they can be useful and, by contrast, when they can be misleading. A parallel with physics can be useful. One of the most important discoveries in the history of sciences is the Newtonian modeling of the freefall of a body subject to a constant acceleration under gravity. A crucial assumption behind this model is that air resistance can be neglected. Is this assumption acceptable by a scientist who wants to study the movement of a falling body? Well, it depends. If the body in question is a lead ball, then the model is excellent. If, by contrast, the body in question is a feather, then the model is appalling. Our objective in the following chapters is to show how decision makers can select among different risk models, depending on the question addressed.

4   The Basic Tools of Risk Modeling

In this book, we adopt the point of view of a corporation seeking to quantify random events that can impact its future profits and losses. A crucial element is quantifiability. In his treatise, "Risk, Uncertainty and Profit" (published in 1921), Knight distinguishes **"risk"** (events to which the decision maker can assess probability distributions) from **"uncertainty"** (events that cannot be expressed in terms of such probabilities). Pure uncertainty corresponds to cases where it is not possible to build a quantitative approach of the severity and the frequency of the risk. Keynes (in his famous article of 1937, "The General Theory of Employment," in the Quarterly Journal of Economics) gives examples, such as: "The prospect of an European war (indeed!),..., or the price of copper and the rate of interest twenty years hence..." True risk modeling is only possible for those random events that can be quantified both in terms of frequency and severity. Note again that risk does not always have a negative connotation—for example, exchange rate fluctuations can generate profits as well as losses.

There are basically two methods for quantifying risks: the frequentist approach, which can be applied in stationary environments when enough past observations are available, or the subjective approach, which has to be applied when there are not enough such observations. We show below how these methods can be combined. We also suggest a way to take care of Knightian uncertainty by the use of "worst-case scenarios." The chapter concludes by a discussion of the dangers of the stationarity assumption: what if the future differs from the past?

4.1 ASSESSING PROBABILITIES: THE FREQUENTIST AND SUBJECTIVE APPROACHES

The frequentist approach relies on the law of large numbers (*see* Chapter 5 for more detail). This law states that in large samples, the frequency of occurrence of independent and identical events is approximately equal to a constant, which is called the **probability** of the event.

For example, the sentence "The probability of drawing heads when throwing a coin is 1/2" just means that if the coin is thrown many times, the frequency of occurrence of heads is very likely to be close to 1/2. This notion of probability is justified by the fact that in a stationary[1] environment, the future frequency of such events can be predicted from that of past events, at least if the samples involved are large. This method has been employed for a long time in the insurance industry.

Example 1: *Insuring car windshields.* Consider an insurer that is covering the motor fleet of a corporation. The fleet consists of 1000 vehicles. Past observations show that the number of windshields broken by year is relatively stable—around 150 for an average annual cost of $12000.

The average cost for one windshield is $\frac{12000}{150} = \$800$. The cost of the cover by car is $\frac{12000}{1000} = \$120$. The frequency of the event is $\frac{150}{1000} = 15\%$. The insurer will monitor the risk by analyzing the evolution of the average cost ($800) and the frequency of the event (15%).[2]

This approach is robust but cannot be used when too few data are available. This is the case for events with a low frequency of occurrence or for new types of coverage. The risk carriers have to estimate ex ante the "probability" of occurrence of the event. Here the interpretation of the word "probability" is very different from the one that derives from the frequentist approach. In particular, it is subjective, as it may differ from one individual to another: it summarizes an "opinion."

Example 2: *Insuring satellite launches.* Consider now the insurance of the launch of commercial satellites. When this activity started in the 1970s, there was obviously no past observation that could be used to compute the frequency of launch failures. The initial assessment of the "probability" of failure was therefore a subjective measure of the "likelihood" of a failure, based on evaluations of the reliability of technology and launching procedures. The premium charged by the insurer of the first commercial satellite was very similar to the odd ratios offered by bookmakers organizing bets on sports events. In a similar fashion, insurance and financial markets aggregate individual assessments (subjective probabilities) in what can be called a market "sentiment." Like bookmakers' odds ratios, market premiums for this kind of risk thus reflect the average opinion of experts on the likelihood of these risks. But this average opinion does not have the objective content of the frequency distribution of losses in a large sample of identical and independent events. And business decisions based on subjective probabilities always have some features of a bet.

In practice, corporations have to deal with combinations of risks that lie in between these two cases: they are more or less reproducible, and more or less data are available. A mixed approach is thus necessary, relying on a very important method that we present now: Bayesian updating.

4.2 BAYESIAN UPDATING

This method is based on the Bayes formula, which shows how to revise subjective probabilities on the basis of new information. As an illustration consider again the example of satellite insurance, and suppose that initially, insurance experts assigned a (subjective) probability of $P_0 = 50\%$ that the technology was safe (in which case the frequency of failures would only be 10%) and a probability of 50% that it was risky (in which case the frequency of failures would be 40%).

This is illustrated by the event-tree Figure 4.1.

Figure 4.1

BOX 4.1 ■ The Bayes Formula

For any couple A, B of stochastic events, the posterior (or conditional) probability of A given B is the ratio of the probability of A and B by the probability of B:

$$Pr(A|B) = \frac{Pr(A \text{ and } B)}{Pr(B)}.$$

The initial assessment of the probability of failure, prior to the first launch (and called the prior probability of failure), would therefore be:

$$\text{Prior Probability of Failure} = \frac{50}{100} \times 10\% + \frac{50}{100} \times 40\% = 25\%.$$

After the first launch, this prior probability has to be revised according to the Bayes formula for conditional probabilities.

Numerical Example

In our example, A is the event "the technology is safe" and B is the outcome of the first launch. If this outcome is a failure, we obtain:

$$Pr(A \text{ and } B) = Pr\,(\text{safe technology and failure}) = 50\% \times 10\% = 5\%,$$

$$Pr(B) = Pr\,(\text{failure}) = 25\%,$$

$$Pr(\text{Safe|Failure}) = \frac{5\%}{25\%} = 20\%.$$

This means that if the first launch is a failure, then the (revised) probability of the technology to be safe is now 20%. This implies a dramatic reduction of the probability that the technology is safe (from 50% to 20%). If, on the contrary, the first launch is a success, then the probability that the technology is safe becomes

$$\text{Pr(Safe|Success)} = \frac{\text{Pr (Safe and Success)}}{\text{Pr (Success)}} = \frac{50\% \times 90\%}{75\%} = 60\%.$$

If the technology for launching satellites was constant over time (this is what we mean by our assumption of "stationary environment"), then successive revisions of subjective probabilities on the basis of more and more observations would converge to the "objective" probability based on the frequency of failures, and the two approaches (frequentist and subjective) would ultimately lead to the same result. However, in practice, environments are never completely stationary:[3] for example, the technology for launching satellites is likely to improve over time (because of "learning by doing"). This means that the Bayes formula has to be amended. A typical method is to compute the past frequency of launch failures and to reduce it by a subjective term corresponding to the "learning-by-doing" factor.

These two examples give a good illustration of the various approaches used by risks carriers, but they are somewhat too simplistic: in reality, risks cannot always be put into one of these two categories. Very often, a good estimation of the cost of the risks requires a combination of the two methods. For example, part of marine insurance risks may be analyzed through a frequentist approach but the occurrence of large catastrophes like the pollution of a shoreline by a tanker must be estimated by a subjective probability approach.

4.3 ESTIMATING LOSS DISTRIBUTIONS

In the examples below, risks are modeled by a random variable $\tilde{x}$ that represents the possible losses[4] associated with the risky activity under study.

> **Simple** risks correspond to a loss L that is known *a priori*. The associated random variable $\tilde{x}$ follows a Bernoulli distribution, as in Figure 4.2.

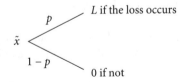

Figure 4.2

> **Complex** risks correspond to situations where the loss itself (conditionally on the occurrence of the risk) is a random variable. If sufficiently many occurrences of the same risk have been observed in the past, it is possible to build the risk histogram by plotting past observations by increasing size. Figure 4.3 represents an example with five categories of risk size.

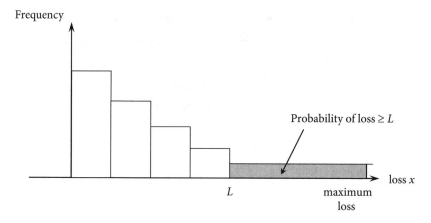

Figure 4.3

For a complex risk, the probability of a loss of size less than x is given by the cumulative distribution function:

$$F(x) = \Pr(\tilde{x} \leq x).$$

It is customary to approximate the histogram by parametrized density functions, which are typically continuous. The advantage of continuous densities is that computations are easy. In particular, like in Figure 4.4 the distribution function is differentiable, and the derivative of F is equal to the density :

$$f(x) = F'(x), \qquad \text{for all} \quad x > 0.$$

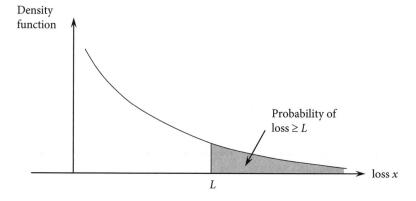

Figure 4.4

Well-known examples of such parametrized distributions are:

- the uniform distribution, represented in Figure 4.5 (parametrized by two numbers a and $b > a$):

$$\begin{cases} f(x) & = \frac{1}{b-a} \text{ for } a \leq x \leq b \\ & = 0 \text{ otherwise} \end{cases}$$

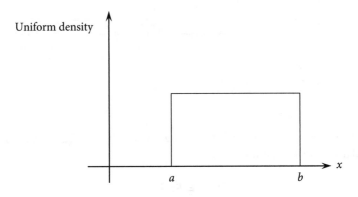

Figure 4.5

- the exponential distribution represented in Figure 4.6 (parametrized by one number $\lambda > 0$): $f(x) = \lambda e^{-\lambda x}$ for $x \geq 0$,

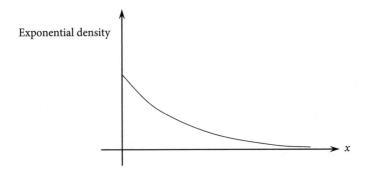

Figure 4.6

- the Normal distribution represented in Figure 4.7 (parametrized by two numbers μ and $\sigma > 0$):

$$f(x) = \frac{1}{\sigma \sqrt{2\pi}} e^{-\frac{1}{2}\left(\frac{x-\mu}{\sigma}\right)^2} \text{ for } x \in \mathbb{R}.$$

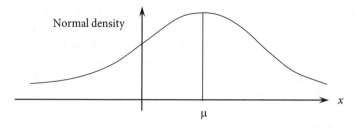

Figure 4.7

BOX 4.2 ■ The Binomial Distribution

One natural example of such complex risks is the binomial distribution, obtained by the independent[5] repetition of simple (Bernoulli) risks. It is parametrized by p, the probability of an individual loss, and n, the number of repetitions. The probability of i losses is given by the binomial formula (hence the name of the distribution)

$$\Pr(i \text{ losses}) = \binom{n}{i} p^i (1-p)^{n-i},$$

where

$$\binom{n}{i} = \frac{n(n-1)(n-2)\ldots(n-i+1)}{i(i-1)(i-2)\ldots 1}.$$

BOX 4.3 ■ The (Univariate) Normal Distribution

If $\tilde{x}$ is normal with parameters μ and σ, then $\tilde{t} = \frac{\tilde{x}-\mu}{\sigma}$ is a standard normal. Thus,

$$\Pr[\tilde{x} \le x] = \Pr\left[\tilde{t} \le \frac{x-\mu}{\sigma}\right] = N\left(\frac{x-\mu}{\sigma}\right).$$

The cumulative distribution function (c.d.f.) of a normal random variable with $\mu = 0$ and $\sigma = 1$ (standard normal) is denoted $N(x)$. By definition:

$$N(x) = \Pr(\tilde{x} \le x) = \frac{1}{\sqrt{2\pi}} \int_{-\infty}^{x} \left(\exp -\frac{1}{2}t^2\right) dt.$$

A typical method for calibrating distribution functions is to choose a family of parametrized density functions (depending on the type of risk to be modeled) and to select the parameter values that provide the best fit to empirical histograms.

In practice, risk professionals and insurers are helped by the development of statistical software that can be run on personal computers. These computer programs analyze numerical data and propose the parametrized density function with the best fit to the observed distribution.

However, histograms are a fundamental tool for assessing how risks are allocated between several counterparties. Indeed, it is often the case that complex risks are sliced into different pieces and each slice is allocated to a different investor or insurer. This method, which is called **layering** in insurance/reinsurance and **tranching** in structured finance, can be represented as shown in Figure 4.8 on the histogram of the underlying risk:

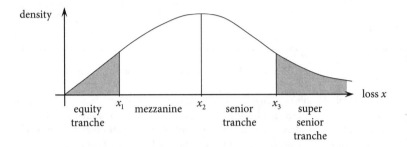

Figure 4.8 Tranching of losses in finance. Retained tranches correspond to the two shaded areas.

Figure 4.8 can illustrate structured finance operations. All losses below x_1 (equity tranche) are often retained by the financial intermediary. The losses between x_1 and x_2 (mezzanine tranche) are borne by a first category of counterparties, who typically specialize on risks that are relatively frequent. If the mezzanine tranche is securitized, its rating is likely to be median. By contrast, the senior tranche (losses between x_2 and x_3) is less risky and is typically designed to obtain a top rating by rating agencies. The supersenior tranche (losses above x_3) is normally very safe, but several episodes of the subprime crisis have shown that it can be exposed to macro-economic shocks, as default risks may become strongly correlated during recessions. x_1, x_2, and x_3 are called the **attachment** points of the structured issue. Structure finance products like CDOs (*see* Box 4.4) use this tranching methodology.

Another example is the layering of claims in insurance, as illustrated by Figure 4.9:

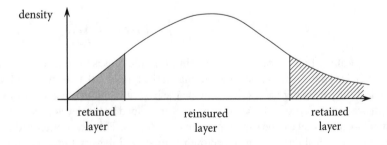

Figure 4.9 An example of layering in insurance (stop-loss reinsurance).

BOX 4.4 ■ Collateralized Debt Obligations[6] (CDOs)

A collateralized debt obligation (CDO) is a structured finance product in which some *ad hoc* legal entity, called a special purpose vehicle (SPV), issues bonds against an investment in an underlying asset pool (typically a portfolio of loans). The claims issued against the collateral pool of assets are prioritized by creating different tranches of debt securities. Senior claims are largely insulated from default risk to the extent that more junior tranches absorb first credit losses.

To be concrete, consider a pool of three identical loans[7] of nominal 1, each with a 10% probability of default and zero recovery in case of default. If defaults are independent,[8] then the histogram of future losses is easy to construct. Indeed, the number of defaults follows a binomial[9] distribution of parameters $p = 10\%$ and $n = 3$:

$$\Pr(i \text{ defaults}) = \binom{n}{i} p^i (1-p)^{n-i}.$$

Thus,

$$\Pr(1 \text{ default}) = \binom{3}{1} (0.1)^1 (0.9)^2 = 3 \times 0.1 \times 0.81 = 24.3\%$$

$$\Pr(2 \text{ defaults}) = \binom{3}{2} (0.1)^2 (0.9) = 3 \times 0.01 \times 0.9 = 2.7\%$$

$$\Pr(3 \text{ defaults}) = \binom{3}{3} (0.1)^3 = 1 \times 0.001 = 0.1\%.$$

Suppose now that this pool of loans is securitized against three tranches of bonds of nominal 1 but of different priorities. The equity tranche bears the losses up to $x_1 = 1$. The mezzanine tranche bears the losses between $x_1 = 1$ and $x_2 = 2$. Finally, the senior tranche bears all the losses above $x_2 = 2$. In this simple example, these tranches behave like bonds with a zero recovery rate and probabilities of default that can be deducted from the above probabilities. Their prices are easy to compute: $P(\text{equity}) = 24.3\%$, $P(\text{mezzanine}) = 2.7\%$ and $P(\text{senior}) = 0.1\%$. Thus, the senior and mezzanine tranches are much safer than the underlying bonds, but the equity tranche is much more risky. In some sense, the CDO allows the shift of risks to the upper tail.

4.4 COMBINING EVENT TREES AND MONTE CARLO METHODS

Because corporations are subject to multiple risks, a complete modeling of these risks necessitates a combination of the basic tools presented above. Event trees are useful to model different scenarios, combining "subjective" assessments of isolated events (e.g., who is going to win the next presidential election in the United States) and "objective" probability distributions based on frequency analysis of rich data sets.

Consider the following example: Suppose that the Republican candidate to the next U.S. presidential election is in favor of restricting trade with country X, whereas his or her opponent is against such restrictions. Assuming firm Y has an important export activity toward country X, the result of the presidential election is a major source of risk for firm Y. One way to model the situation would be to assess a "subjective" probability p to the election of the Republican candidate but to combine it with "objective" forecasts of earnings, separating activity with country X, denoted by the random variable $\tilde{x}_1$, from those with the rest of the world, denoted by another random variable $\tilde{x}_2$. We obtain the event tree shown in Figure 4.10:

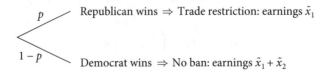

Figure 4.10

Event trees allow estimation of combined distributions of earnings, which mix "subjective" probabilities and "objective" forecasts, as illustrated in Figure 4.11.

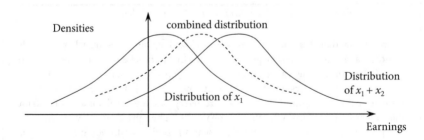

Figure 4.11

The combined cumulative distribution function (c.d.f.) is simply the weighted sum of the c.d.f. of x_1 and $x_1 + x_2$, as illustrated in Figure 4.12

$$\Pr(\tilde{x} \leq x) = p\Pr(\tilde{x}_1 \leq x) + (1 - p)\Pr(\tilde{x}_1 + \tilde{x}_2 \leq x).$$

Monte Carlo methods are another important tool: they allow to simulate cumulative distribution functions (c.d.f.) of large models, which may involve many different risks, related by complex correlation structures. Analytical computations of the cumulative distribution functions (c.d.f.) are impossible because of the high dimensionality of such models. However, once the model has been calibrated, it is always possible to use a random number generator (RNG) and simulate the final outcomes of the model. When the number of such simulations increases, plotting

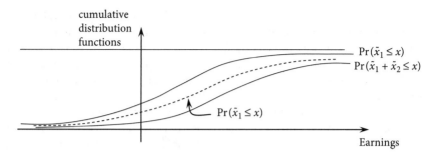

Figure 4.12

the results of these simulations gives a good approximation of the cumulative distribution function of the variables of interest, as if we had accumulated a large number of empirical observations.

Consider as an illustration the case of a plane manufacturer who wants to invest in a new plant to develop a new model of plane. The characteristics of the project are:

- overall investment: $1.5 billion
- time to build the plant: 2 years
- time to develop and build the first prototypes: 3 years

Identification of risks:

- Currency risk: fluctuation of the euro/dollar exchange rate
- Exogenous risk: fire or property damage in the plant during a 5-year period
- Economic risk: possibility of a recession that can reduce the demand from airlines
- Operational risk: social tensions with the workers of the new plant that may cause strikes and create delays

One can find adequate models for each of these risks, but it is not possible to compute an explicit formula for the global cumulative distribution function.

A Monte Carlo approach will consist of the calibration of a model for each risk and then the use of a RNG to simulate the global results. This method has been made popular by the development of personal computers that give easy access to large capacities of computation.

Note, however, that Monte Carlo simulations are also confronted with model risk: If the parameters of the model have been improperly calibrated, then the final outcome will be erroneous (*see* illustration in Section 5.4).

4.5 THE DANGERS OF THE STATIONARITY ASSUMPTION

"In a strict sense, there wasn't any risk—if the world had behaved as it did in the past."—Merton Miller, commenting on the LTCM debacle[10]

As we explain in more detail in Chapter 9, LTCM was a hedge fund that was created in 1993 to exploit arbitrage opportunities on international bond markets. For several years, it was very successful. It was able to offer huge returns (and limited risks) to its investors because of the extremely sophisticated investment models that were developed by its founders, the would-be Nobel laureates Myron Scholes and Robert Merton and the star bond trader John Meriwether. But in August 1998, the environment changed radically when Russia defaulted on its sovereign debt. The sophisticated models of LTCM revealed being disastrous in this new environment: In less than a month, LTCM lost almost all its equity capital, forcing a rescue package coordinated by the New York Fed.

This complete inaccuracy of sophisticated probabilistic models, even when they have been carefully designed and calibrated by some of the best risk specialists, is a recurrent feature of financial crises. Consider, for example, the models used by Credit Rating Agencies, for the rating of structured products generated by the securitization of subprime mortgages. Some of these models completely ignored the possibility that real estate prices could fall simultaneously in all U.S. regions, on the grounds that such an event had never occurred in the recent past!

In fact, the sophisticated probabilistic models used in finance rely too much on the assumption that the environment is stationary: They assume that the world will always behave as it has in the past. This assumption works well for lab experiments and casino games, but it is largely inaccurate for economic environments, especially in the medium-to-long run. Even if the best economic models typically provide good forecasts[11] in the short run, they fail to do so for longer horizons, in a way that is very reminiscent of weather forecast models. The best approach for modeling financial risk seems to be the use of "regime shifting" models whereby the environment is described by a finite set of possible scenarios. In each of these scenarios, risks can be quantified with a reasonable accuracy, but there is always a possibility that a new scenario (or regime) prevails. If sufficiently large data sets are available, one may try to assess the probability of such regime changes. However, in most situations, it is probably more reasonable to adopt the approach proposed by Knight and consider that the probability of these regime changes cannot really be quantified. A prudent modeling then is to use "Worst-Case Scenarios"—that is, incorporating a further branch to the event tree to which no probability is assigned but that can be taken into account in the decision-making process of the firm. Thus, aside from the most likely scenarios that can be assigned a subjective probability, and thus incorporated in the expected present value computation (*see* Chapter 4 for detail), the decision maker will be alerted to the consequences of his/her choice, should an unlikely but catastrophic event occur.

5   Statistical Risk Measures

In practice it is too complex to work with the entire distribution function of losses. This is why several types of risk measures have been designed to summarize relevant information about risks. These measures were developed by mathematicians and actuaries. They are widely used by risk practitioners in finance, insurance, and risk management. The simplest of these measures are:

- The expected loss, computed as the mean (or expectation) of $\tilde{x}$: $\mathcal{E}[\tilde{x}]$
- The variance of $\tilde{x}$: var $[\tilde{x}]$
- The linear correlation between two risks, $\tilde{x}_1$ and $\tilde{x}_2$: cor $(\tilde{x}_1, \tilde{x}_2)$
- The Value at Risk of $\tilde{x}$ at level α: $VaR_\alpha[\tilde{x}]$.

More recently, statisticians have proposed more sophisticated tools, such as copulas or abstract risk measures. This chapter successively describes these different measures and shows how they can be used to derive some simple rules for risk management. It also illustrates their dangers, when they are used without precaution. A mathematical appendix provides an introduction to extreme value theory.

5.1 THE EXPECTATION OR MEAN

For simple risks, the size of the loss L (if it occurs) is perfectly anticipated. Then the expected loss (denoted by the symbol $\mathcal{E}(\tilde{x})$) equals the probability of loss multiplied by the size of the loss, as illustrated by Figure 5.1.

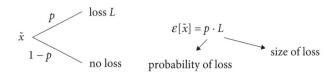

Figure 5.1

For example, the simplest credit risk models assume a fixed Loss Given Default on a loan, implying a simple formula for expected loss:

$$\text{Expected Loss} = (\text{Probability of Default}) \times (\text{Loss Given Default}).$$

Using standard acronyms, this becomes: $EL = PD \times LGD$.

For complex risks, the expected loss is equal to the probability of loss multiplied by the average loss. When the distribution of losses in discrete, the expected loss is the sum of all possible losses multiplied by their respective probabilities.

Example 1: *Expected loss of a binomial distribution.* Take the binomial distribution $B(3, 0.1)$ considered in Box 4.4 of Chapter 4 (three loans of nominal 1 and probability of default 10%). Because of the assumption of zero recovery rate, the LGD is just equal to the number of defaults (that can be 1, 2, or 3). Thus, the expected loss is:

$$\mathcal{E}(\tilde{x}) = \Pr(1 \text{ default}) + 2\Pr(2 \text{ defaults}) + 3\Pr(3 \text{ defaults})$$

$$= 24.3 + (2 \times 2.7) + (3 \times 0.01) = 30\%.$$

For a general loss size L and binomial distribution $B(n, p)$, the formula becomes

$$\mathcal{E}(\tilde{x}) = L \sum_{i=1}^{n} i \binom{n}{i} p^i (1-p)^{n-i}.$$

A simple computation shows that $\mathcal{E}(\tilde{x})$ is equal to npL.

When the distribution of losses is continuous the expected loss is computed by the following integral:

$$\mathcal{E}[\tilde{x}] = \int x f(x) dx,$$

where $f(\cdot)$ is the density function of the risk.

Example 2: *Computation of the actuarial premium for an insurance contract.* If $\tilde{x}$ represents the claim on an insurance contract, the actuarial premium on the contract is equal by definition to the expectation of $\tilde{x}$. For example, if the probability of accident is p and the size of the claim has an exponential distribution of parameter λ, we have:

$$f(x) = p\left[\lambda e^{-\lambda x}\right], \text{ for } x > 0.$$

$$\mathcal{E}(\tilde{x}) = p \int_0^\infty \lambda x e^{-\lambda x} dx,$$

or

$$\mathcal{E}(\tilde{x}) = \frac{p}{\lambda}.$$

$L = \frac{1}{\lambda}$ is thus the average loss (conditionally on the occurrence of the risk), and the actuarial premium is the product of L by the probability of accident p.

Numerical Example:

Recall Example 1 of windshield insurance in Chapter 4: the probability of accident p is estimated by the past frequency of claims $p = 15\%$. The average loss is $L = 800$ (in \$). The actuarial premium is

$$\pi = 15\% \times 800 = 120.$$

The first rule of risk management is to ensure that **expected losses are sufficiently provisioned:**

Basic Rule n° 1 (one-period version): The first basic rule of risk management is that provisions should be (at least) equal to expected losses.

This condition ensures that, on average, the firm will have enough reserves to cover future losses. The justification for this rule can be found in a mathematical result that lies at the heart of premium computation in actuarial calculus—namely, the law of large numbers. This result applies to large portfolios of risks $\tilde{x}_1, \cdots, \tilde{x}_n$ that are **mutually independent**[1] and **identically distributed**. We first explain the meaning of these two assumptions:

The random variables $\tilde{x}_i$ and $\tilde{x}_j$ are mutually independent when the **joint** distribution function $F_{ij}(x_i, x_j)$ defined as the probability that $\tilde{x}_i \leq x_i$ and $\tilde{x}_j \leq x_j$ is for all (x_i, x_j) the **product** of the **marginal** distribution functions $F_i(x_i) = \Pr(\tilde{x}_i \leq x_i)$ and $F_j(x_j) = \Pr(\tilde{x}_j \leq x_j)$:

$$F_{ij}(x_i, x_j) = F_i(x_i) F_j(x_j).$$

The random variables $\tilde{x}_i$ and $\tilde{x}_j$ are identically distributed when their distribution functions are identical: for all x,

$$F_i(x) = F_j(x).$$

The intuitive meaning of the LLN is clearly illustrated by a simple experiment. If one draws repeatedly a fair coin, the probability that heads and tails do not become equally frequent (as the number of draws goes to infinity) is zero. To obtain a formal statement, let us introduce some notation. Because all $\tilde{x}_i$ are identically distributed, they have the same expectation, which we denote $\mu : \mu = \mathcal{E}(\tilde{x}_i)$. Denote the average loss by $\bar{X}_n = \frac{\tilde{x}_1 + \tilde{x}_2 + \cdots \tilde{x}_n}{n}$. $\bar{X}_n$ also has the same expectation:

$$\mathcal{E}(\bar{X}_n) = \frac{\mathcal{E}(\tilde{x}_1) + \mathcal{E}(\tilde{x}_2) + \cdots \mathcal{E}(\tilde{x}_n)}{n} = \mu.$$

Now the precise meaning of the LLN is that the probability that $\bar{X}_n$ does not converge to μ, when n tends to infinity, is zero.[3]

BOX 5.1 ∎ The Law of Large Numbers (LLN)

The average loss from a portfolio of n independent and identically distributed risks with finite variance[2] converges with probability one to the expectation of these risks when the number of risks, n, becomes arbitrarily large.

This is the mathematical formulation of an important property that constitutes the basis of traditional insurance activities: by having a large portfolio of independent risks, an insurance company decreases the uncertainty on its average liability.

In a multiperiod context, future losses (or gains) have to be discounted. Consider, for example, a multiperiod insurance contract. The future claims on this contract (that will have to be paid by the insurer) can be represented by a sequence of random variables $\tilde{x}_1, \tilde{x}_2, \ldots, \tilde{x}_T$ at dates $t = 1, 2, \ldots, T$. The insurance company wants to compute the minimum provision that has to be kept in reserve at date 0 to cover the average losses over the whole life of the contract. If r denotes the actualization rate that is used to evaluate the remuneration of the reserves of the company, the average losses of period t will be covered by a provision $\mathcal{E}\left(\frac{\tilde{x}_t}{(1+r)^t}\right)$ at date zero.

By adding these terms from $t = 1$ to $t = T$, we obtain the Expected Present Value (EPV) of futures losses:

$$\text{Expected Present Value} = \mathcal{E}\left[\frac{\tilde{x}_1}{1+r} + \frac{\tilde{x}_2}{(1+r)^2} + \cdots + \frac{\tilde{x}_T}{(1+r)^T}\right].$$

Thus, we obtain the general formulation of Basic Rule n° 2:

Basic Rule n° 1 (general version): Provisions for future losses should be at least equal to the EPV of these future losses.

Example 3: *Computation of the default spread on a loan.* Consider a one-period loan of volume V, with nominal rate R, probability of default PD and expected loss given default LGD, as illustrated by Figure 5.2.

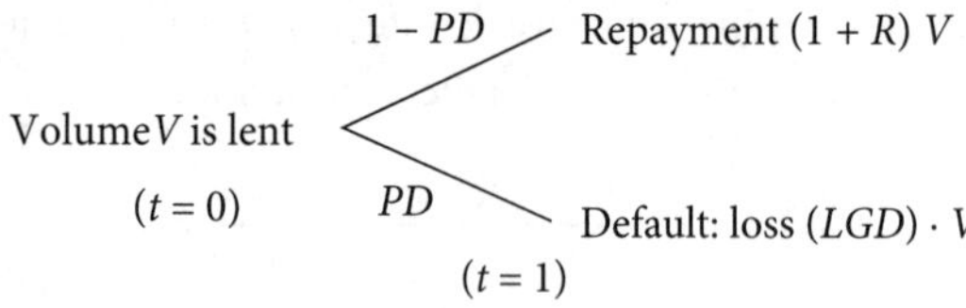

Volume V is lent

$(t = 0)$ PD

$1 - PD$ — Repayment $(1 + R) V$

Default: loss $(LGD) \cdot V$

$(t = 1)$

Figure 5.2

The expected present value of future repayments from this loan can be computed easily:

$$EPV = \frac{V}{1+r}(1+R)(1 - PD \times LGD).$$

This EPV corresponds to the break-even point of the bank that grants the loan. Assuming that the bank's operating expenses are small, the EPV of the future repayments is indeed the maximum amount that can lent by the bank without losing money in expectation. If competition on the loan market is fierce, banks' profits will be driven down to almost zero and this expected present value will approximately equal the volume of the loan:

$$EPV \sim V,$$

leading to the condition :

$$(1 + R)(1 - PD \times LGD) \sim 1 + r.$$

When PD is small, this condition can be approximated further by a simpler condition:

$$R \sim r + PD \times LGD.$$

Thus, up to a first-order approximation, the competitive default spread $R - r$ is equal to the product of the probability of default PD by the expected loss given default LGD.

Numerical Example:

Take $r = 5\%$, $PD = 1\%$ and $LGD = 20\%$. The exact formula for R is

$$R = \frac{1 + r}{1 - PD \times LGD} - 1 = \frac{1.05}{1 - 0.002} - 1 = 5.21\%.$$

The exact spread $R - r$ is thus of 21 basis points, whereas the approximation $PD \times LGD$ gives 20 basis points.

5.2 THE VARIANCE

Variance is the simplest measure of the dispersion of losses (or gains): it is the expectation of the square of the deviation of $\tilde{x}$ from its mean $\mathcal{E}(\tilde{x})$ as illustrated by Figure 5.3

$$\text{var}\,[\tilde{x}] = \mathcal{E}\left[\{\tilde{x} - \mathcal{E}(\tilde{x})\}^2\right] = \int [x - \mathcal{E}(\tilde{x})]^2 f(x)\,dx.$$

It is always non-negative and zero only when $\tilde{x}$ is completely concentrated in $\mathcal{E}(\tilde{x})$ and therefore not random. It should not be confused with the Value at Risk (VaR), which we present in Section 5.5.

Standard deviation is the square root of the variance: $\sigma = \sqrt{\text{var}\,[\tilde{x}]}$.

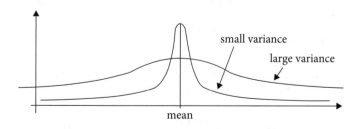

small variance

large variance

mean

Figure 5.3 Comparison of variances for two distributions with the same mean.

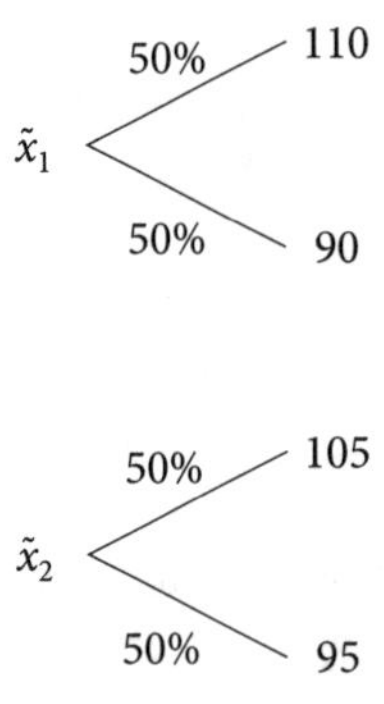

$$50\% \diagup 110 \qquad \mathcal{E}[\tilde{x}_1] = 100$$

$$\tilde{x}_1 <$$

$$50\% \diagdown 90 \qquad \begin{array}{l} \text{var}[\tilde{x}_1] = \frac{1}{2}(110 - 100)^2 + \frac{1}{2}(90 - 100)^2 = 100 \\ \sigma_1 = \sqrt{100} = 10 \end{array}$$

$$50\% \diagup 105 \qquad \mathcal{E}[\tilde{x}_2] = 100$$

$$\tilde{x}_2 <$$

$$50\% \diagdown 95 \qquad \begin{array}{l} \text{var}[\tilde{x}_2] = \frac{1}{2}(105 - 100)^2 + \frac{1}{2}(95 - 100)^2 = 25 \\ \sigma_2 = \sqrt{25} = 5 \end{array}$$

Figure 5.4

Numerical Example:

Consider the example of two simple risks as in Figure 5.4:

They have the same mean: $\mathcal{E}(\tilde{x}_1) = \mathcal{E}(\tilde{x}_2) = 100$, *but* $\tilde{x}_1$ *is more dispersed than* $\tilde{x}_2$. *Thus,* $\tilde{x}_1$ *has a larger variance (and a larger standard deviation).*

The second basic rule of risk management (in its simplest form) is that **the firm should keep, as a protection against bad luck, a capital buffer at least equal to the product of the standard deviation of this risk with a safety coefficient determined in advance:**

Basic Rule n° 2: The second basic rule of risk management is that a minimum level of capital E should be kept as a buffer against unexpected losses. This minimum level (called economic capital) is equal to a multiple s of the standard deviation of the portfolio of risks: $E \geq s\sigma$. The number s is called the safety coefficient. It is chosen by the firm.[4]

This basic rule can be justified by Chebyshev's inequality, which gives a (conservative) estimate of the probability that losses $\tilde{x}$ exceed the sum of provisions $\mathcal{E}(\tilde{x})$ (expected losses) and the equity capital buffer E. Chebyshev's inequality is:

$$\Pr[\tilde{x} \geq \mathcal{E}(\tilde{x}) + E] \leq \frac{\text{var}[\tilde{x}]}{E^2} \qquad \text{[Chebyshev's inequality]}$$

The left-hand side of this inequality represents the probability that losses exceed provisions plus capital E. Thus, if $E \geq 10\sigma$, then:

$$\Pr[\tilde{x} \geq \mathcal{E}(\tilde{x}) + E] \leq \frac{\text{var}[\tilde{x}]}{E^2} = \frac{\sigma^2}{E^2} \leq \left(\frac{1}{10}\right)^2 = 1\%.$$

This inequality shows that the probability that the firm defaults (this occurs when losses exceed the sum of provisions $\mathcal{E}(\tilde{x})$ and capital E) can be reduced to less than 1% if the capital buffer E is at least 10σ. However, for all practical purposes, this estimate is too conservative.

A more precise estimate can be obtained if the distribution of losses is Normal (*see* Box 4.3 in Chapter 4):

$$\Pr(\tilde{x} \geq \mathcal{E}(\tilde{x}) + E) = \Pr\left(\frac{\tilde{x} - \mathcal{E}(\tilde{x})}{\sigma} \geq \frac{E}{\sigma}\right) = 1 - N\left(\frac{E}{\sigma}\right).$$

Thus, if the manager wants to limit the probability of default to less than $1 - \alpha$,

$$1 - N\left(\frac{E}{\sigma}\right) \leq 1 - \alpha,$$

then he has to hold a capital buffer E such that

$$E \geq \sigma N^{-1}(\alpha) \equiv \sigma q_\alpha. \tag{5.1}$$

q_α is called the **α quantile** of the standard Normal distribution. The table below gives some usual quantiles of the standard normal:

TABLE 5.1.   *Some Quantiles of the Standard Normal*

Threshold α	95%	99%	99.5%	99.9%
α quantile $N^{-1}(\alpha)$	1.65	2.33	2.90	3.1

The estimate of economic capital given by formula (5.1) is much smaller than the very conservative estimate deduced from Chebyshev's inequality. When $\alpha = 1\%$, for example, Chebyshev's inequality gives $E \geq 10\sigma$, whereas formula (5.1) gives $E \geq 2.33\sigma$.

Chapter 9 will show that normality assumptions are sometimes very dangerous. However, in the case of a large number of independent risks, the Normal approximation is justified by the Central Limit Theorem:

BOX 5.2   ■   The Central Limit Theorem

Consider, like in the law of large numbers, a portfolio of n independent and identically distributed risks, each having standard deviation σ. When n is large, the difference between the actual loss on the portfolio and the expected loss follows approximately a Normal distribution with mean 0 and standard deviation $\sigma\sqrt{n}$.

The Central Limit Theorem shows that normality is a good approximation for large samples of independent risks with finite variance. It also allows to adjust the level E of capital (or the safety coefficient s) to the size of the portfolio. Suppose that the objective of the firm is to guarantee its survival with probability α (say, 99%).[5] Neglecting operating expenses and financial revenues, the net income of the insurer at the end of the period will equal the sum of collected premiums nP minus the sum of all losses $\tilde{x}_1, \tilde{x}_2, \ldots, \tilde{x}_n$ on the portfolio of risks. This net income can be negative if total losses $\tilde{x}_1 + \tilde{x}_2 + \cdots + \tilde{x}_n$ exceed the sum of premiums. In this case, the insurer incurs a deficit. Failure occurs when this deficit $\tilde{y}_n$ (total losses $\tilde{x}_1 + \tilde{x}_2 + \cdots + \tilde{x}_n$ minus the sum of premiums nP) exceeds equity capital E:

$$E < \tilde{x}_1 + \tilde{x}_2 + \cdots + \tilde{x}_n - nP \equiv \tilde{y}_n. \tag{5.2}$$

If premiums are actuarially fair $(P = \mathcal{E}(\tilde{x}_1) = \mathcal{E}(\tilde{x}_2) = \ldots = \mathcal{E}(\tilde{x}_n))$, then the deficit $\tilde{y}_n$ is exactly the difference between the actual loss and the expected loss. By the Central Limit Theorem, the deficit $\tilde{y}_n$ follows approximately, when n is large, a Normal distribution with mean 0 and standard deviation $\sigma \sqrt{n}$.

To see how Normal quantiles can be used to approximate the probability of failure of the insurer, we just have to define the normalized deficit on the portfolio:

$$\tilde{Z}_n = \frac{\tilde{y}_n}{\sigma \sqrt{n}},$$

obtained by dividing the deficit $\tilde{y}_n$ by its standard deviation. The Central Limit Theorem implies that $\tilde{Z}_n$ follows approximately a standard Normal distribution. Moreover, dividing the inequality 5.2 by $\sigma \sqrt{n}$, we see that failure occurs exactly when

$$\tilde{Z}_n > \frac{E}{\sigma \sqrt{n}}.$$

Thus the probability of failure is less than $(1 - \alpha)$ whenever

$$\frac{E}{\sigma \sqrt{n}} \geq q_\alpha, \quad \text{or} \quad E \geq (q_\alpha \sqrt{n})\sigma.$$

Numerical Example:

Go back to Example 1 (windshield insurance) in Chapter 4. The probability of accident is $p = 15\%$ and the loss in case of accident is $L = \$800$. The variance of the loss is $\sigma^2 = pL^2 - p^2 L^2 = p(1 - p)L^2$. Thus, the standard deviation is $\sigma = \sqrt{p(1 - p)}L \sim \$286$. Consider a portfolio of n independent risks. To guarantee a probability of survival of $\alpha = 99\%$, the equity capital buffer should be at least

$$E = N^{-1}(\alpha)\sigma \sqrt{n} = 2.33 \times 286\sqrt{n} \sim \$665\sqrt{n}.$$

The following table shows the impact of **mutualizing** risks (i.e., increasing n) on economic capital per risk (i.e., $\frac{E}{n}$).

We see that $\frac{E}{n}$, the economic capital per risk, decreases very fast when the number of risks grows. This is a first illustration of the mutualization principle: a collective management of risks reduces the variance of average losses. This principle (and its limits) are developed in Section 5.6.

TABLE 5.2. *The Impact of Mutualizing Risks*

Number of risks (n)	100	10.000
Economic capital per risk $\left(\dfrac{E}{n}\right)$ in \$	66.5	6.65

The law of large numbers allows to compute the safety coefficient s as a function of the size n of the portfolio and the target probability of survival α. Chapter 6 extends this approach by presenting Ruin Theory and how it can be used to compute the economic capital of a firm, defined as the "adequate" amount of equity capital that the firm should maintain for covering it risky activities.

5.3 LINEAR CORRELATION

With the exception of very special cases, risks of losses on different industrial or financial activities cannot be modeled as statistically independent. This means that the joint distribution of these risks is not simply equal to the product of the marginal distributions. Consider, for simplicity, the case of two risks, $\tilde{x}_1$ and $\tilde{x}_2$. The joint distribution of these two risks is

$$F(x_1,x_2) = \Pr\{\tilde{x}_1 \leq x_1, \tilde{x}_2 \leq x_2\},$$

whereas the marginal distributions are

$$F_i(x_i) = \Pr\{\tilde{x}_i \leq x_i\}, \quad i = 1,2.$$

By definition, $\tilde{x}_1$ and $\tilde{x}_2$ are said to be statistically independent whenever the joint distribution is the product of the two marginals:

$$F(x_1,x_2) = F_1(x_1)F_2(x_2).$$

However if $\tilde{x}_1$ and $\tilde{x}_2$ are not independent, then this property is not true.

Statisticians have traditionally used simple measures of dependence, such as the covariance, defined as

$$\mathrm{cov}\,(\tilde{x}_1, \tilde{x}_2) = \mathcal{E}(\tilde{x}_1 \tilde{x}_2) - \mathcal{E}(\tilde{x}_1)\mathcal{E}(\tilde{x}_2).$$

This covariance is a number that is zero when $\tilde{x}_1$ and $\tilde{x}_2$ are independent. This number can vary between $-\sigma(\tilde{x}_1)\sigma(\tilde{x}_2)$ and $+\sigma(\tilde{x}_1)\sigma(\tilde{x}_2)$, where $\sigma(\tilde{x}_i)$ denotes the standard deviation of $\tilde{x}_i$ ($i = 1,2$). It is therefore natural to norm this measure by dividing it by the product of the two standard deviations. We obtain the (linear) correlation between $\tilde{x}_1$ and $\tilde{x}_2$:

$$\rho(\tilde{x}_1, \tilde{x}_2) = \frac{\mathrm{cov}\,(\tilde{x}_1, \tilde{x}_2)}{\sigma(\tilde{x}_1) \cdot \sigma(\tilde{x}_2)} = \frac{\mathcal{E}(\tilde{x}_1 \tilde{x}_2) - \mathcal{E}(\tilde{x}_1)\mathcal{E}(\tilde{x}_2)}{\sigma(\tilde{x}_1) \cdot \sigma(\tilde{x}_2)}.$$

This coefficient varies between -1 and $+1$.

To understand the meaning of the covariance and the linear correlation, consider the linear regression of $\tilde{x}_2$ on $\tilde{x}_1$ in the simple case of distributions that have a zero mean: $\mathcal{E}(\tilde{x}_1) = \mathcal{E}(\tilde{x}_2) = 0$. This linear regression is by definition the multiple $a^*\tilde{x}_1$ of the random variable $\tilde{x}_1$ that minimizes the expected squared deviation with $\tilde{x}_2$—that is, $\mathcal{E}([\tilde{x}_2 - a\tilde{x}_1]^2)$. By developing the square and using the linearity of expectations, this expected square deviation is equal to

$$\varphi(a) = \mathcal{E}(\tilde{x}_2^2) - 2a\mathcal{E}(\tilde{x}_1\tilde{x}_2) + a^2\mathcal{E}(\tilde{x}_1^2) = \sigma^2(\tilde{x}_2) - 2a\mathcal{E}(\tilde{x}_1\tilde{x}_2) + a^2\sigma^2(\tilde{x}_1).$$

The minimum of this expression is obtained when the derivative of φ is zero:

$$\varphi'(a) = -2\mathcal{E}(\tilde{x}_1\tilde{x}_2) + 2a\sigma^2(\tilde{x}_1) = 0.$$

The value a^* that satisfies this property—namely:

$$a^* = \frac{\mathcal{E}(\tilde{x}_1\tilde{x}_2)}{\sigma^2(\tilde{x}_1)}$$

is by definition the regression coefficient of $\tilde{x}_2$ on $\tilde{x}_1$.

When $\mathcal{E}(\tilde{x}_1) = \mathcal{E}(\tilde{x}_2) = 0$, and $\sigma(\tilde{x}_1) = \sigma(\tilde{x}_2)$, this coefficient is also equal to $\rho(\tilde{x}_1, \tilde{x}_2)$. Thus, when $\tilde{x}_1$ and $\tilde{x}_2$ have the same variance, the linear correlation between $\tilde{x}_1$ and $\tilde{x}_2$ can be interpreted as the coefficient of the linear regression of $\tilde{x}_2$ on $\tilde{x}_1$. Now if we insert the value of a^* in the expression of the expected square deviation $\varphi(a)$, we find:

$$\min_a \mathcal{E}((\tilde{x}_2 - a\tilde{x}_1)^2) = \varphi(a^*) = [1 - (a^*)^2]\sigma^2(\tilde{x}_2),$$

where we have used again the property that $\sigma^2(\tilde{x}_1) = \sigma^2(\tilde{x}_2)$. We find that the fraction of the variance of $\tilde{x}_2$ that remains unexplained by its linear regression on $\tilde{x}_1$—namely, $\frac{\varphi(a^*)}{\sigma^2(\tilde{x}_2)}$—is exactly $1 - \rho^2(\tilde{x}_1, \tilde{x}_2)$. This can be zero only when $\rho(\tilde{x}_1, \tilde{x}_2)$ is equal to ± 1 (perfect correlation between $\tilde{x}_1$ and $\tilde{x}_2$). By contrast, it is one when $\rho(\tilde{x}_1, \tilde{x}_2) = 0$ ($\tilde{x}_1$ and $\tilde{x}_2$ are uncorrelated). To some extent, the explanatory power of the linear regression of $\tilde{x}_2$ over $\tilde{x}_1$ is thus measured by $\rho^2(\tilde{x}_1, \tilde{x}_2)$.

A very useful property of linear correlations is that they allow us to compute the variance of a portfolio of risks by a simple quadratic formula. Consider, for example, a portfolio with θ_1 units of $\tilde{x}_1$ and θ_2 units of $\tilde{x}_2$. We have:

$$\text{var}\,(\theta_1\tilde{x}_1 + \theta_2\tilde{x}_2) = \theta_1^2\text{var}\,(\tilde{x}_1) + 2\theta_1\theta_2\,\text{cov}\,(\tilde{x}_1, \tilde{x}_2) + \theta_2^2\text{var}\,(\tilde{x}_2).$$

The matrix $V = \begin{pmatrix} \text{var}\,(\tilde{x}_1) & \text{cov}\,(\tilde{x}_1, \tilde{x}_2) \\ \text{cov}\,(\tilde{x}_1, \tilde{x}_2) & \text{var}\,(\tilde{x}_2) \end{pmatrix}$ is called the variance–covariance matrix of $(\tilde{x}_1, \tilde{x}_2)$. It allows to write the variance of the portfolio $\theta_1\tilde{x}_1 + \theta_2\tilde{x}_2$ in a synthetic way:

$$\text{var}\,(\theta_1\tilde{x}_1 + \theta_2\tilde{x}_2) = (\theta_1, \theta_2)\,V\begin{pmatrix}\theta_1 \\ \theta_2\end{pmatrix} = \theta^t V\theta,$$

where $\theta^t = (\theta_1, \theta_2)$ is the transposed (row) vector of the column vector $\theta = \begin{pmatrix}\theta_1 \\ \theta_2\end{pmatrix}$.

In the case where $\tilde{x}_1$ and $\tilde{x}_2$ have the same variance σ^2 and ρ denotes the correlation between $\tilde{x}_1$ and $\tilde{x}_2$, the formula becomes

$$\text{var}\,(\theta_1\tilde{x}_1 + \theta_2\tilde{x}_2) = \sigma^2\left(\theta_1^2 + 2\theta_1\theta_2\rho + \theta_2^2\right).$$

For example, if $\theta_1 = \theta_2 = 1/2$, we find

$$\mathrm{var}\left(\frac{\tilde{x}_1 + \tilde{x}_2}{2}\right) = \frac{\sigma^2}{2}(1+\rho) \leq \sigma^2,$$

with equality only when $\rho = 1$ (perfect correlation). Thus, the variance of a diversified portfolio $\frac{\tilde{x}_1 + \tilde{x}_2}{2}$ is always smaller than that of each separate risk $\tilde{x}_1$ or $\tilde{x}_2$.

This formula is the basis of the diversification principle that is discussed in detail in Section 5.6. However, this principle relies on the presumption that the variance of a portfolio is a good measure of its risk. As we explain in detail in Chapter 9, this is true for Gaussian risks, which are stable by linear combinations and also are completely characterized by their mean and variance.[6] This property is not true for more general distributions of practical importance (*see* Section 5.7). In the same fashion, using covariance and linear correlation to measure statistical dependence is correct for Gaussian distributions but can be completely misleading for more general distributions. These two important remarks are developed in Section 5.6 below. Before this, we need to give the definition of a multivariate Normal distribution:

Definition 5.1. *Multivariate Normal Distribution*
A random vector $\tilde{x}$ in $\mathbb{R}^n$ has a multivariate Normal distribution with mean vector μ and (non-singular) variance–covariance matrix V if it has a density on $\mathbb{R}^n$-given by:

$$f(x_1, x_2, \ldots, x_n) = \frac{1}{\sqrt{(2\pi)^n \det V}} \exp -\frac{1}{2}(x-\mu)^t V^{-1}(x-\mu),$$

where V^{-1} is the inverse of matrix V and $\det V$, its determinant.

For multivariate Normal distributions, the linear correlation is a simple and adequate measure of statistical dependence. Consider, for example, the computation of the economic capital that is needed to cover losses on a portfolio $\tilde{x}_1 + \tilde{x}_2$ of two identical risks with means 0, variance σ^2 and correlation ρ. If the couple $(\tilde{x}_1, \tilde{x}_2)$ is Normal, the computation is easy:

$$\mathrm{var}\,(\tilde{x}_1 + \tilde{x}_2) = 2\sigma^2(1+\rho).$$

Thus, for any safety level α, the economic capital given by the LLN (*see* Box 5.1) is

$$E = \sqrt{\mathrm{var}\,(\tilde{x}_1 + \tilde{x}_2)}N^{-1}(\alpha) = \sigma\sqrt{2(1+\rho)}N^{-1}(\alpha),$$

to be compared with formula (5.1), which gives the economic capital needed to cover each risk separately (at the same level α):

$$E_1 = E_2 = \sigma N^{-1}(\alpha).$$

Assessing E is thus easy: it is enough to compute the coefficient ρ of the regression of $\tilde{x}_2$ on $\tilde{x}_1$ (the correlation of $\tilde{x}_1$ and $\tilde{x}_2$) and multiply the stand-alone capital by $\sqrt{2(1+\rho)}$.

BOX 5.3 ■ For Multivariate Normal Distributions Zero Correlation Implies Independence

Consider a bivariate Normal $(\tilde{x}_1, \tilde{x}_2)$, assumed for simplicity to have zero means and unit variances. Its variance–covariance matrix is $V = \begin{pmatrix} 1 & \rho \\ \rho & 1 \end{pmatrix}$, where ρ is the linear correlation between $\tilde{x}_1$ and $\tilde{x}_2$. Thus, $\det V = 1 - \rho^2$ and $V^{-1} = \frac{1}{1-\rho^2} \begin{pmatrix} 1 & -\rho \\ -\rho & 1 \end{pmatrix}$. By the above definition, the joint density of $(\tilde{x}_1, \tilde{x}_2)$ is:

$$f(x_1, x_2) = \frac{1}{2\pi\sqrt{1-\rho^2}} \exp - \frac{1}{2(1-\rho^2)} (x_1^2 - 2\rho x_1 x_2 + x_2^2).$$

By definition, $\tilde{x}_1$ and $\tilde{x}_2$ are independent if and only if their joint density can be written as the product of the two marginals $f_1(x_1)f_2(x_2)$. The above density satisfies this property if and only if $\rho = 0$. In this case indeed:

$$f(x_1, x_2) = \left[\frac{1}{\sqrt{2\pi}} \exp - \frac{x_1^2}{2} \right] \cdot \left[\frac{1}{\sqrt{2\pi}} \exp - \frac{x_2^2}{2} \right].$$

When $\rho \neq 0$, such a factorization of f is impossible. Thus for a (jointly) Normal distribution, independence is equivalent to zero correlation. Of course independence always implies zero correlation because in this case

$$\mathcal{E}(\tilde{x}_1 \tilde{x}_2) = \mathcal{E}(\tilde{x}_1)\mathcal{E}(\tilde{x}_2) \text{ and thus } \rho(\tilde{x}_1, \tilde{x}_2) = 0.$$

However, as shown in Subsection 5.6.1, the converse is not true for other distributions: in general, linear correlation is not a good measure of statistical dependence.

TABLE 5.3. *Impact of Correlation on Economic Capital*

Correlation (ρ)		-1	-0.5	0	0.5	1
total capital stand-alone capital	$\left(\dfrac{E}{E_1} \right)$	0	1	1.41	1.73	2

Table 5.3 illustrates how correlation influences the ratio $\frac{E}{E_1}$ of total capital over stand-alone capital E_1:

For a perfect negative correlation ($\rho = -1$) no capital is needed (perfect diversification) whereas for a perfect positive correlation ($\rho = 1$) there are no gains: $E = E_1 + E_2$. Correlation also matters for portfolio choices (see Chapter 9).

5.4 COPULAS

Suppose now that we want to model statistical dependence for a portfolio of risks $(\tilde{x}_1, \tilde{x}_2)$ for which the marginal distributions F_1 and F_2 are known and differ from the normal. This is particularly important for portfolios of loans,[7] for which marginals are easy to estimate but risks are clearly not independent. Consider, for example, the case where $\tilde{x}_1$ and $\tilde{x}_2$ are uniformly distributed on $[0,1]$: $F_1(x_1) = x_1$, $F_2(x_2) = x_2$, and denote by C the joint distribution function of the couple $(\tilde{x}_1, \tilde{x}_2)$:

$$C(x_1, x_2) = \Pr(\tilde{x}_1 \leq x_1, \tilde{x}_2 \leq x_2).$$

When $\tilde{x}_1$ and $\tilde{x}_2$ are independent, $C(x_1, x_2)$ is just the product $x_1 x_2$. But this is a very peculiar case. Many different forms of dependence can occur, associated to different types of functions C. However, C is not completely arbitrary, because it is a bivariate distribution function with uniform marginals on $[0, 1]$. This implies:

$$C \text{ is zero if } x_1 \text{ or } x_2 \text{ is equal to zero.} \tag{5.3}$$

$$\text{For all } y, \ C(y, 1) = C(1, y) = y. \tag{5.4}$$

Moreover, when C is differentiable, it is equal to the integral of its derivative, and we can write:

$$C(x_1, x_2) = C(x_1, x_2) - C(0, x_2) = \int_0^{x_1} \frac{\partial C}{\partial x_1}(t_1, x_2)\, dt_1,$$

where the first equality results from (5.3): $C(0, x_2) = 0$. Similarly, when $\frac{\partial C}{\partial x_1}$ is differentiable, it is also equal to the integral of its derivative:

$$\frac{\partial C}{\partial x_1}(t_1, x_2) = \frac{\partial C}{\partial x_1}(t_1, x_2) - \frac{\partial C}{\partial x_1}(t_1, 0) = \int_0^{x_2} \frac{\partial^2 C}{\partial x_1 \partial x_2}(t_1, t_2)\, dt_1\, dt_2$$

where the first equality also results from (5.3): $C(x_1, 0) \equiv 0 \Rightarrow \frac{\partial C}{\partial x_1}(t_1, 0) \equiv 0$.
Thus, C can be written as the double-integral of its density:

$$C(x_1, x_2) = \int_0^{x_1} \int_0^{x_2} \frac{\partial^2 C}{\partial x_1 \partial x_2}(t_1, t_2)\, dt_1\, dt_2.$$

Because a probability density is always non-negative, we must have:

$$\text{For all } (x_1, x_2), \quad \frac{\partial^2 C}{\partial x_1 \partial x_2}(x_1, x_2) \geq 0. \tag{5.5}$$

It turns out that the three conditions (5.3), (5.4), and (5.5) fully characterize smooth copulas. For non-smooth copulas, condition (5.5) must be replaced by the following property:

$$C(b_1, b_2) + C(a_1, a_2) \geq C(b_1, a_2) + C(a_1, b_2), \tag{5.6}$$

for all $0 \leq a_1 \leq b_1 \leq 1, 0 \leq a_2 \leq b_2 \leq 1$.
The three properties (5.3), (5.4), and (5.6) characterize the set of distribution functions on $[0, 1]^2$ that have uniform marginals. As we have seen, any such distribution satisfies these three properties, but the converse is also true: For any function C that satisfies properties (5.3), (5.4), and (5.6), it is possible to find a random vector $(\tilde{x}_1, \tilde{x}_2)$ on $[0, 1]^2$ having C as its cumulative distribution functions, as well as uniform marginals.

Definition 5.2. *A bidimensional copula is a function $C : [0,1]^2 \rightarrow [0,1]$ that satisfies the following properties:*

- *C is zero if x_1 or x_2 is equal to zero. (5.3)*
- *For all y $C(y,1) = C(1,y) = y$. (5.4)*
- *For all $a_1 \leq b_1$, $a_2 \leq b_2$:*
  $C(b_1, b_2) + C(a_1, a_2) \geq C(b_1, a_2) + C(a_1 + b_2)$. (5.6)

In other words, C is a copula if and only if it is the distribution function of a random vector with uniform marginals. This tool can be used to model any type of statistical dependence between random variables $\tilde{x}_1$ and $\tilde{x}_2$ that have arbitrary marginal distributions $F_i(x_i) = \Pr(\tilde{x}_i \leq x_i)$, $i = 1, 2$. Indeed, Sklar's Theorem[8] shows that for any copula C and any couple of marginal distributions F_1 and F_2, the function $F(x_1, x_2) = C(F_1(x_1), F_2(x_2))$ is the joint distribution function of a couple of random variables $(\tilde{x}_1, \tilde{x}_2)$ having marginals F_1 and F_2. Conversely, if F is the joint distribution of $(\tilde{x}_1, \tilde{x}_2)$ and F_1, F_2 are the marginal distributions of $\tilde{x}_1, \tilde{x}_2$, the copula of $(\tilde{x}_1, \tilde{x}_2)$ is the function C defined implicitly by:

$$F(x_1, x_2) = C[F_1(x_1), F_2(x_2)].$$

So, the copula is the most general instrument that can be designed for modeling statistical dependence.[9] However, one has to find a copula $C(y_1, y_2)$ that lends itself to simple simulations. One popular example is the Gaussian copula, defined by[10]

$$C(N(x_1), N(x_2))$$

$$= \frac{1}{2\pi(1-\rho^2)} \int_{-\infty}^{x_1} \int_{-\infty}^{x_2} \exp{-\frac{1}{2(1-\rho^2)}(t_1^2 - 2\rho t_1 t_2 + t_1^2)} dt_1 \, dt_2.$$

When $\tilde{x}_1$ and $\tilde{x}_2$ are standard normal, the joint distribution is Normal with correlation ρ because by definition

$$F(x_1, x_2) = C(N(x_1), N(x_2)) = \int_{-\infty}^{x_1} \int_{-\infty}^{x_2} f(t_1, t_2) dt_1 \, dt_2,$$

where f is the Normal density given in Box 5.3. Thus, the Gaussian copula allows one to generalize the Gaussian dependence structure to situations where the marginals are not Gaussian. Other than that, the Gaussian copula does not seem to be particularly well-adapted to risk management problems. In particular, this copula gives raise to weak tail dependence and does not fit well financial and insurance data. Another copula that fits better these data is the Gumbel copula, parametrized by a number β in $(0,1)$:

$$C_\beta(u_1, u_2) = \exp\left[-\{(-\ln u_1)^{1/\beta} + (-\ln u_2)^{1/\beta}\}^\beta\right].$$

The following figure compares the scatter plot of two bivariate distributions with standard Normal marginals and correlation 0.7. The left panel corresponds to the Gaussian Copula $C_{0.7}^N$, whereas the right panel is generated by the Gumbel copula $C_{0.7}$.

We see that upper tail correlation is much more pronounced in the right panel, in conformity with most financial and insurance data. Indeed, the very "acute"

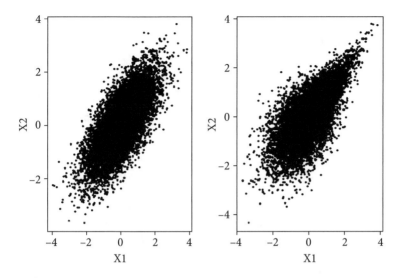

Figure 5.5 Simulated data from two bivariate distributions with same marginal distributions and correlation, but different dependence structures.[11]

BOX 5.4 ■ The rise and fall of the Gaussian copula

The Chinese Actuary David X. Li became famous in 2000 for his article "On Default Correlation: A Copula Function Approach", where he proposed to use the Gaussian copula for pricing CDO tranches. This method was so simple that it was immediately adopted by many credit risk analysts and more importantly by the major credit rating agencies. However, it turned out that the Gaussian copula could not account for the very high upper tail correlation exhibited by homeowners defaults when U.S. real estate prices started to plummet. After having been revered by the financial community, David Li became a scapegoat. He was heavily criticized for his formula, despite having repeatedly warned credit analysts against the dangers of relying too much on this formula. In an interview with the Wall Street Journal[12] in 2005 (2 years before the start of the subprime crisis), he wrote: "The current copula framework gains its popularity owing to its simplicity... However, there is little theoretical justification of the current framework...".

---

shape of the data in the "north-east" corner of the right panel (as compared with the left panel) clearly shows a high correlation in upper tail events.

5.5 THE VALUE AT RISK

The Value at Risk (VaR) is a very important concept in risk management. It was popularized in the 1990s by Dennis Weatherstone, then the CEO of the U.S. investment bank J.P. Morgan. Weatherstone did not feel confortable with the idea of going home every evening without having an assessment of the global market

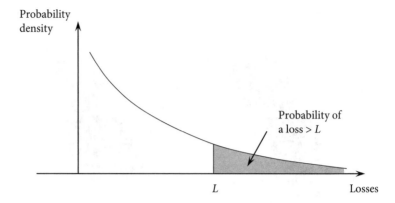

Figure 5.6 The surface of the gray area corresponds to the probability of a loss exceeding L. When this surface equals $(1 - \alpha)$, L is the VaR_α of the density.

risk taken by his bank. He wanted to have a simple measure of the bank's exposure on its entire trading portfolio. His risk managers came out with the notion of VaR. In fact, the VaR was not really new but just a particular case of the notion of Economic Capital developed by actuaries in their Ruin Theory (*see* Chapter 6). It corresponds to the classical notion of quantiles in Statistics.

For any level α (typically 95% or 99%), the *VaR* at level α is by definition the threshold $L = VaR_\alpha$ such that losses $\tilde{x}$ on this portfolio remain below VaR_α exactly with probability α:

$$\Pr(\tilde{x} \leq VaR_\alpha) = \alpha.$$

It can be constructed easily from the distribution function of losses $\tilde{x}$, defined by: $F(x) = \Pr(\tilde{x} \leq x)$. Indeed

$$\Pr(\tilde{x} \leq \text{Var } R_\alpha) = F(\text{Var } R_\alpha) = \alpha \Leftrightarrow VaR_\alpha = F^{-1}(\alpha),$$

The following two figures represent a typical distribution function F and its inverse the *VaR* (or quantile function)

The quantile function is obtained from this figure by swapping the axes:

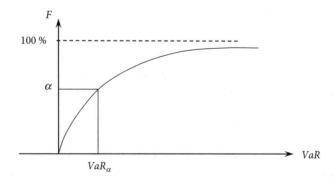

Figure 5.7 A typical cumulative distribution function F. It increases from 0 to 100%.

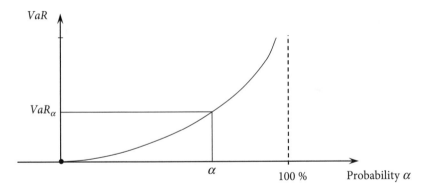

Figure 5.8 The associated quantile or *VaR* function.

Thanks to the *VaR* measure, the probability of tail events that provoke failure can be limited to a predetermined threshold $(1 - \alpha)$. This can be done by covering losses up to the level VaR_α—for example, through a minimum capital requirement.[13]

For a Normal distribution, the VaR is a linear function of the mean μ and the standard deviation σ. This is because the c.d.f. of any Normal distribution can be easily deduced from the c.d.f. of a standard normal, which we denote by $N(.)$. It suffices to substract the mean μ and divide by the standard deviation σ:

$$\Pr[\tilde{x} \leq L] = \Pr\left(\frac{\tilde{x} - \mu}{\sigma} \leq \frac{L - \mu}{\sigma}\right) \equiv N\left(\frac{L - \mu}{\sigma}\right).$$

When this number is equal to α, L is equal to VaR_α.
Thus:

$$VaR_\alpha = \mu + \sigma N^{-1}(\alpha)$$

where $N^{-1}(\alpha)$ is the $\alpha-$ quantile of the standard Normal distribution.

In accord with the Basic Rule n⁰ 1 of risk management (*see* Section 5.1), the expected loss μ corresponds to the level of provisions. Therefore the level of equity capital that is needed to complement these provisions is just $\sigma N^{-1}(\alpha)$ (Basic Rule n⁰2, Section 5.2). Thus, we can view the *VaR* method as a simple generalization of our two basic rules for risk management. When losses (or returns) are Normal, the two rules coincide exactly. The safety coefficient is equal to $N^{-1}(\alpha)$.

However *VaR* methods are more general because they allow to deal with non-Normal returns and skewed or heavy-tailed distributions. Indeed, most portfolios of risks clearly have non-Normal distributions. Using mean and variance to approximate the VaR can then be misleading. An example are heavy-tailed distributions, illustrated by the Figure 5.9:

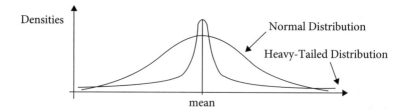

Densities

Normal Distribution

Heavy-Tailed Distribution

mean

Figure 5.9 Comparison of the densities of two distributions with same mean and variance.

BOX 5.5 ■ Heavy-Tailed Distributions

A distribution is heavy-tailed if the probability of large event (i.e., $\Pr(|\tilde{x}| > x)$ for x large) converges to zero **very slowly** when x tends to infinity, for example like $\left(\frac{1}{x}\right)^{a}$ with $a < 2$. When $a = 1$ we have the Cauchy distribution, which has the density

$$f(x) = \frac{\sigma}{\pi(\sigma^2 + x^2)}, \quad x \in \mathbf{R},$$

where σ is a parameter that measures the dispersion of the distribution (*see* Figure 5.10), like the standard deviation for a Normal distribution. However σ is **not** the standard deviation of the Cauchy distribution: this distribution has an infinite variance as illustrated in Figure 5.10.

Another example is obtained when $a = 1/2$, for which we have the Lévy distribution (which takes only positive values):

$$f(x) = \sqrt{\frac{\sigma}{2\pi x^3}} \exp\left(-\frac{\sigma}{2x}\right), \quad x > 0.$$

The Lévy distribution has an infinite mean. Benoit Mandelbrot was a pioneer in the use of heavy-tailed distributions. He showed[14] that daily changes of cotton prices were best described by an heavy-tailed distribution with $a \sim 1.7$. Another popular example is Zipf's distribution for firms sizes[15] or cities sizes.[16]

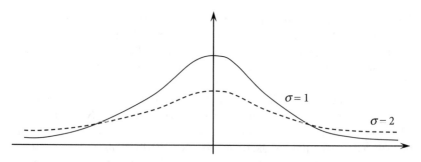

$\sigma = 1$

$\sigma = 2$

Figure 5.10 Two Cauchy distributions with different dispersion parameters: $\sigma = 1$ for the solid line, $\sigma = 2$ for the dotted line.

Numerical Example: The VaR of a Cauchy Distribution

Suppose that the losses on some portfolio have a Cauchy distribution of mean zero and dispersion parameter σ. From Box 5.5, the density of these losses is

$$f(x) = \frac{\sigma}{\pi(\sigma^2 + x^2)}.$$

The distribution function is obtained by integrating this density function on $]-\infty, x]$. It is a simple transformation of the arctan function, the reciprocal of the tangent:

$$F(x) = \int_{-\infty}^{x} \frac{\sigma\, dt}{\pi(\sigma^2 + t^2)} = \frac{1}{\pi}\left[\arctan\frac{x}{\sigma} - \arctan(-\infty)\right]$$

$$= \frac{1}{\pi}\arctan\frac{x}{\sigma} + \frac{1}{2}.$$

The VaR_α is obtained by solving the equation

$$\alpha = F(\text{VaR}_\alpha) = \frac{1}{\pi}\arctan\left(\frac{\text{VaR}_\alpha}{\sigma}\right) + \frac{1}{2}.$$

The solution is:

$$\text{VaR}_\alpha = \sigma\tan\left[\pi\left(\alpha - \frac{1}{2}\right)\right].$$

Thus, the VaR of a Cauchy distribution is proportional to the scale parameter σ, which plays the same role as the standard deviation for a Normal distribution. However, the safety coefficient that multiplies σ—namely $s_\alpha = \tan\left[\pi\left(\alpha - \frac{1}{2}\right)\right]$—is much bigger than $N^{-1}(\alpha)$, as shown by Table 5.4.

The figures given by Table 5.4 are striking. For same safety level α, the amount of capital needed to cover losses is much higher (up to hundred times when $\alpha = 99.9\%$!) for a Cauchy distribution than for a normal. Making normality assumptions when the distributions are fat-tailed can lead to catastrophes!

The following figure compares the right-tail distributions of a Normal distribution and an heavy-tailed distribution with same means and variances.[17]

Other examples where normality assumptions are inappropriate are asymmetric (or skewed) distributions for which (as illustrated by the diagram below) the probability density is not symmetric around the peak (which is called the mode of

TABLE 5.4. *Comparing* VaR_α
for Normal and Cauchy
distributions with $\sigma = 1$

VaR_α	α 95%	99%	99.9%
Normal	1.65	2.33	3.1
Cauchy	6.31	31.82	318.3

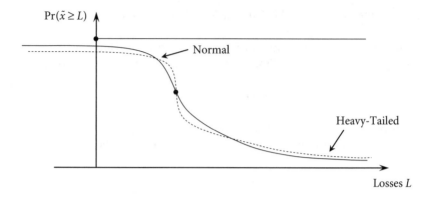

Figure 5.11 Comparison of two right-tail distributions.

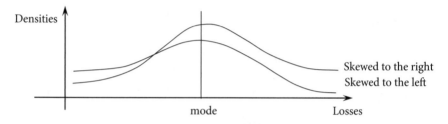

Figure 5.12 Skewed distributions.

the distribution). Here again, a Normal approximation of the VaR would be misleading: too low if the distribution is skewed to the right, too high if it is skewed to the left as illustrated by Figure 5.12.

5.6 MUTUALIZATION AND DIVERSIFICATION

We have seen how two simple statistical measures (mean and VaR) could lead to two basic rules for risk management: (*see* Figure 5.13):

- **Provisions** for future losses should equal the expected present value of these future losses.
- The level of equity **capital** should be such that the sum of capital and provisions is (at least) equal to the *VaR* computed on a prespecified horizon T for a prespecified level α. In the Normal case, this capital buffer is proportional to the standard deviation of losses.

The mutualization principle asserts that in general, a collective management of risks should decrease the amount of capital needed to cover each of these risks. There are two problems: this principle is not always valid, and the above two rules are silent about the coverage of tail risks.

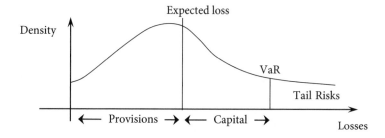

Figure 5.13 The first two rules of Risk Management.

This section starts by a presentation of the mutualization principle (SubSection 5.6.1). We then discuss the limits to mutualization (SubSection 5.6.2) and the management of tail risks (SubSection 5.6.3).

5.6.1 The Mutualization Principle

Primitive forms of insurance involved mutuals covering *a posteriori* the losses of their unlucky members (i.e., the ones that had been injured) through a contribution of the lucky ones. This is in line with the motto of Lloyd's of London, the famous reinsurer: "The contribution of the many to the misfortune of the few." Modern insurance started in the seventeenth century with the invention of statistical methods and actuarial calculus. This allowed calculation in advance of the contribution of each individual agent as a function of its risk. However, the management of the mutuality remained the first objective of insurance companies. Thus, for an insurer, the price of a risk does not exist without reference to the mutuality to which this risk belongs. To explain how this mutualization works, the following notation is useful:

- $\tilde{x}_i$ = individual loss for agent $i = 1, \ldots, n$. By assumption, its variance is the same for all i and is denoted σ^2.
- $\tilde{x} = \dfrac{1}{n} \displaystyle\sum_{i=1}^{n} \tilde{x}_i$: average loss.

Because the covariance operator is bilinear, the variance of the average loss $\tilde{x}$ is equal to the sum of the covariances of its components:

$$\mathrm{var}\,(\tilde{x}) = \mathrm{cov}\left(\frac{1}{n}\sum_{i=1}^{n}\tilde{x}_i, \frac{1}{n}\sum_{j=1}^{n}\tilde{x}_j\right) = \sum_{i=1}^{n}\sum_{j=1}^{n}\mathrm{cov}\left(\frac{\tilde{x}_i}{n}, \frac{\tilde{x}_j}{n}\right).$$

Each of these covariance terms cannot be greater than the (common) variance of $\frac{\tilde{x}_i}{n}$ and $\frac{\tilde{x}_j}{n}$—that is, $\frac{\sigma^2}{n^2}$:

$$\mathrm{cov}\left(\frac{\tilde{x}_i}{n}, \frac{\tilde{x}_j}{n}\right) \le \frac{\sigma^2}{n^2}.$$

Because there are exactly n^2 such terms, this inequality implies that

$$\text{var} (\tilde{x}) \leq \sigma^2.$$

Thus, the variance of the average loss cannot exceed the variance of individual losses. Moreover, in general, var $(\tilde{x})$ is much smaller than σ^2. For example, if the risks are independent, the variance of the average loss is n times smaller than the variance of individual losses:

$$\text{var} [\tilde{x}] = \text{var} \left[\frac{1}{n} \sum_{i=1}^{n} \tilde{x}_i \right] = \frac{1}{n^2} \sum_{i=1}^{n} \sum_{j=1}^{n} \text{cov} (\tilde{x}_i, \tilde{x}_j) = \frac{1}{n^2} \sum_{i=1}^{n} \text{var} (\tilde{x}_i) = \frac{\sigma^2}{n}.$$

This is because cov $(\tilde{x}_i, \tilde{x}_j) = 0$ when $i \neq j$, whereas cov $(\tilde{x}_i, \tilde{x}_i) = var(\tilde{x}_i) = \sigma^2$ for all i.

Thus, when economic capital is proportional to the standard deviation of losses (this is true when risks are Normal), it is reduced by diversification.[18]

Basic Rule n° 3: Mutualization of Risks
A collective management of risks (i.e., increasing n) reduces the variance of average losses and is therefore (in general) an efficient tool for risk management.

The principle of mutualization (managing many independent risks together) explains why having a sufficient size is crucial for insurance companies; it also justifies several forms of organizations such as insurance pools or coinsurance treaties. It is a particular form of the principle of managing different risks together diversification of risks.

The **diversification principle** is a variant of the mutualization principle. It recommends to spread risks by investing into different assets that are negatively correlated.

Consider, for example, a financial intermediary that needs to allocate equity capital to two business units $i = 1, 2$, which are characterized by identical loss distributions $N(\mu, \sigma^2)$. We have seen that the basic rules of risk management suggest to keep provisions μ and capital $s\sigma$ for each of these units (where $s = N^{-1}(\alpha)$ is the safety coefficient chosen by top management). Now if these two units are merged (or if their risks are managed together), diversification will generally allow savings on equity capital while maintaining the same level of safety. To measure this gain from diversification, assume indeed that the **joint** distribution of $\tilde{x}_1$ and $\tilde{x}_2$ is also Normal with covariance ρ. As we have seen above, the standard deviation of $\tilde{x}_1 + \tilde{x}_2$ is (weakly) less than 2σ:

$$\sqrt{\text{var} (\tilde{x}_1 + \tilde{x}_2)} = \sigma \sqrt{2(1 + \rho)} \leq 2\sigma.$$

BOX 5.6 ■ The Two Dimensions of Insurance

Insurance claims are always paid by the insurer **after** the premiums have been collected: this is called the **inversion of the production cycle**. Thus, the profitability of an insurer results from two dimensions:

- selection and pricing of risks (technical dimension), and
- investment of the premiums that have been collected (financial dimension).

A classical way to measure the insurer's efficiency on the first dimension is to compute the **loss ratio** LR:

$$LR = \frac{C}{P} = \frac{\text{Total amount of claims}}{\text{Total amount of premiums}}.$$

To measure the insurer's efficiency on the second dimension, one needs to split the claims according to the date of their settlement: $k = 1, \ldots, T$. Let a_k denote the proportion of total claims paid on year k. The present value of claim payments is thus:

$$PVC = \left(\sum_k \frac{a_k}{(1+r)^k} \right) C.$$

The global profitability of the insurer can be measured by the ratio of PVC over premiums

$$\frac{PVC}{P} = \left(\sum_k \frac{a_k}{(1+r)^k} \right) \left(\frac{C}{P} \right).$$

The term in the first parenthesis measures the financial component of insurance. The term in the second parenthesis measures its technical dimension.

Thus, there is need for less equity capital $\left(2s\sigma\sqrt{\frac{1+\rho}{2}} \right.$ instead of $2s\sigma$) and the (relative gain from diversification $1 - \sqrt{\frac{1+\rho}{2}}$ only depends on the covariance of $\tilde{x}_2$ and $\tilde{x}_1$, given that $\tilde{x}_1$ and $\tilde{x}_2$ have the same variance.

Covariance ρ		−1	0	0.5	1
Gains from diversification $\left(1 - \sqrt{\frac{1+\rho}{2}}\right)$		100%	29.3%	66.7%	0

5.6.2 The Limits to Mutualization

Mutualization of risks is the founding principle of insurance and a powerful tool to manage risks. It works well under two conditions: independence of risks and absence of heavy-tails. However, these conditions are not always satisfied in practice. We now show how risk practitioners have to adapt their approaches and methodologies when risks are not independent or have heavy tails.

The first case is the correlation of risks within one given type of insurance business. An obvious example is a catastrophic event that may generate many claims in one geographical area—for example, in 1992 Hurricane Andrew struck a large proportion of Florida buildings; for a property insurer in Florida, claims generated by different individual insurance contracts cannot be considered as independent and the model proposed above is no longer valid. Examples can be found in other types of insurance. Consider, for example, the pharmaceutical industry. With the development of generic products (that all have the same active molecule) two different drug manufacturers can suffer correlated claims; again, independence of risks is not satisfied.

Insurance and re-insurance practitioners have developed interesting techniques to analyze the impact of correlated risks on their portfolio and to price these correlated risks. Box 5.7 describes a methodology applicable to catastrophic events such as earthquakes, hurricanes, and tsunamis. It can easily be adapted to other risks.

The development of such techniques has allowed the insurance industry to enlarge the range of its products and offer to its clients the coverage of certain cor-related risks that were previously uninsurable. However, for risks like earthquakes and hurricanes, the zones exposed to these catastrophic risks are not always well-known. It is sometimes hardly possible to form a mutuality grouping enough risks; the consequence is an increase in the price of coverage.

Correlation between different types of insurance (or lines of business) is more difficult to handle properly. September 11th catastrophic events have illustrated the fact that different lines of business (life insurance, property insurance, avia-tion insurance, asset risks, business interruption) could be impacted by a single

---

BOX 5.7 ■ Assessment of Catastrophic Risks

Definition of geographic zones
(e.g., CRESTA zones used for earthquakes)
↓
Calculation of exposures for each zone
(values of buildings, contents, business interruption)
↓
Scenario of events
(e.g., probability of an earthquake of a given intensity)
↓
Impact of events
(% of damage caused by an earthquake of a given intensity)
↓
Premium Calculation
(for each risk or each reinsurance treaty)

event. The management of these hidden correlations is very complex for insurers and reinsurers. A solution that is currently at an early stage of development is re-insurance treaties that encompass several lines of business. We believe that a more fruitful approach would be that insurers apply to their portfolios the risk management techniques presented in this book: risk mapping, scenario planning, and Monte Carlo methods. Here again, critical size seems to be a key factor of success, as it reinforces diversification.

However diversification can have counterproductive effects when individual risks are heavy-tailed. This comes from a very surprising property of heavy-tailed distributions,[19] which we illustrate in the two particular cases that we have already studied.

Cauchy distributions: If $\tilde{x}_1$ and $\tilde{x}_2$ have independent, identical Cauchy distributions (*see* Box 5.5) with dispersion parameter σ, $\frac{\tilde{x}_1+\tilde{x}_2}{2}$ also has a Cauchy distribution with the **same** dispersion parameter σ! Thus, diversification does not help for Cauchy distributions.

Levy distributions: If $\tilde{x}_1$ and $\tilde{x}_2$ have independent, identical Levy distributions (*see* Box 5.5) with dispersion parameter σ, $\frac{\tilde{x}_1+\tilde{x}_2}{2}$ has a Levy distribution with a **double** dispersion parameter 2σ. Thus, diversification actually **hurts** for Levy distributions!

These examples illustrate that diversification, which is a fundamental tool of risk management, only works well for risks distributions that are not too far from the Normal distribution (more on this in Section 9.8).

5.6.3 The Management of Tail-Events

A final question is what happens when a catastrophe (tail-event) occurs. Most executives would argue that they should not be concerned with such events because they occur with small probabilities and, moreover, shareholders are protected by limited liability.

As we will show in Chapter 13, this attitude is consistent with (selfish) shareholder value maximization, but it hurts public interests, because these catastrophic losses will ultimately be borne by the victims or by the taxpayers. This is an example of what economists call an externality—that is, when actions taken by some economic agents hurt other economic agents. When this externality cannot be internalized (e.g., when polluting firms cannot be forced to compensate fully their victims), which is typically the case when the size of the damage exceeds the financial capacity of the firm, a collective risk management policy has to be designed, either through spontaneous cooperation between private economic agents or through regulation by the government.

Examples of cooperation between private economic agents for risk management are easy to find. If several corporations are located along the same river, they have to coordinate their environmental and waste management policies. Otherwise, if the river is polluted, public authorities may decide to stop the activity of all these firms.

Government intervention can also occur *a priori*, by deciding how risks should be allocated between different stakeholders. This is an interesting way to build an efficient risk management policy. One of the best examples is how several countries have elaborated specific insurance systems to facilitate the production of electricity through the use of civil nuclear plants.

The main obstacle to the development of civil applications of nuclear energy was the management of risks and, more specifically, the allocation of risks between all parties: designers of the plants, utility companies, and the government. Considering the enormous potential damages, it was difficult to convince any corporation to invest in such a project, as shareholders and managers considered that the amount of equity needed to cover the risk of a nuclear accident was likely to be very high and, in any case, very difficult to assess. The traditional risks carriers like insurance and re-insurance companies had no appetite for this activity for the same reasons. Another complexity came from the fact that a nuclear accident could contaminate many countries as demonstrated in 1986 by the Chernobyl accident.

Several governments worked together to design an interesting legal framework for the liability of the civil nuclear industry. This regulation was formalized in several international conventions in the early 1960s and has been revised many times since. The main ideas of this regulation are:

- to impose a strict liability on the utility company;
- to limit the amount of this liability;

BOX 5.8 ■ Re-insurance

Re-insurance is an activity by which a re-insurer (a specialized company or a direct insurer) assumes some fraction of risks underwritten by another insurer (the "cedent") in exchange for a certain compensation. The two main forms of re-insurance are: facultative re-insurance and treaty re-insurance.

- **Facultative re-insurance** considers the insurer's risks on an individual basis. The re-insurance company looks at each individual risk and determines whether to accept or decline their coverage.
- **Treaty re-insurance** is a global participation of the re-insurer in certain sections of the insurer's business as agreed by a contract called a treaty.

Re-insurance treaties specify how losses are shared between the insurer and the re-insurer. The most frequent forms of re-insurance treaties are: quota share, excess of loss, and stop loss.

- **Quota-share re-insurance:** The re-insurer covers the same percentage of all risks held by the insurer (in a specific line of business). In this case, premiums and claims are shared proportionally by the insurer and re-insurer:
- **Stop-loss re-insurance:** The re-insurer cover all losses over some threshold (the insurer's retention)
- **Excess of loss re-insurance:** The re-insurer cover all losses above a first threshold and below a second threshold.

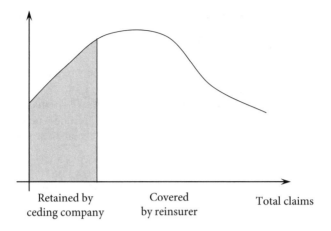

Figure 5.14 Stop-loss reinsurance.

- to limit the duration of the liability to the time needed by victims to claim for their damages;
- to impose to the utility company to cover a first tranch of its liability through insurance contracts; and
- to give a governmental and multi country warranties above this threshold.

This regulation determines the allocation of risks between all stakeholders and removes the uncertainty around liabilities. Thus, it creates the conditions for the development of an insurance market for these risks. Without some guarantee provided by the government very large or catastrophic risks would not be insurable.

Finally, an important instrument for sharing large losses is **re-insurance**. The main mechanisms of reinsurance are presented in the next box.

5.7 THE DANGERS OF USING SIMPLE RISK MEASURES

The necessities of pragmatism often force risk managers to content themselves with the simple risk measures that we have presented in this chapter: mean, variance, linear correlations, and values at risk. This section briefly points at the dangers of using these simple measures without precaution. As already mentioned, variances can be misleading measures of risks when distributions of risks are not Normal or elliptical.[20] Similarly, covariances and linear correlations can be misleading measures of statistical dependence, even when marginal distributions are normal, as soon as the joint distribution is not. In Chapter 6 we discuss in detail the dangers of the "normal" vision of the world.

5.7.1 Zero Correlation Does not Necessarily Imply Independence

It is easy to find examples of random variables that are uncorrelated but not independent. Take, for example, $\tilde{x}_1$ and $\tilde{x}_2 = \tilde{x}_1^2$ and assume that the distribution of $\tilde{x}_1$ is symmetric around 0. This implies that $\mathcal{E}(\tilde{x}_1) = \mathcal{E}(\tilde{x}_1^3) = 0$ so that

$$\mathcal{E}(\tilde{x}_1 \cdot \tilde{x}_2) = \mathcal{E}(\tilde{x}_1^3) = 0 = \mathcal{E}(\tilde{x}_1) \cdot \mathcal{E}(\tilde{x}_2).$$

What is more surprising is that this can also happen when both $\tilde{x}_1$ and $\tilde{x}_2$ are Normal (but not jointly so).

Consider the following example:[21] $\tilde{x}_1$ follows a standard normal, and $\tilde{x}_2 = \tilde{u}\tilde{x}_1$ where $\tilde{u}$ takes values $+1$ and -1 with probability $\frac{1}{2}$ and is independent from $\tilde{x}_1$. A first remark is that $\tilde{x}_2$ also follows a standard normal. This can be seen immediately by computing its distribution function:

$$\Pr(\tilde{x}_2 \leq x) = \frac{1}{2}\Pr(\tilde{x}_1 \leq x|\tilde{u} = 1) + \frac{1}{2}\Pr(-\tilde{x}_1 \leq x|\tilde{u} = -1).$$

Because $\tilde{x}_1$ and $\tilde{u}$ are independent, we have

$$\Pr(\tilde{x}_1 \leq x|\tilde{u} = 1) = \Pr(\tilde{x}_1 \leq x) = N(x)$$

and

$$\Pr(-\tilde{x}_1 \leq x|\tilde{u} = -1) = \Pr(-\tilde{x}_1 \leq x) = \Pr(\tilde{x}_1 \geq -x) = 1 - N(-x).$$

Because the Normal distribution is symmetric, we have

$$1 - N(-x) = N(x) \text{ and thus } \Pr(\tilde{x}_2 \leq x) = \frac{1}{2}N(x) + \frac{1}{2}(1 - N(-x)) = N(x).$$

Thus, both $\tilde{x}_1$ and $\tilde{x}_2$ are (separately) normal, but their **joint** distribution is not, because it is concentrated on the two lines[22] $x_2 = x_1$ and $x_2 = -x_1$. This property also implies that $\tilde{x}_2$ and $\tilde{x}_1$ cannot be independent because the conditional distribution of $\tilde{x}_2$ given $\tilde{x}_1$ can only take two values. However, $\tilde{x}_1$ and $\tilde{x}_2$ are uncorrelated. To see this, note first that

$$\mathcal{E}(\tilde{x}_1\tilde{x}_2) = \frac{1}{2}\mathcal{E}(\tilde{x}_1^2|\tilde{u} = 1) + \frac{1}{2}\mathcal{E}(-\tilde{x}_1^2|\tilde{u} = -1).$$

Again by independence of $\tilde{x}_1$ and $\tilde{u}$, we have

$$\mathcal{E}(\tilde{x}_1^2|\tilde{u} = 1) = \mathcal{E}(\tilde{x}_1^2) = 1,$$

and

$$\mathcal{E}(-\tilde{x}_1^2|\tilde{u} = -1) = -\mathcal{E}(\tilde{x}_1^2) = -1.$$

Thus, $\mathcal{E}(\tilde{x}_1 \cdot \tilde{x}_2) = 0$. Because $\mathcal{E}(\tilde{x}_1) = \mathcal{E}(\tilde{x}_2) = 0$ we have established that $\rho(\tilde{x}_1, \tilde{x}_2) = 0$. Thus, $\tilde{x}_1$ and $\tilde{x}_2$ have zero correlation but they are not independent.

5.7.2 Linear Correlations May Overestimate Diversification Benefits

Consider a portfolio of two risks where losses $(\tilde{x}, \tilde{y})$ are:

- independent and uniformly distributed on $[0, 1]$ during "normal" times,

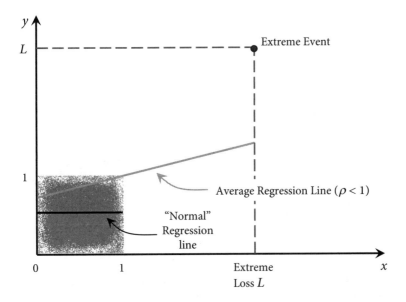

Figure 5.15 Linear correlations and extreme losses.

- perfectly correlated during crisis times (which have probability slightly above 1%), in which the loss are $L_x = L_y = L > 1$.

It is clear that the 99% VaR on each risk (on a stand alone basis) is L. To compute the economic capital needed to cover the portfolio of both risks, one might be tempted to use the "normal" method (*see* Section 5.3) and multiply L by $\sqrt{2(1+\rho)}$, where ρ is the regression coefficient of $\tilde{y}$ over $\tilde{x}$. This would be legitimate if $(\tilde{x}, \tilde{y})$ were jointly Normal and would imply a diversification gain (because $\rho < 1$, as shown in Figure 5.15). However, it is also clear from the picture that $VaR(\tilde{x} + \tilde{y}) = 2L$: if a crisis occurs (this has probability 1%), the total loss is $2L$. Thus, at the 99% level, there is absolutely no diversification gain. This example shows that using linear correlation in the computation of the VaR would suggest a (spurious) diversification gain. This illustrates the well-documented phenomenon that tail dependence (i.e., high statistical dependence during turbulent times) is much higher than "Normal" dependence (as measured by linear correlation).

5.7.3 The VaR May Violate the Diversification Principle

When risks are not jointly normal, the VaR is not always decreased by diversification. In other words, it may happen that

$$VaR(\tilde{x}_1 + \tilde{x}_2) > VaR(\tilde{x}_1) + VaR(\tilde{x}_2).$$

Consider, for example, two independent Bernoulli variables with the same distribution, described by Figure 5.16.

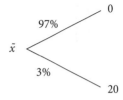

Figure 5.16

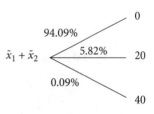

Figure 5.17

At the 95% level, $VaR(\tilde{x}_1) = VaR(\tilde{x}_2) = 0$. However, the probability of a loss on $\tilde{x}_1 + \tilde{x}_2$ is larger than 5% as shown in Figure 5.17.

Thus, $VaR(\tilde{x}_1 + \tilde{x}_2) = 20 > VaR(\tilde{x}_1) + VaR(\tilde{x}_2)$. In this example, the VaR does not satisfy the diversification principle.[23] This has motivated some mathematicians to look for alternative risk measures that always satisfy this principle. These risk measures are presented in Subsection 5.7.6.

5.7.4 The Value at Risk is Manipulable

Alfred Galichon ("The VaR at Risk" available at SSRN: http://ssrn.com/abstract= 1287807) puts forward what we consider as the most devastating critique of the VaR: by cutting **any** risk into sufficiently many pieces, one can make the total VaR not only decrease but, in fact, completely **vanish**! Risk is still there but cannot be seen anymore. The intuition behind this devastating result is remarkably simple. We are going to explain it in a few lines. Take any risk $\tilde{x}$ and compute its VaR at a certain level, say $\alpha = 95\%$. By definition:

$$VaR_\alpha = F^{-1}(\alpha),$$

where F^{-1} is the quantile function—that is, the inverse of the distribution function F. Now, cut the risk $\tilde{x}$ into 20 pieces $\tilde{x}_1,\ldots,\tilde{x}_{20}$ defined by "attachment points" associated with the 20 quantiles of $\tilde{x}$ at 5%, 10%,...up to 100%

$$\begin{cases} \tilde{x}_i = \tilde{x} \text{ if } a_{i-1} \le \tilde{x} < a_i & i = 1,\ldots,20 \\ \quad = 0 \text{ otherwise,} \end{cases}$$

where $a_0 = F^{-1}(0)$, $a_1 = F^{-1}(0.05),\ldots, a_{20} = F^{-1}(1)$. In practice, this corresponds to excess of loss re-insurance contracts or digital options. This is illustrated in Figure 5.18.

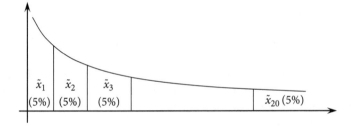

Figure 5.18 The total *VaR* vanishes when *x* is tranched into 20 digital options.

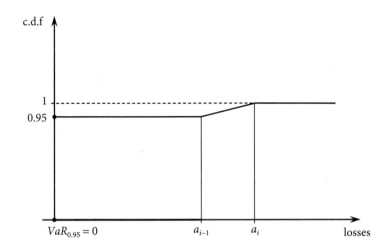

Figure 5.19

It is immediate that for all i, the probability that $\tilde{x}_i \neq 0$ is $1 - \alpha = 5\%$. Indeed, contract $\tilde{x}_i$ only loses money when the overall loss $\tilde{x}$ falls behind a_i and a_{i-1}. By the choice of the attachment points a_i and a_{i-1}, this has exactly probability 5%:

$$\Pr(\tilde{x}_i \neq 0) = F(a_i) - F(a_{i-1}) = 5\%.$$

Therefore, the probability that $\tilde{x}_i = 0$ is $\alpha = 95\%$, which means that $VaR_\alpha(\tilde{x}_i) = 0$!

To see why, consider the cumulative distribution function of losses associated with each of these contracts or options. It has the shape shown in Figure 5.19.

Indeed, the loss is zero with probability 95%, and it is equal to $\tilde{x}$ when $\tilde{x} \in (a_{i-1}, a_i)$. Thus, by definition of the Value at Risk, $VaR_{0.95}(\tilde{x}_i) = 0$.

Thus, we have been able to cut any risk $\tilde{x}$ (with an arbitrarily large VaR) into 20 risks $\tilde{x}_1, \ldots, \tilde{x}_{20}$ that have exactly a value at risk of zero! Tranching[24] is like a magician's trick: it gives you the impression that the risk has vanished, but of course it is still there! You see it initially when the VaR is measured on the whole risk $\tilde{x}$. You don't see it anymore when you compute the sum of the VaRs associated with the different pieces.

5.7.5 The Value at Risk Does Not Capture Tail-Risk

The above example shows that the VaR encourages managers to hide the risks "underneath the rug" or, more accurately, in the upper tail of the loss distribution. No event, even the most devastating one, that happens with probability less than $(1 - \alpha)$ is taken into account in VaR calculations. This is why statisticians recommend replacing the VaR by the Tail VaR, also called the Expected Shortfall. By definition, the expected shortfall at level α, denoted ES_α is equal to the conditional expectation of losses, given that they exceed VaR_α:

$$ES_\alpha = \mathcal{E}\left(\tilde{x} | \tilde{x} \geq VaR_\alpha\right)$$

$$= \frac{1}{1-\alpha} \int_{VaR_\alpha}^{\infty} x dF(x).$$

By changing variables, and using $t = F(x)$ instead of $x = VaR_t$ we see that ES_α is also equal to the average of the VaR corresponding to all thresholds t above α:

$$ES_\alpha = \frac{1}{1-\alpha} \int_\alpha^1 VaR_t \, dt.$$

This formula can be interpreted by saying that the decision maker is only concerned about tail-events that occur with a probability $t \leq 1 - \alpha$ and gives them equal weight $\frac{1}{1-\alpha}$. The expected shortfall at level α is the average VaR for all such tail-events.

Consider, for example, a uniform distribution $\tilde{x} \sim [0, L]$. L is the maximum loss and all losses smaller than L are equally likely. The associated distribution function is

$$F(x) = \frac{x}{L} \quad \text{for} \quad 0 \leq x \leq L,$$

and the quantile function is

$$VaR_\alpha(\tilde{x}) = F^{-1}(\alpha) = \alpha L.$$

The expected shortfall at level α is just

$$ES_\alpha(\tilde{x}) = \frac{1}{1-\alpha} \int_\alpha^1 tL \, dt = \frac{1+\alpha}{2} L.$$

If, for example, $\alpha = 95\%$ and $L = 1000$, $VaR_\alpha = 950$, and $ES_\alpha = 975$.

In this example, the difference between ES_α and VaR_α is really small, but this is because $\tilde{x}$ has a uniform distribution. For Normal random variables, the difference between the tail VaR or expected shortfall is more significant, but it simply amounts to increase slightly the safety coefficient (see Table 5.5).

With thicker tails, the difference can be much bigger and even infinite in the case of heavy-tailed distributions like the Cauchy or the Levy distributions (*see* Box 5.5).

More importantly, the expected shortfall cannot be manipulated easily by tranching risks as in the Galichon construction. In the example of a uniform

TABLE 5.5. *Comparison of VaR and ES for Normal random variables*

α	95%	99%	99.5%
VaR_α	1.65	2.33	2.58
ES_α	2.07	2.67	2.90

distribution on $[0, L]$, with $L = 1000$, the VaR at 95% is 950 but we saw that the total VaR on the portfolio of tranches $\tilde{x}_i = \tilde{x}\mathbf{I}\left\{\frac{(i-1)L}{20} \leq \tilde{x} \leq \frac{iL}{20}\right\}$, $(i = 1,\ldots,20)$ was zero! For the expected shortfall (ES), the manipulation does not work:

$$ES_{95\%}(\tilde{x}_i) = \frac{(i-1/2)}{20}L.$$

In this case, the expected shortfall is just the median loss. Thus, if we add these numbers for all i:

$$ES_{95\%}(\tilde{x}_1) + \cdots + ES_{95\%}(\tilde{x}_{20}) = 10L = 10,000.$$

Thus, the total expected shortfall on the portfolio of losses is actually much bigger than that on the initial risk! Contrarily to the VaR, ES discourages manipulation. This is because, contrarily to the VaR, ES satisfies the diversification principle: the ES on a portfolio is always less than the sum of the ES on the components of the portfolio. Some statisticians have tried to find other risk measures by adopting an abstract approach. They have explored the family of all risk measures that satisfy the diversification principle (which they call sub-additivity) together with other axioms, considered as reasonable. This defines the notion of coherent risk measures, which we present now.

5.7.6 Are Coherent Risk Measures the Solution?

Disappointed with the VaR, Artzner, Delbaen, Eber, and Health (1999)[25] have put forward a list of four properties that they consider reasonable for risk measures to have. Adopting a systematic approach they first define the notion of an **abstract risk measure** ρ—namely, a mapping that associates to any random variable $\tilde{x}$ a real number $\rho(\tilde{x})$. Then they call an abstract risk measure ρ **coherent** if it satisfies the four properties listed below.

For any numbers $\lambda > 0$ and n, and any random variables $\tilde{x}$ and $\tilde{y}$:

1. $\rho(\lambda\tilde{x}) = \lambda\rho(\tilde{x})$ (positive homogeneity)
2. $\rho(\tilde{x}+\tilde{y}) \leq \rho(\tilde{x})+\rho(\tilde{y})$ (sub-additivity)
3. $\tilde{x} \leq \tilde{y} \Rightarrow \rho(\tilde{x}) \leq \rho(\tilde{y})$ (monotonicity)
4. $\rho(\tilde{x}+n) = \rho(\tilde{x})+n$ (translation invariance)

For continuous distributions, the expected shortfall is the simplest example of a coherent risk measure. The more general example of spectral risk measures has been proposed by Acerbi (2002):[26] To any increasing function $g(\cdot)$, one can associate a spectral risk measure M by setting:

$$M = \int_0^1 g(t)\, VaR_t\, dt.$$

A natural interpretation of this formula is that $g(t)$ is the weight given by the decision maker to a right-tail event of probability $1 - t$. The higher t, the more extreme the event, and the higher the weight given to it. Expected shortfall at level α corresponds to a particular case of this formula, obtained by setting:

$$\begin{cases} g(t) = \frac{1}{1-\alpha} & \text{if} \quad t \geq \alpha, \\ \quad\;\; = 0 & \text{if} \quad t < \alpha. \end{cases}$$

Coherent risk measures, especially spectral ones, are very appealing to mathematicians, because they are almost as tractable as the VaR, while satisfying four properties that are reasonable from a mathematical point of view.

However these risk measures are "normative," which means that they describe how risk "should" be measured from a social perspective, say by a scientist or a regulator. Our purpose here is more "positive": how to design measures that can be useful for managing risks in the best interest of the shareholders of large corporations. Adopting this perspective, some of the axioms above are not reasonable. Take, for example, axiom 1) (positive homogeneity). From the point of view of a corporation, it does not seem reasonable to consider that managing the 10-fold multiple of a risk $10\tilde{x}$ is exactly 10 times more costly to manage than $\tilde{x}$. On the contrary, the subprime crisis has revealed that even risks that could be considered as acceptable by a given bank or insurer (on a reasonable scale) can become lethal if they are scaled up 10 times or more. Thus, the homogeneity axiom of coherent risk measures does not make much sense for a corporation. Similarly, the axiom of translation invariance may be reasonable for a mathematician or a regulator, it is certainty not for a corporate risk manager. Indeed if a very large (deterministic) loss n is added to some risk $\tilde{x}$, it is unlikely that the impact on the corporation will be additive. Most probably, it will provoke the death of the corporation, which will have exactly the same consequences for the shareholders (they will lose their stake in the company) independently of the realization of $\tilde{x}$.

Put differently, even if they are good normative measures, coherent risk measures cannot be applied fruitfully by corporate risk managers because they do not account for two basic facts of corporate life:

- shareholders have limited liability and therefore are not concerned with losses that exceed the own funds of the corporation;
- risks assessments by corporations (supposedly the motivation for constructing abstract risk measures) and subsequent risk management decisions cannot be independent of the current financial situation of the corporation—notably, its leverage and its cash position.

In Chapter 12 we show how to construct a new type of risk measures, which we call **shareholder risk measures**, that account for these two basic facts of corporate life.

APPENDIX: EXTREME VALUE THEORY

Extreme Value Theory (EVT) provides the mathematical modeling of **catastrophic** events—that is, the largest losses among a large number of observations. It is becoming equally important as the law of large numbers and the central limit theory that are the mathematical tools for modeling **averages** of a large number of observations. Modern methods of EVT are essentially based on peaks-over-threshold (POT) models that study all the observations that exceed some high threshold given *a priori*. Consider, for example, the daily losses $X_1, X_2, \ldots, X_N$ (for days $n = 1, 2, \ldots, N$), on a portfolio and assume that the random variables X_n are independent with the same distribution function $F(x) = \Pr\{X_n \leq x\}$. Because F does not depend on n, we simplify the formulas by dropping the index n: $F(x) = \Pr\{X \leq x\}$.

Our objective is to estimate the VaR and the expected shortfall on the portfolio for a given confidence level α:

$$VaR_\alpha = F^{-1}(\alpha)$$

$$ES_\alpha = \frac{\int_\alpha^1 VaR_t \, dt}{1 - \alpha} = \mathcal{E}[X | X > VaR_\alpha].$$

The Distribution of Excess Losses

For a high threshold u, the distribution of excess losses over u is defined by:

$$F_u(x) = \Pr[X - u \leq x | X > u].$$

This distribution of excess losses is therefore a conditional probability that can be computed by the Bayes Formula:

$$\Pr[A|B] = \frac{\Pr(A \text{ and } B)}{\Pr B}.$$

Using this formula, F_u can be easily deduced from F, the distribution function of X:

$$F_u(x) = \frac{\Pr[u < X \leq u + x]}{\Pr[X > u]} = \frac{F(x + u) - F(u)}{1 - F(u)}. \tag{5.7}$$

A key result in EVT is the extreme limit theorem. This theorem states that for a very large class of distributions F (including all common continuous distributions), the excess distribution F_u can be approximated, when u is large, by a generalized Pareto distribution:

$$G_{\xi,\beta}(x) = 1 - \left(1 + \frac{\xi x}{\beta}\right)^{-1/\xi} \quad \text{for } x \geq 0,$$

where ξ and β are positive[27] parameters. The case where $\xi = 0$ is also possible and corresponds to the exponential distribution:

$$G_{0,\beta}(x) = 1 - \exp\left(-\frac{x}{\beta}\right), \quad x \geq 0.$$

The parameters ξ and β can be estimated by maximum likelihood methods.

Estimating Extreme Risks

Inverting formula (5.7) allows us to compute the tail distribution of losses as a function of the distribution of excess losses F:

$$F(x + u) = [1 - F(u)]F_u(x) + F(u).$$

The extreme limit theorem allows us to approximate $F_u(x)$ by $G_{\xi,\beta}(x)$. Moreover $1 - F(u)$ can be estimated by the frequency n_u of observations that lie above u. Thus, we obtain, for u large and $x \geq 0$,

$$F(x + u) \sim n_u G_{\xi,\beta}(x) + 1 - n_u = 1 - n_u\left[1 - G_{\xi,\beta}(x)\right].$$

By inverting this formula, we can obtain an estimate of VaR_α (for $\alpha > u$)

$$\alpha = F(VaR_\alpha) \sim 1 - n_u\left[\left(1 + \frac{\xi(VaR_\alpha - u)}{\beta}\right)^{-1/\xi}\right]$$

After simplifications we get:

$$VaR_\alpha \sim u + \frac{\beta}{\xi}\left[n_u^\xi(1 - \alpha)^{-\xi} - 1\right]. \tag{5.8}$$

Similarly, ES_α can be approximated as follows. Recall that:

$$ES_\alpha = \frac{\int_\alpha^1 VaR_t\, dt}{1 - \alpha}.$$

Now, by formula (5.8):

$$VaR_t \sim u + \frac{\beta}{\xi}\left[n_u^\xi(1 - t)^{-\xi} - 1\right].$$

Thus:

$$ES_\alpha \sim u + \frac{\beta}{\xi}\left[n_u^\xi \frac{\int_\alpha^1(1 - t)^{-\xi}\, dt}{1 - \alpha} - 1\right].$$

After computing the integral we obtain:

$$ES_\alpha \sim u + \frac{\beta}{\xi}\left[n_u^\xi \frac{(1 - \alpha)^{-\xi}}{1 - \xi} - 1\right]. \tag{5.9}$$

Comparing with formula (5.8) we see that we can relate ES_α to VaR_α in a simple way. Indeed, formula (5.8) gives:

$$\frac{\beta}{\xi}n_u^\xi(1 - \alpha)^{-\xi} \sim VaR_\alpha - u + \frac{\beta}{\xi}.$$

Thus

$$ES_\alpha \sim u + \frac{1}{1 - \xi}\left[VaR_\alpha - u + \frac{\beta}{\xi}\right] - \frac{\beta}{\xi}.$$

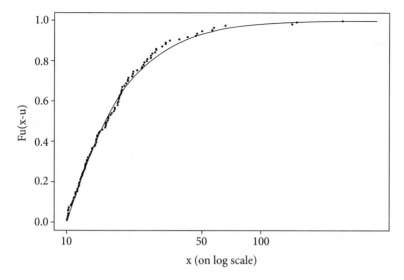

Figure 5.20 Modeling the excess distribution.

After simplifications we obtain:

$$ES_\alpha \sim \frac{1}{1 - \xi} \left[VaR_\alpha + \beta - \xi u \right].$$

McNeil (1999)[28] uses data on 2156 large industrial fire insurance claims in Denmark (sample period 1980–1990) to estimate this model. For a threshold $u = 10$ million (Danish kroner), he finds parameter estimates $\xi = 0.50$ and $\beta = 7.0$. The fit between extreme events and the general Pareto distribution is shown in Figure 5.20.

For $\alpha = 99\%$, he finds the following estimates: $VaR_\alpha \sim 27.3$ million and $ES_\alpha \sim 58.2$ million.

6   Leverage and Ruin Theory

Entrepreneurs have always tried to magnify their returns on investment by **leveraging** their positions, which means borrowing at a fixed rate a large part of their financing needs. This allows them to keep for themselves their excess returns on assets—that is, the part of these returns that exceed the fixed rate required by the lender. But leverage also magnifies the losses and thus generates default risk. In fact, many commentators have argued that one of the most important reasons behind the subprime crisis was the generalized "pressure for yield" that forced bank managers to leverage as much as they could to deliver the highest possible returns to their shareholders.

Thus, it is natural to inquire into the appropriate level of economic capital for a firm—that is, the fraction of its financing that should come from its owners. A natural tool for this is ruin theory, which was developed by actuaries to determine the economic capital of an insurance company. This economic capital is defined as minimum level of equity capital needed to ensure that the probability of ruin of the insurance company remains below some given 'acceptable' value. This theory is widely used both by risk managers, prudential regulators, and insurance/reinsurance practitioners. It is very close in spirit to the "Value at Risk" methods that were discussed in Chapter 5. All these methods may involve high-tech modeling tools, but they hinge on the same simple principles. This chapter starts by recalling the link between leverage and return on equity (6.1) and proceeds by showing how Ruin Theory can be applied to determine the economic capital needed by a bank (6.2) and an insurance company (6.3). The chapter concludes by showing the dangers of Ruin Theory, when it is used without precaution, as illustrated by the fall of the U.K. bank Northern Rock in September 2007.

6.1 LEVERAGE AND RETURN ON EQUITY

In this section, we recall the basic relation between return on equity (ROE) and leverage when default risk can be neglected. Consider the balance sheets of a firm at two different dates:

Assets A	Equity E
	Debt D

current date
$(t = 0)$

Assets A_T	Equity E_T
	Debt D_T

horizon date
$(t = T)$

Net return on assets is defined as $ROA = \frac{A_T}{A} - 1$.
Net return on equity is defined as $ROE = \frac{E_T}{E} - 1$.

As of date 0, these returns are uncertain: they are thus modeled as random variables.

Using balance sheet equalities, one can easily compute the return on equity:

$$ROE = \frac{E_T}{E} - 1 = \frac{A_T - D_T}{E} - 1 = \frac{A_T}{A}\left(\frac{A}{E}\right) - \frac{D_T}{D}\left(\frac{D}{E}\right) - 1. \qquad (6.1)$$

Leverage is usually measured by the first term between brackets—that is, the ratio λ of assets over equity:[1]

$$\lambda = \frac{A}{E}.$$

Note that $D = A - E$, so that the second term between brackets is

$$\frac{D}{E} = \lambda - 1.$$

If we denote by R the interest rate on debt we have by definition:[2] $\frac{D_T}{D} = R + 1$. After rearranging (6.1), we obtain in this case:

$$ROE = (ROA + 1)\lambda - (R + 1)(\lambda - 1) - 1.$$

Excess return on equity is thus given by:

$$\boxed{ROE - R = \lambda \cdot (ROA - R).} \qquad (6.2)$$

Formula (6.2) expresses that the (realized) excess return on equity ($ROE - R$) equals the (realized) excess return on assets ($ROA - R$) multiplied by leverage λ. Because leverage is greater than one, this formula shows that (realized) excess return on equity is **magnified** by leverage. This, of course, is also true for expected excess return on equity, which can be estimated at date $t = 0$ by the managers of the firm. By taking expectations, we see that because leverage is greater than one, the return on equity has a greater expectation μ_E than the return on assets (if the firm is profitable—that is, if the expected return on assets μ_A exceeds R):

$$\boxed{\mu_E - R = \lambda \cdot (\mu_A - R).} \qquad (6.3)$$

Because $\lambda > 1$, this is greater than $\mu_A - R$ if $\mu_A > R$.

Note also that risk is increased: the standard deviation σ_E of the return on equity is also a multiple of the standard deviation σ_A of the return on assets:

$$\boxed{\sigma_E = \lambda \sigma_A.} \qquad (6.4)$$

Numerical Example:

Suppose, for example, that the expected return on assets is $\mu_A = 10\%$, the interest rate on debt is $R = 5\%$ and leverage is $\lambda = 4$. The return on equity is magnified by leverage:

$$\mu_E = 5 + (4)(10 - 5) = 25\%.$$

But risk is also magnified: if the volatility of assets' return is $\sigma_A = 10\%$, the volatility of equity's return is:

$$\sigma_E = 4(10) = 40\%.$$

Thus, increasing leverage is double-sided: it magnifies excess returns on assets (when they are positive), but it also magnifies risk.

6.2 ECONOMIC CAPITAL FOR A BANK

Recall from Chapter 5 that for a given horizon T and level α, the VaR on a portfolio is defined as the amount needed to cover the losses on the portfolio with probability α as illustrated by Figure 6.1.

When applied to the global portfolio of assets of a bank, the VaR allows us to compute the amount of equity capital needed to limit the probability of default of the bank to a maximum of $1 - \alpha$. Consider a bank with the following (simplified) balance sheet:

| Assets A | Equity E |
| | Deposits D |

Neglecting the interests paid on deposits and other liabilities, we have that the bank is insolvent at horizon T whenever the value of its assets A_T is less than the value of its liabilities D:

$$\Pr(\text{Insolvency}) = \Pr(A_T < D).$$

The return on assets of the bank is defined as:

$$ROA = \frac{A_T}{A} - 1.$$

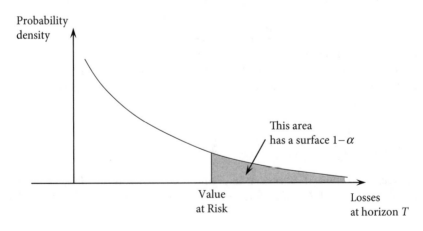

Figure 6.1 Value at Risk.

Thus, the probability of insolvency of the bank can also be written:

$$\Pr(\text{Insolvency}) = \Pr\left(ROA \leq \frac{D}{A} - 1\right)$$

$$= \Pr\left(ROA \leq -\frac{E}{A}\right).$$

Alternatively, one can define the losses on the portfolio as $\tilde{x} = -ROA$ (the opposite of the Return on Assets). Then,

$$\Pr(\text{Insolvency}) = \Pr\left(\tilde{x} \geq \frac{E}{A}\right).$$

Let us denote by q_α the α quantile of the statistical distribution of the losses on assets. It is defined implicitly by:

$$\Pr(\tilde{x} \leq q_\alpha) = \alpha.$$

The above formulas show that the probability of insolvency of the bank at horizon T will be less than $1 - \alpha$ if and only if

$$\frac{E}{A} \geq q_\alpha.$$

In other words $E^* = A \cdot q_\alpha$ is the minimum amount of capital needed to limit the probability of failure of the bank to $1 - \alpha$. The VaR at level α is thus equal to

$$VaR_\alpha = A \cdot q_\alpha.$$

Numerical Example:

Suppose losses are normally distributed with mean zero and (weekly) volatility $\sigma = 3\%$.

The 99% quantile of the standard normal is $N^{-1}(\alpha) = 2.33$. Thus, the 99% quantile of the bank's return on assets is $q_{99\%} = 3 \times 2.33\% \sim 7\%$. For a total portfolio $A = \$100$ million and a confidence level $\alpha = 99\%$, the VaR is approximately $\$7$ million.

6.3 ECONOMIC CAPITAL FOR AN INSURANCE COMPANY

6.3.1 A Basic Model

Although the economic capital of a bank is a multiple of its volume of assets, the economic capital of property casualty insurance company is often based on its volume of premiums. To see why, consider the simplified profit and loss account and balance sheet of an insurance company:

<table>
<tr><td colspan="2" align="center">Profit and Loss</td><td colspan="2" align="center">Balance sheet</td></tr>
<tr><td>Claims C</td><td>Premiums P</td><td>Assets A</td><td>Equity E</td></tr>
<tr><td>Expenses</td><td>Financial revenues</td><td></td><td>Technical Reserves T</td></tr>
</table>

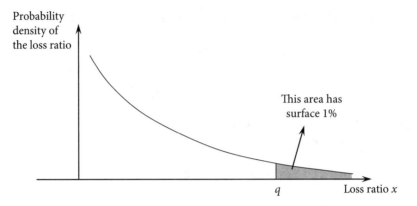

Figure 6.2 The 99% quantile of the loss ratio.

The insurance industry uses the loss ratio $\frac{\text{Claims}}{\text{Premiums}}$ as a measure of technical profitability. We denote this loss ratio by $\tilde{x}$ and assume that $\mathcal{E}(\tilde{x}) = 1$. This means that premiums are actuarially fair:

$$P = \mathcal{E}(\text{claims}).$$

We neglect asset risk and thus assume that the assets of the company consist of a riskless asset, with net return r_F. For simplicity, we also normalize r_F and operating expenses to zero.

At the end of the reference period, failure occurs when the value of claims exceeds the value of assets A. In a stationary regime, the average duration for claim settlement is constant. This implies that technical reserves should be proportional to expected claims and thus to P: $T = dP.$[3]

Provided the level of technical reserves is appropriately computed, failure occurs when:

$$P\tilde{x} > A = E + T = E + dP.$$

Dividing by P, we see that ruin (failure) is characterized by the stochastic event

$$\tilde{x} > \frac{E}{P} + d.$$

Therefore, if the probability distribution $F(\cdot)$ of the loss ratio $\tilde{x}$ is estimated by statistical methods, the probability of ruin equals

$$PR = \Pr\left(\tilde{x} > \frac{E}{P} + d\right) = 1 - F\left(\frac{E}{P} + d\right)$$

If q represents the 99% quantile of the probability distribution of $\tilde{x}$, defined by $F(q) = 99\%$, and illustrated by Figure 6.2, imposing a minimum margin requirement (equity over premiums) of $(q - d)$ limits the probability of failure below 1%:

$$\frac{E}{P} \geq q - d \Leftrightarrow PR = 1 - F\left(\frac{E}{P} + d\right) \leq 1 - F(q) = 1\%.$$

Economic capital at 99% level is thus equal to $(q - d)$ times the total volume of premiums P. Ruin Theory essentially aims at solving more sophisticated, dynamic versions of this model to estimate the minimum solvency margin needed to obtain a survival probability of at least 99% over a given, possibly large, time horizon.

6.3.2 An Extended Model

Let us enrich the elementary model of Ruin Theory by modeling the insurance portfolio more explicitly. Consider an insurer with equity E, who manages a portfolio of n independent and identically distributed risks. Denote by $\tilde{x}_i$ the random variable representing the loss associated with risk i, during the relevant time period, and for $i = 1, \ldots, n$. We assume that each $\tilde{x}_i$ has mean 1 and standard deviation σ. Each risk is covered by a premium $1 + \lambda$, where $\lambda > 0$ represents the loading factor (net of reinsurance premiums).

The probability of ruin PR is thus

$$PR = \Pr(E + n(1 + \lambda) < \tilde{x}_1 + \tilde{x}_2 + \ldots + \tilde{x}_n)$$
$$= \Pr(\tilde{x}_1 + \tilde{x}_2 + \ldots + \tilde{x}_n - n1 > E + n1\lambda).$$

By the Central Limit Theorem, (*see* Section 5.2) this probability of ruin can be approximated by $1 - N\left(\frac{E+n\lambda}{\sigma\sqrt{n}}\right)$ where $N(\cdot)$ is the c.d.f. of the standard normal.

This expression shows that there are several ways to reduce the probability of ruin: increasing the capital buffer E of course is one, but other methods are possible, like reducing σ or increasing λ and n.

Let us now account for the riskiness of assets as follows. Consider a situation where the insurer is invested in two types of assets: a riskless asset with net return r_F (that we normalize to zero) and a risky asset with a random net return $\tilde{r}$. If we neglect the insurer's expenses, the $P \& L$ and balance sheet of the insurer becomes:

P & L		Balance sheet	
Claims C	Premiums P	Riskless asset A_0	Technical Reserves T
	Financial income	Risky asset A_1	Equity E

In this case, failure is avoided when:

$$C = P\tilde{x} < A_0 + A_1(1 + \tilde{r}).$$

Assuming again that $T = dP$, we obtain a simpler condition:

$$P\tilde{x} < A_1\tilde{r} + E + dP,$$

or

$$\tilde{y} < E,$$

where $\tilde{y} = P(\tilde{x} - d) - A_1\tilde{r}$ denotes unexpected net operating losses (difference between net claims and financial income).

If $\tilde{y}$ can be approximated by a normal distribution[4] of mean 0 and variance σ_y^2, the probability of survival is approximated by $N\left(\frac{E}{\sigma_y}\right)$, where N is the cumulative distribution function of a standard normal variable. Denoting by $q = 2.33$ the 99% lower quantile of this distribution, the probability of failure will be less than 1% if E is at least equal to $q\sigma_y$. The interest of this method is that the standard deviation σ_y can be computed easily, especially if asset risks and liability risks are supposed to be independent. We can use the formula derived in Section 5.3:

$$\sigma_y^2 = \text{var } (\tilde{y}) = \text{var } (A_1\tilde{r}) + \text{var } (P\tilde{x}) = A_1^2 \text{ var } (\tilde{r}) + P^2 \text{ var } (\tilde{x}),$$

therefore:

$$\sigma_y = \sqrt{A_1^2\sigma_r^2 + P^2\sigma_x^2},$$

where σ_r^2 denotes the variance of asset risks and σ_x^2 denotes the variance of the loss ratio (liability risks). The economic capital of the insurer (minimum level of equity needed to limit the probability of failure to a predetermined threshold) is thus given by $9\sigma_y$. This formula is the basis for the risk-based capital (RBC) regulation used by U.S. insurance regulators.

However, the independence of technical and financial risks underlying such ratios seems a heroic assumption. Indeed, casual evidence suggests that distressed insurance companies tend to experience simultaneously financial and operational difficulties, so that assuming these risks being positively correlated seems more realistic. This correlation is, of course, related to the fact that both risks are driven by common factors—namely, the organizational inefficiency of the company and the poor quality of its governance. Another source of correlation comes from the fact that in many lines of insurance, technical results deteriorate during recessions. An obvious example is credit insurance.

Another practical difficulty is the estimation of σ_x (the standard deviation of the claims ratio $\tilde{x}$) because of the lack of market statistics in many lines of insurance. Moreover, even if a market standard is available, this market standard should not be applied to insurance companies that are close to financial distress.

Let us conclude this section by stressing the practical limits to capital requirements. Even if Ruin Theory provides theoretical foundations for margin requirements and for the RBC type formulas used by regulators, these formulas do not seem particularly good in practice at predicting failures or financial distress. Several scholars have studied the predictive power of the RBC and also the FAST scores, designed by U.S. insurance supervisors for forecasting failure or financial distress of U.S. insurance companies. All their studies have concluded that this predictive power is very weak. Other methods, based on cash flows simulations, seem to work better.

6.4 THE LIMITS OF RUIN THEORY

Ruin Theory (in its simpler version) and the VaR can be useful tools for choosing the appropriate amount of economic capital for an insurance company or a bank. However, they can also be very dangerous tools, when used without precaution, as illustrated by the example of Northern Rock presented below in Subsection 6.4.1. The main reason behind the Northern Rock disaster was that refinancing risk was completely neglected: standard Ruin Theory and simple VaR models only consider risks on assets, not on liabilities. Even when both asset risks and liability risks are taken into account, like in the U.S. RBC ratio for insurance companies, they are assumed to be independent, which is not a good assumption. Moreover, modern financial institutions rely extensively on short-term financing, which runs the risk of not being renewed. Simultaneously, interest risk fluctuations expose these financial institutions to transformation risk. Subsection 6.4.2 presents a simple tool for measuring this transformation risk and incorporating it into VaR calculations.

6.4.1 Northern Rock

In September 2007, Northern Rock was viewed as one of the most successful mortgage lenders in the United Kingdom. Its business model was very simple: invest on (apparently) safe tranches of Residential Mortgage Back Securities (RMBS) and finance these investments by short-term deposits (mostly uninsured wholesale deposits). This strategy was very profitable, because the interest rates on (long-term) mortgages were much higher than those on short-term wholesale deposits. Moreover, this strategy seemed reasonably safe because assets were well-rated and Northern Rock seemed reasonably capitalized (at least to its supervisors). As of June 2007, Northern Rock had total assets $A = £113$ bn and equity $E = £2.2$ bn. Its leverage was thus around 51, which is huge, but the FSA (the British regulator) allowed it because most of Northern Rock's assets were considered almost riskless. The regulatory capital requirement, computed by the FSA by using the VaR method, was only £1.5 bn, well below the actual level of capital of $E = £2.2$ bn.

However, on September 15, 2007, and following rumors about a risk of recession in the United States, the depositors of Northern Rock panicked, which resulted in the first bank run on a U.K. bank since the nineteenth century: first, professional investors did not renew their large deposits, then there were long lines of depositors waiting to withdraw their money, which prompted massive injections of liquidity by the Bank of England. Ultimately, the U.K. Treasury had to nationalize the bank and recapitalize it through taxpayers' money. On total, U.K. authorities had to inject £23 bn—that is, 15 times the amount of capital required by regulators!

The main reason behind this disaster was that financial authorities had focused on limiting **leverage** (through capital requirements based on the default risk of assets) but completely neglected another fundamental risk of banking—namely, **transformation risk**. We now discuss how this transformation risk can be measured and incorporated into VaR calculations.

6.4.2 Duration and Asset Liability Management

Duration is a simple notion that was invented to measure the risk of a portfolio of fixed income securities (bonds) or a life insurance portfolio. In a nutshell, it is defined as the time to maturity (or duration, hence the name) of a zero coupon bond that has the same sensitivity to interest rate risk than the portfolio of bonds. It is computed as follows. Recall that when the interest rate is r, the (theoretical) price of a zero-coupon bond of time to maturity T is

$$B(r) = \frac{1}{(1+r)^T}.$$

The sensitivity of this price to interest rate fluctuations is by definition equal to:

$$\frac{B'(r)}{B(r)} = \frac{-T}{1+r}. \tag{6.5}$$

The sensitivity is thus proportional to the duration T of the bond.

Consider now a portfolio of bonds, characterized by the cash flows that it will deliver in the future:[5]

Future dates	t_1	$\cdots$	t_n
Future cash flows	c_1	$\cdots$	c_n

If interest rates are constant (equal to r) on the relevant period (from $t = t_1$ to $t = t_n$) and if markets are frictionless, the price of this portfolio should be equal to the sum of the present values of these cash flows:

$$P(r) = \frac{c_1}{(1+r)^{t_1}} + \cdots + \frac{c_n}{(1+r)^{t_n}}.$$

The sensitivity of this price to interest rate fluctuations is by definition:

$$\frac{P'(r)}{P(r)} = -\left[\frac{c_1 t_1}{(1+r)^{t_1+1} P(r)} + \cdots + \frac{c_n t_n}{(1+r)^{t_n+1} \cdot P(r)} \right].$$

By rearranging terms, this is also equal to:

$$\frac{P'(r)}{P(r)} = -\frac{\alpha_1 t_1 + \cdots + \alpha_n t_n}{1+r}, \tag{6.6}$$

where $\alpha_i \equiv \frac{c_i}{(1+r)^{t_i} P(r)}$ represents the fraction of the current value of the portfolio that comes from the i-th cash flow. The duration δ of the portfolio is defined as the numerator of (6.6)—that is, a weighted sum of the dates of the future cash flows, where the weights are equal to the α_is:

$$\delta = \alpha_1 t_1 + \cdots + \alpha_n t_n.$$

The sensitivity of the value P of the portfolio is thus equal to $-\frac{\delta}{1+r}$ (the minus sign comes from the fact that asset prices go down when interest rates go up).

Duration can also give a simple approximation of the *VaR* of a portfolio of fixed income securities, at least on a short horizon. Suppose indeed that the probability that interest rates increase by more than Δr_α on this horizon is $(1 - \alpha)$. If this horizon is small enough, then Δr_α is also small and the loss on the portfolio of bonds can be approximated by $-P'(r)\Delta r_\alpha$, which is also equal (*see* formula (6.6)) to $P(r) \cdot \frac{\delta}{1+r} \cdot \Delta r_\alpha$: this is the value at risk of the portfolio at level α.

Duration can also be used for asset liability management. Consider, for example, a bank whose simplified balance sheet at some horizon t_0 is:

Assets A	Equity E
	Deposits D

The market value of assets A and deposits D fluctuate with the interest rate r. Therefore, the market value of equity is also sensitive to interest rate risk. Formally,

$$E(r) = A(r) - D(r).$$

The sensitivity of equity to interest rate risk is thus

$$\frac{E'(r)}{E(r)} = \frac{A'(r) - D'(r)}{E(r)}.$$

This can be rewritten as:

$$\frac{E'(r)}{E(r)} = \frac{A'(r)}{A(r)}\left[\frac{A(r)}{E(r)}\right] - \frac{D'(r)}{D(r)}\left[\frac{D(r)}{E(r)}\right].$$

Let us introduce some notation:

$$\delta_E = -(1+r)\frac{E'(r)}{E(r)} : \text{ duration of equity.}$$

$$\delta_A = -(1+r)\frac{A'(r)}{A(r)} : \text{ duration of assets.}$$

$$\delta_D = -(1+r)\frac{D'(r)}{D(r)} : \text{ duration of deposits.}$$

$$\lambda = \frac{A(r)}{E(r)} : \text{ leverage.}$$

Note that,

$$\frac{D(r)}{E(r)} = \frac{A(r) - E(r)}{E(r)} = \lambda - 1.$$

This allows to transform the above formula:

$$\delta_E = \delta_A \lambda - \delta_D(\lambda - 1) = \delta_D + \lambda(\delta_A - \delta_D).$$

This formula shows that the sensitivity of a bank's equity to interest rate fluctuations comes from two sources:

- transformation—that is, the fact that the duration of assets is typically much larger than the duration of deposits ($\delta_A \gg \delta_D$)
- leverage λ, which magnifies the duration of assets.

Numerical Example:

Consider, for example, a bank like Northern Rock with leverage $\frac{A}{E} = \frac{113}{2.2} \sim 51$. If the average duration of assets is $\delta_A = 7$ years and the duration of deposits is $\delta_D = 1$ year, then the duration of equity of the bank is huge:

$$\delta_E = 7 \times (51) - 50 = 307 \text{ years!}$$

This means that if interest rate r increases by 20 basis points from, say, 5% to 5.2%, then the market value of the bank's equity is going to fall by about

$$-\frac{E'(r)}{E(r)} \Delta r = \frac{\delta_E}{1+r} \Delta r = \frac{307}{1.05} \times 0.2\% \sim 58.5\%,$$

which is huge!

PART THREE

The Perfect Markets Hypothesis and Its Dangers

The third part of the book presents two very important tools developed by financial economists for measuring risks. One is **risk neutral valuation**, a method initially developed for pricing stock options but was revealed extremely general and very elegant. It has generated an enormous academic literature in mathematical finance, but it relies on a very unreasonable assumption: the perfect markets hypothesis. This hypothesis requires that financial markets are complete (all risks are traded on active markets) and frictionless (trade is costless and efficient). This hypothesis, together with the risk neutral valuation method and its dangers, is presented in Chapter 7. A less demanding set-up is presented in Chapter 8, where it is still assumed that markets are frictionless but not complete. In this case, risk premiums are more complicated to compute because they require a detailed knowledge of the fundamentals of the economy: technology, available resources, and preferences. Chapter 9 examines the only tractable example of incomplete markets: the "Normal" world. When the joint distribution of assets returns is Normal, investors' preferences can be represented by a mean–variance criterion and risk premiums are very easy to compute; this is the celebrated Capital Asset Pricing Model (CAPM) methodology. Moreover, in the Normal world, all risk management decisions (portfolio choices, hedging, capital allocation,...) can be modeled by linear-quadratic optimization problems that have linear solutions. Unfortunately, the normality assumption is often rejected by financial data: the world is not "Normal." At the end of Chapter 9, we give some concrete examples of the dangers of viewing the world as Normal, despite the empirical evidence.

7 Risk Neutral Valuation

Risk neutral valuation (RNV) is a very elegant method for pricing risky securities. It was elaborated for the pricing of options and other derivatives, but it can be applied to many other questions such as determining the profitability of a risky investment or assessing the value of complex securities. The reasons for the popularity of RNV are its simplicity and, more importantly, the fact that it allows determination of risk premiums (how much financial markets require to bear different risks) without any knowledge of economic fundamentals. But this is too good to be true. The method relies on two assumptions that are completely unrealistic: all risks are traded on active markets (market completeness) and trade is efficient (no frictions nor transaction costs).

This chapter explores the magic of perfect markets and shows that these two assumptions imply that the RNV method is indeed valid. However, it also shows the mirages of the perfect markets world: putting too much faith into these assumptions leads to some crude fallacies: "maturity transformation is not risky," "leverage does not matter," and "risk management is useless!"

7.1 THE EXPECTED PRESENT VALUE CRITERION

The simplest tool used in finance to evaluate an investment is to compute the expectation of the net present value of future cash flows generated by this investment—for example, a project that needs an investment of $I = 100$ and provides expected cash flows of 60 in each of the next 2 years. Its expected (net) present value is:

$$EPV(r) = \frac{60}{1+r} + \frac{60}{(1+r)^2} - 100.$$

When the interest rate, r, used to discount future cash flows is 5%, we obtain a positive value:

$$EPV(5\%) = 11.56.$$

This suggests that the investment should be undertaken. However this computation does not take into account the risk of future cash flows, because a random cash flow $\tilde{x}$ is valued identically to a certain cash flow with the same mean $\mathcal{E}(\tilde{x})$.

In practice, investors usually require a higher rate of return on risky investments. For example, stocks, which are more volatile than bonds, typically have higher returns (on average, over a long period). The difference is called a risk premium. Similarly, corporate bonds, which are subject to default risk, have higher nominal returns than government bonds, which are normally immune to default.[1] The difference in returns is called the corporate spread: it is usually bigger than what a simple estimation of the probability of default would imply.

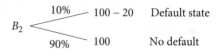

Figure 7.1

Numerical Example:

Consider two bonds that promise to repay the same amount (100) in a 1 year time. Bond 1 is a government bond with yield $r = 5\%$: This means that the price of this bond is:

$$B_1 = \frac{100}{1.05} \simeq 95.2.$$

By contrast, bond 2 is a corporate bond issued by some firm X, characterized by an estimated probability of default $PD = 10\%$ and a loss given default $LGD = 20\%$.

Bond 2 has a higher yield $R = 10\%$ and thus a lower price $B_2 = \frac{100}{1.1} \simeq 90.9$.

Bond 2 being risky, its liquidation value can be modeled as a Bernoulli variable as shown in Figure 7.1.

The expected return of bond 2 is thus

$$\mu = \frac{(0.1)(80) + (0.9)(100)}{90.9} - 1 \simeq 7.8\%.$$

This is higher than the expected return on the risk-free bond, which is only 5%. If the corporate bond had an expected return of 5%, its price would be given by the expected present value of its future repayments:

$$EPV = \frac{(0.1)(80) + (0.9)(100)}{1.05} \simeq 93.3.$$

The price $B_2 = 90.9$ of the bond is smaller than this EPV because most investors are risk-averse.[2] The difference between the expected return of the risky bond B_2 and that of the risk-free bond B_1 is called a **risk premium**.

Assessing risk premiums is in principle a delicate exercise, requiring good forecasts of future returns on the risky asset, as well as on the future economic situation. However, when sufficiently many financial assets are traded actively, their market prices reveal implicitly the risk premiums required by investors for different types of risks. This is the magic of perfect markets, which we now explain.

7.2 THE MAGIC OF PERFECT MARKETS

Suppose that on the top of the two bonds considered above, a new financial instrument is traded, namely a credit default swap.

This CDS is a contract that guarantees the payment of a fixed sum, say $1, if firm X defaults. To estimate the reasonable premium P that the protection seller can charge to the CDS buyer is in principle a complex exercise, requiring analysis of the financial situation of firm X and forecast of the future situation of the overall economy.

BOX 7.1 ■ Credit Default Swaps

A credit default swap (CDS) is a contract between two parties. The **protection buyer** pays a periodic premium to the **protection seller** who, in exchange for this premium, commits to pay a fixed sum if a credit instrument (a bond or a loan) goes into default. The mechanism is very similar to insurance, but there are two important differences:

- The protection buyer does not necessarily own the credit instrument that is insured by the CDS contract. CDS contracts may therefore be used for **speculating** as well as **hedging**.
- The protection seller is not necessarily a regulated entity.

The CDS market has grown tremendously since the beginning of the twenty-first century. By the end of 2007, the world CDS market had a (notional)[3] value of more than \$45 trillion! However, the subprime crisis has precipitated a dramatic compression of this market. Regulators are also deeply concerned with the opacity of this market, which made exposures of large financial institutions difficult to monitor. For example, the U.S. insurance giant AIG lost more than \$100 billion on CDS contracts in 2008 (*see* Box 1.1).

The magic of the complete markets world is that the CDS premium P can in fact be computed without any further knowledge just by using the **no arbitrage principle**, which is simply a sophisticated version of the law of one price. Indeed, if one constitutes a portfolio comprising one corporate bond B_2 (of nominal 100 and loss given default of 20) and 20 *CDS* contracts, the total payoff of this portfolio is 100, independently of whether firm X defaults.

States Values	Corporate Bond (B_2)	20 *CDS* contracts	Total portfolio
Default of firm X	80	20	100
No default	100	0	100

This portfolio is exactly equivalent to a risk-free bond. Therefore, the price of the portfolio must equal the price of the risk-free bond, (otherwise an arbitrage is possible):

$$B_2 + 20P = B_1.$$

Using the numerical values $B_1 = 95.2$ and $B_2 = 90.9$, we obtain the unique value of the *CDS* premium P that is compatible with the no arbitrage principle:

$$P = \frac{95.2 - 90.9}{20} = 21.5\%.$$

If we compare P with the actuarially fair premium

$$P_0 = \frac{PD}{1+r},$$

we see that the probability of default that would be necessary to justify such a high level of the *CDS* premium is

$$\widehat{PD} = (1+r)P = (1.05) \times (0.215) \simeq 22.6\%.$$

This is more than the double of the "true" probability of default—that is, the one that is estimated on historical data

$$PD = 10\%.$$

$\widehat{PD}$ is called the risk neutral (*RN*) probability of default.[4] This name comes from the fact that when the expected present value of the corporate bond B_2 (this is also true for any security) is computed under this *RN* probability (we call it the risk neutral value [*RNV*]), it matches the price of B_2 observed in the market

$$RNV = \frac{1}{1+r} [\widehat{PD} \times 80 + (1 - \widehat{PD}) \cdot 100],$$

$$= \frac{1}{1.05} [(0.226) \times 80 + (0.774) \cdot 100] = 90.9.$$

Thus, $RNV = B_2$.

The spread between the risk-adjusted probability of default $\widehat{PD}$ and the historical probability of default PD reflects the market's risk aversion and investors' expectations about the future state of the economy. As a result, it may vary a lot over time.

We can now summarize our findings.

The modern tool of risk neutral valuation is thus a rigorous way to take risk into account while maintaining the simplicity of expected present value computations. The idea is to modify probabilities in such a way that they incorporate risk premia. The modified probabilities, called risk neutral probabilities, can be computed from market prices. Arbitrage pricing methods (initially used to price options but now applied to all sorts of financial computations) show that in the absence of arbitrage opportunities, it is always possible to find such risk neutral probabilities. Moreover, if financial markets are complete, there is a unique way to compute them.

7.3 COMPLETE MARKETS AND ABSENCE OF ARBITRAGE OPPORTUNITIES

To explain the principle of absence of arbitrage opportunities, we need to introduce some notation. Consider a two-period model of a financial market.

At date 0, N financial assets are traded at prices $p_1, \ldots, p_N$.

Uncertainty is modeled by an ordered tree that has one node at date 0 (today) and S nodes at date 1 (tomorrow), corresponding to the different possibilities (called the states of the world) that can occur at that date (*see* Figure 7.2):

At date 1, asset n pays off a value v_{sn} that depends on the state of the world, s, at that date. The matrix $V = (v_{sn})_{\substack{s \leq S \\ n \leq N}}$ has S rows and N columns, where S is

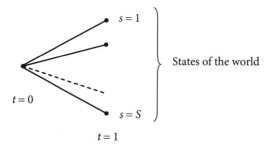

Figure 7.2 Modeling uncertainty by a tree.

the number of states of the world at date 1. A portfolio θ is any vector $(\theta_1, \ldots, \theta_N)$ in $\mathbb{R}^N$, θ_n representing the number of assets n in the portfolio. Note that θ_n can be negative, which means that shortsales are possible. Each portfolio $\theta \in \mathbb{R}^N$ costs $p \cdot \theta = p_1\theta_1 + \cdots + p_N\theta_N$ at date 0 and delivers payoff $m_s = \sum_n v_{sn}\theta_n$ at date 1 if state s prevails. The payoff vector, m, is thus equal to $V\theta$.

Definition 7.1. *The market is arbitrage-free* $\Leftrightarrow \forall \theta \in \mathbb{R}^N$, $V\theta \in \mathbb{R}_+^S \Rightarrow p \cdot \theta \geq 0$.

An arbitrage would correspond to a portfolio θ that has a negative cost ($p \cdot \theta < 0$) at date 0 and a non-negative payoff vector ($m = V\theta \geq 0$) at date 1.

In the absence of frictions or transaction costs, the market will be (close to) arbitrage-free, as any arbitrage opportunity will be immediately exploited.

Note that in an arbitrage-free market, two portfolios θ_1 and θ_2 that generate the same payoff vector at date 1 (and therefore are such that $V\theta_1 = V\theta_2$) must necessarily have the same price at date 0 (and therefore are such that $p \cdot \theta_1 = p \cdot \theta_2$). This is the **replicating portfolio principle**. We now introduce a second important notion.

Definition 7.2. *The market is complete* $\Leftrightarrow \forall m \in \mathbb{R}^S$, $\exists \theta \in \mathbb{R}^N$, $V\theta = m$.

Thus, a market is complete if and only if the rank of matrix V is S. This means that the space spanned by payoff vectors $V \cdot \theta$ (for all possible portfolios θ) has full dimension S. In other words, any vector, m, in $\mathbb{R}^S$ can be generated as the payoff vector of some portfolio θ in $\mathbb{R}^M$.

Proposition 7.1 (Arbitrage Pricing). *If the market is arbitrage-free and complete, there exists a unique vector π in $\mathbb{R}_+^S$ (called the vector of state prices) such that for any asset, n:*

$$p_n = \sum_s \pi_s v_{sn}.$$

Thus, the price of any asset is equal to the sum of what it pays in all states of the world, weighted by the vector of state prices.

The proof of Proposition 7.1 is easy: If markets are complete (rank $V = S$), it must be that $N \geq S$ and that a non-singular $S \times S$ matrix of "fundamental" assets can be extracted from V. All other assets can be replicated by portfolios of

---

BOX 7.2 ■ The Principle of Risk Neutral Valuation

When financial markets are perfect (i.e., arbitrage-free and complete), all financial assets can be priced by computing the expectation of the present value (PV) of their future cash flows under a fictitious probability distribution that neutralizes risk premia.This probability distribution is called the **risk neutral probability**, and the expectation is called the RNV of cash flows. It has been used successfully for option pricing (Black Scholes) and bond pricing (Merton). A particularly simple example is the binomial model of Cox, Ross, and Rubinstein.

---

these S fundamental assets. Moreover, for each s there is a unique portfolio of fundamental assets that gives a payoff of 1 in state s and 0 is all other states. Since the market is arbitrage-free, the price π_s of this portfolio must be non-negative. This ends the proof of Proposition 7.1.

Proposition 7.1 shows how to compute the price of any security in this model. Consider, in particular, the price of a riskless bond of nominal 1. Because the payoff of this bond is by definition 1 in all states of the world ($v_{sn} \equiv 1$) the price of this bond (given by Proposition 7.1) must be equal to

$$\frac{1}{1+r} = \sum_s \pi_s.$$

Now, we can define a probability distribution $Q = (q_1, \ldots, q_s)$ by setting (for all $s = 1, \ldots, S$): $q_s = (1+r)\pi_s$.

This allows us to define the related notion of RNV:

Proposition 7.2 (Risk neutral valuation). *If the market is arbitrage-free and complete, there exists a unique probability distribution Q on $\{1, \ldots, S\}$ (i.e., a vector $[(q_1, \ldots, q_S)]$ in $\mathbb{R}_+^S$ with $\sum_s q_s = 1$) such that, for any asset n:*

$$p_n = \frac{1}{1+r} \sum_s q_s v_{sn}.$$

Proposition 7.2 is an immediate consequence of Proposition 7.1 obtained by replacing π_s by $\frac{q_s}{1+r}$.

7.4 A BINOMIAL EXAMPLE

As a second example of the RNV method, consider the binomial model of Cox, Ross, and Rubinstein (1979). This model can be seen as the elementary version of the Black Scholes model in the sense that it gives the economic intuition behind option pricing methods without any need to use the complex techniques of stochastic calculus. This economic intuition can be stated literarily as follows: in the absence of frictions on financial markets, the risk premiums that financial markets assign to different contingencies can be deduced from the observation of the prices of sufficiently many securities.

The Cox-Ross-Rubinstein model allows the simplest possible formulation of this argument. In this model, there are only two dates ($t = 0, 1$) and two contingencies (states of the world) at date 1, say a boom (state up) and a recession (state down). As soon as there are two different securities that are traded, the prices of these securities determine the risk premium required by investors on any other security and thus the "fair" price of any other security. Suppose, for example, that the two traded securities are a riskless bond with (gross) return $1 + r$ and a stock with (gross) return u in state up and d in state down (with $d < u$). If $u < 1 + r$ or $d > 1 + r$, one asset dominates the other. For both assets to be traded, it is necessary that $d \leq 1 + r \leq u$. If p denotes the probability of state up (and $1 - p$ the probability of state down), the expected return on the stock is higher than the riskless return when:

$$pu + (1 - p)d > 1 + r.$$

The risk premium on the stock equals, by definition, the difference between the expected return on the stock and the riskless return ($1 + r$):

$$\pi = pu + (1 - p)d - (1 + r).$$

However, because $d \leq 1 + r \leq u$ (otherwise, one of the two assets is dominated by the other) there always exists a (unique) $q \in [0, 1]$ such that

$$qu + (1 - q)d = 1 + r. \tag{7.1}$$

Consider the probability distribution Q that assigns probability q to state "up" (boom) and probability $1 - q$ to state "down" (recession). This probability distribution Q is called the risk neutral probability distribution because it neutralizes risk premia. Under Q, the expected (net) return on all assets is equal to the risk-free return r.

Numerical Example: $u = 1.2$, $r = 5\%$, $d = 1$, $p = 1/2$;

$$\pi = pu + (1 - p)d - (1 + r) = \frac{1}{2}(1.2) + \frac{1}{2}(1) - 1.05$$

$$= 5\%.$$

The risk neutral probability of state up—that is, q—is the unique solution of

$$q \times (1.2) + (1 - q) \times (1) = 1.05 \quad \Rightarrow \quad q = 1/4.$$

The risk neutral probability distribution $Q = (1/4, 3/4)$ can be viewed as more "pessimistic" that the "true" or "historical" probability distribution $P = (1/2, 1/2)$ because the probability of the "favorable" event u is reduced from $1/2$ to $1/4$.

What is remarkable is that this risk neutral probability always exists (unless there are arbitrage opportunities). It is unique as soon as markets are complete.[5] Once Q is determined (in our binomial example it suffices to solve (7.1), which gives $q = \frac{1+r-d}{u-d}$ and $1 - q = \frac{u-(1+r)}{u-d}$), it is easy to compute the "fair" prices of all assets that pay future cash flows contingent on the stock's returns.

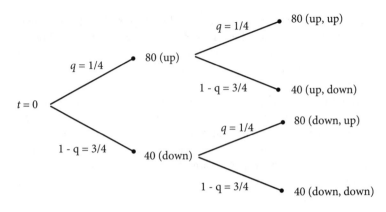

Figure 7.3

Let us come back to our initial example of an investment of $I = 100$ that provides expected cash flows of 60 in each of the next 2 years. If the interest rate is 5% and the cash flows are not risky, we saw that the investment should be undertaken, because its NPV is positive:

$$NPV = \frac{60}{1.05} + \frac{60}{(1.05)^2} - 100 \sim 11.56.$$

If cash flows are risky, the computation has to be modified. Suppose, for example, that cash flows $\tilde{C}$ follow a Bernoulli process, as in the Cox-Ross-Rubinstein model illustrated in Figure 7.3:

Expected cash flows per period are

$$\frac{1}{2}(80) + \frac{1}{2}(40) = 60.$$

However, the risk neutral expectation of cash flows is lower:

$$\mathcal{E}(\tilde{C}) = \frac{1}{4}(80) + \frac{3}{4}(40) = 50.$$

In fact, the risk neutral expected present value becomes negative:

$$RNV = \frac{50}{1.05} + \frac{50}{(1.05)^2} - 100 < 0.$$

Therefore, once risk premia are taken into account, the risky investment should **not** be undertaken! This reverses the previous conclusion, which was based on the EPV method, which neglects risk premia.

7.5 THE MIRAGES OF THE PERFECT MARKETS WORLD

A well-known anecdote[6] illustrates perfectly the dangers of the perfect markets hypothesis: A finance student and her professor find a $100 bill lying on the ground. The student wants to pick it up, but the finance professor tells her: "Don't bother: if it were a real $100 bill, it would not be here."

To some extent, the illusion that financial markets are close to be perfect (i.e., arbitrage-free, complete, and frictionless) has been responsible for the generalized excess in risk taking by financial institutions that was one of the main characteristics of the subprime crisis. This section develops three examples of fallacies generated by the perfect market assumption: maturity transformation is not risky (7.5.1), leverage does not matter (7.5.2) and risk management is useless (7.5.3).

7.5.1 Fallacy 1: Maturity Transformation is not Risky

One of the major economic functions of banks is to collect deposits from the public and transform then into loans to firms and households. The maturity of the loans is typically larger than a year, whereas that of deposits can be very short (often 1 week or even 1 day). This economy function of banks is called maturity transformation. It exposes banks to the risk of a run by depositors: if, for some reason or another, deposits are not renewed, the bank may be forced to liquidate its long-term assets at a loss, which may even provoke its default.

However, if markets were perfect and banks' assets were reasonably safe, then this situation would never occur, because the liquidation of these assets (whenever needed) would never entail a loss with respect to their fundamental value. Bank defaults would still be possible, but they would be provoked by solvency, rather than liquidity, problems.

In the real world, markets are not perfect, and banks can be exposed to liquidity problems as illustrated below.

Consider a bank that has the following business model (very much in the spirit of Northern Rock): borrow short term at the risk-free interest rate r, and invest long term (say at maturity T) in a (reasonably) safe asset that returns R per period. The (initial) balance sheet of the bank is

	Equity
Assets	(E)
(A)	Deposits
	(D)

Thus, all the bank's debt is in the form of deposits. The bank is subject by regulation to a capital requirement:

$$E \geq kA.$$

After T periods, assets are liquidated for a value $A(1+R)^T$. Deposits only last one period, so that the bank has to borrow

$$D_t = D(1+r)^t$$

at date t to repay the amount $D_{t-1} = D(1+r)^{t-1}$ borrowed at date $t-1$, plus the interests. If markets are perfect, then shareholders are sure to obtain at date

T the difference between the asset value $A(1+R)^T$ and the final debt obligation $D(1+r)^T$. The present value of the gain for shareholders is

$$\pi = \left[A \left(\frac{1+R}{1+r} \right)^T - D \right] - E.$$

Using the fact that $D + E = A$, and assuming that $R > r$, we obtain a positive return on equity

$$ROE = \frac{\pi}{E} = \frac{A}{E} \left[\left(\frac{1+R}{1+r} \right)^T - 1 \right],$$

which illustrates well the classical sources of profit for shareholders: leverage $\frac{A}{E}$ and transformation $\left(\frac{1+R}{1+r} \right)^T - 1$, which increases in T. When leverage is limited by regulation (the capital requirement implies that $A/E \leq 1/k$) shareholders can increase their expected ROE by increasing T, hence the motivation for maturity transformation.

Suppose now that a grain of sand is introduced into the wheels of the perfect markets world: at each period, there is a probability λ that the bank is not able to refinance, either because financial markets are dysfunctional or because investors are suspicious about the real quality of the bank's assets. The probability that the bank will be able to survive the T cycles of refinancing is $(1 - \lambda)^T$. If instead the bank has a (re)financing problem at one of the dates $t = 0, \dots T - 1$, then shareholders lose everything. The expected return on equity becomes

$$ROE = \frac{A}{E} \left[\left\{ (1 - \lambda) \left(\frac{1+R}{1+r} \right) \right\}^T - 1 \right].$$

This is negative if $(1 - \lambda) \left(\frac{1+R}{1+r} \right) < 1$, which is equivalent to $\lambda > \frac{R-r}{1+R}$.

Numerical Example: $R = 5\%$ $R - r = 0.5\%$.
   The expected return on equity is negative if

$$\lambda > \frac{R - r}{1 + R} = \frac{0.5}{105} \simeq 0.474\%.$$

Thus, a very small probability of market dysfunctionality is sufficient to make the Northern Rock strategy unprofitable.

7.5.2 Fallacy 2: Leverage Does not Matter

Consider a firm with cash reserves m, who invests I in some assets that will generate a stream of future earnings. When financial markets are perfect, the value of the investments is measured by the risk neutral (present) value of these future earnings, which we denote by A. We assume that the investment is profitable: A exceeds the amount invested, I. Shareholders want to determine the optimal way to finance this investment. If $m > I$, they can fully self-finance their investment and distribute the excess cash $(m - I)$ in the form of dividends. In this case, shareholder value[7] (with self-financing) is given by:

$$SV_0 = m - I + A. \tag{7.2}$$

An alternative solution is to borrow D against the promise to repay a certain stream of future coupons and repayments (financial expenses), which allows us to distribute a larger dividend $d = m + D - I$ at $t = 0$. However, the ex-dividend value of equity is reduced to some lower value, E, and total shareholder value becomes (with debt financing):

$$SV_1 = m + D - I + E. \tag{7.3}$$

A natural question is: Which type of financing (self-finance or debt) or more generally what financial structure (i.e., combination of debt and equity) maximizes shareholder value?

To compare SV_1 with the shareholder value SV_0 obtained when $D = 0$ (complete self-finance), we have to evaluate E. This can be done easily when financial markets are perfect (efficient and complete). In this case, E is given by the risk neutral present value of future dividends:

$$E = \mathcal{E}_Q[\text{Discounted Future Dividends}], \tag{7.4}$$

where $\mathcal{E}_Q$ represents the expectation operator under the risk neutral probability Q. Similarly, the amount D borrowed at $t = 0$ is equal to the risk neutral expectation of future coupons and debt repayments (financial expenses):

$$D = \mathcal{E}_Q[\text{Discounted Future Financial Expenses}]. \tag{7.5}$$

In the absence of frictions, the sum of the two terms between brackets must be equal to future earnings,[8] thus:

$$E + D = \mathcal{E}_Q[\text{Discounted Future Earnings}] = A.$$

Comparing (7.2) and (7.3) we see that shareholder value is the same under self-financing (SV_0) or under debt financing (SV_1)!

Thus, we have established the following, paradoxical result:

Result 7.1. *(The Modigliani-Miller Theorem) When financial markets are perfect, leverage has no impact on shareholder value.*

This counterintuitive result is called the Modigliani-Miller theorem. The famous economists Modigliani and Miller, who were the first to prove it, were obviously dissatisfied with it. They showed that when corporate taxes are taken into account, leverage matters. The reason is that in most countries, interest expenses are tax deductible.

Thus, corporations have an incentive to increase leverage to minimize taxes. However, increasing leverage also increases the probability that the firm goes bankrupt, and bankruptcy costs are non-negligible. Using the same methodology as in the previous section, we can write a new formula for shareholder value, which incorporates taxes and bankruptcy costs:

$$SV = SV_0 - \mathcal{E}_Q[\text{Discounted Future Taxes}]$$
$$- \mathcal{E}_Q[\text{Discounted Future Bankruptcy Costs}],$$

where SV_0 represents the shareholder value computed above, in a world without taxes nor bankruptcy costs.

Generally speaking, the trade-off between tax optimization and bankruptcy costs implies an optimal level of debt. This optimal level is obtained by minimizing the expected sum of taxes and bankruptcy costs.

7.5.3 Fallacy 3: Risk Management is Useless

An equally paradoxical result can be deduced from the perfect markets assumption: Risk transfers can only **reduce** shareholder value at least for a large firm that is held by a large number of diversified shareholders.

As an illustration, consider the following (fictitious) example. Companies A and B sell sports items, such as soccer jerseys of national teams. Company A specializes in European teams, whereas company B only sells the jerseys of the Brazilian national team. Given that sales increase dramatically for the national team that wins the FIFA World Cup final, company B considers insuring against the risk that Brazil does not win the next World Cup final. This makes sense if company B is held by its manager. It is a nonsense if companies A and B are publicly listed. By holding equal[9] numbers of shares of companies A and B, each investor can costlessly hedge the risk: the gains on the winner will exactly offset the losses of the loser.

However, note that as we already pointed out, the manager of the firm may have different views than shareholders. In particular, he may attach more weight to downside risk than shareholders. Indeed, if the firm makes unexpected profits, this will essentially benefit shareholders. By contrast, the manager incurs the risk of having to find a new job if the firm goes bust or if he is fired after unexpected losses made by the firm. The risk cannot be perfectly insured by market instruments that cover this risk. Thus, the manager has a strict preference for self-financing investments and limiting leverage to a minimum (and more generally for financial strategies that reduce downside risks) to minimize the probability of bankruptcy of the firm.

The generality of the uselessness of risk management within the perfect markets world can be established very easily. Any risk transfer operation (through a market instrument like futures, options,... or an insurance contract) has a zero risk neutral present value (at best: it will in fact be negative if intermediation costs or market power are present). Thus, using the Modigliani-Miller formula first before the risk transfer

$$\text{Shareholder Value} = \mathcal{E}_Q[\text{Discounted Future Earnings}]$$
$$- \mathcal{E}_Q[\text{Discounted Financial Expenses}]$$

and then after the risk transfer:

$$\text{Shareholder Value} = \mathcal{E}_Q[\text{Discounted Future Earnings}]$$
$$- \mathcal{E}_Q[\text{Discounted Financial Expenses}]$$
$$+ \mathcal{E}_Q[\text{Risk Transfer Payments}],$$

we see that the two values coincide so that risk management[10] is useless.

8 The Case of Incomplete Markets: Relating Risk Premiums to Economic Fundamentals

As already mentioned, the risk neutral valuation (RNV) method is too good to be true: It is not reasonable to consider that **any** risky asset can be priced without some knowledge of economic fundamentals such as supply and demand for consumption goods, investment goods and savings. But to incorporate such fundamentals one needs to model the behavior of consumers and investors toward risks. This chapter starts by presenting the expected utility criterion, which solves the famous St Petersburg paradox. This criterion can be very useful in several circumstances: modeling insurance decisions by individuals (Section 8.2) or modeling equilibrium prices in the markets where risks are exchanged (Section 8.3). However, the equilibrium approach to the assessment of risk premiums also has its limits, which are discussed in Section 8.4.

8.1 SOLVING THE ST. PETERSBURG PARADOX

This chapter examines the methods used by economists to value risks in isolation—that is, outside the magic world of complete markets where valuations can be deduced from market prices. The difficulties of valuing risks outside this magic world are well-illustrated by the St. Petersburg paradox, proposed in the eighteenth century by Nicolas Bernoulli and solved by his cousin Daniel Bernoulli. Consider the following lottery: Draw a coin several times, until the first head is obtained. If n draws have been necessary (which means that $[n-1]$ successive tails were obtained before the first head), then the lottery gives a prize of 2^n ducats. The question asked by Bernoulli is: How much should a rational decision maker value the right to participate in such a lottery? A little introspection shows that this number should not be much higher than a few ducats. However, because the probability of winning 2^n ducats is exactly $\frac{1}{2^n}$, the expected value[1] is infinite:

$$\mathcal{E}(\text{gain}) = \left(\frac{1}{2} \times 2\right) + \left(\frac{1}{4} \times 4\right) + \left(\frac{1}{8} \times 8\right) + \cdots = +\infty.$$

Thus, there seems to be contradiction between the most natural criterion that can be used to value a lottery (the expectation or actuarial value of the gains) and what common sense would recommend.

Among the different solutions imagined to solve this paradox, the most reasonable was offered by Daniel Bernoulli, and axiomatized much later by Von Neumann and Morgenstern. It consists in computing the expected **utility** of gain, a method we now explain.

Bernoulli proposed to solve the St. Petersburg paradox by introducing psychological aspects. He claimed that the (marginal) satisfaction of winning one more ducat was inversely proportional to the amount already won, leading him to measure the total satisfaction (or utility as it is now called) of winning x ducats by a quantity that is proportional to the integral:

$$\int_1^x \frac{dt}{t},$$

which is equal to $\log x$, the logarithm of x.

With a logarithmic utility, the maximum price one should be ready to pay for participating in the St Petersburg lottery is exactly 4 ducats. Indeed, the expected utility of this lottery is equal to:[2]

$$\frac{1}{2}\log 2 + \frac{1}{4}\log 4 + \cdots \frac{1}{2^n}\log 2^n + \cdots = \log 4.$$

Now, if $u(x) = \log x$, we can write

$$\mathcal{E}u(\text{gain}) = u(4).$$

Thus, an investor characterized by a logarithmic utility has the same utility by participating in the St. Petersburg lottery or by holding exactly 4 ducats with probability 1.

In 1944, Von Neumann and Morgenstern developed an axiomatic justification of a more general criterion, which allows one to account for the specific characteristics of the decision maker. Von Neumann and Morgenstern proposed to allow any increasing function $u(x)$ to represent the utility of winning x ducats (or dollars to make it more modern). $u(.)$ is called the Von Neumann Morgenstern (in short, VNM) utility function of the decision maker.

It turns out that when u is concave, the expected utility of any lottery $\tilde{\ell}$ is always smaller than the utility of the expectation of this lottery:

$$u \quad \text{concave} \Rightarrow \mathcal{E}u(\tilde{\ell}) \leq u(\mathcal{E}\tilde{\ell}).$$

This is the risk aversion property: A decision maker with preferences associated with a concave VNM utility function always gains by replacing a lottery $\tilde{\ell}$ by

---

BOX 8.1 ∎ The Expected Utility Criterion

To any increasing function, u, one can associate a ranking $\succ$ among lotteries (represented by random variables $\tilde{\ell}_1, \tilde{\ell}_2$ characterizing the associated gains):

$$\tilde{\ell}_1 \succ \tilde{\ell}_2 \Leftrightarrow \mathcal{E}u(\tilde{\ell}_1) \geq \mathcal{E}u(\tilde{\ell}_2)$$

Lottery $\tilde{\ell}_1$ is preferred to lottery $\tilde{\ell}_2$ if and only if the expected utility of $\tilde{\ell}_1$ is greater than the expected utility of $\tilde{\ell}_2$.

BOX 8.2 ■ The Risk Aversion Property

For any concave increasing VNM utility function, u, and any lottery, $\tilde{\ell}$, with a finite expectation $\mathcal{E}\tilde{\ell}$, the expected utility is smaller or equal to the utility of the expectation:

$$\mathcal{E}u(\tilde{\ell}) \leq u(\mathcal{E}\tilde{\ell}).$$

This means that the decision maker prefers a deterministic payment equal to $\mathcal{E}\tilde{\ell}$ to the stochastic payment $\tilde{\ell}$.

---

a non-random payment equal to the expectation of $\tilde{\ell}$. Without risk aversion of policyholders, insurance would not be a viable economic activity. Suppose, indeed, that the lottery $\tilde{\ell}$ represents the difference between an individual's wealth W and some insurable loss $\tilde{x}$:

$$\tilde{\ell} = W - \tilde{x}.$$

The expectation of $\tilde{\ell}$ equals the difference between the policyholder's wealth W and the actuarial premium $P = \mathcal{E}(\tilde{x})$ associated with the insurance of $\tilde{x}$. The insurance of this loss is a viable economic activity when the policyholder is ready to pay at least P to get rid of $\tilde{x}$:

$$u(W - \mathcal{E}(\tilde{x})) \geq \mathcal{E}u(W - \tilde{x}).$$

This is only guaranteed when u is concave.

In the polar case where u is convex, the reverse inequality is satisfied: for any convex function u and any lottery $\tilde{\ell}$, we have that

$$\mathcal{E}u(\tilde{\ell}) \geq u(\mathcal{E}\tilde{\ell}).$$

In this case, the decision maker is eager to take fair bets—that is, prefers any lottery $\tilde{\ell}$ to a non-random payment equal to the expectation of $\tilde{\ell}$.

8.2 CERTAINTY EQUIVALENT

For a given lottery (characterized by a random gain $\tilde{\ell}$) and a given decision maker (characterized by a VNM utility function $u(\cdot)$), the certainty equivalent (CE) is defined as the amount of money that gives the same utility to the decision maker (DM in the sequel) as participating in the lottery:

$$u(CE) = \mathcal{E}u(\tilde{\ell}).$$

In the example of the St. Petersburg lottery and the logarithm utility ($u(x) = \ln x$), the certainty equivalent is easy to obtain because we have seen in Section 8.1 (*see* footnote 2) that $\mathcal{E}\ln(\tilde{x}) = \ln 4$. Thus,

$$\ln(CE) = \ln 4,$$

which gives $CE = 4$. An agent having a logarithmic utility is ready to pay up to 4 ducats for participating in the St Petersburg lottery.

Other results are obtained with alternative specifications of u. One of the most popular of these alternative specifications is the **exponential utility**: $u(x) = t\left[1 - \exp -\frac{x}{t}\right]$, where $t > 0$ is a parameter that characterizes the risk tolerance of the decision maker. It is very popular because, when coupled with normality assumption on $\tilde{\ell}$, it gives raise to simple, explicit formulas. Indeed, when $\tilde{\ell}$ follows a normal distribution with mean μ and variance σ^2, one obtains:

$$\mathcal{E}\left(\exp -\frac{\tilde{\ell}}{t}\right) = \exp\left(-\frac{\mu}{t} + \frac{\sigma^2}{2t^2}\right).$$

Therefore:

$$\mathcal{E}u(\tilde{\ell}) = t\left[1 - \mathcal{E}\left(\exp -\frac{\tilde{\ell}}{t}\right)\right] = t\left[1 - \exp\left(-\frac{\mu}{t} + \frac{\sigma^2}{2t^2}\right)\right]$$

$$= u\left(\mu - \frac{\sigma^2}{2t}\right).$$

This gives a simple formula for the certainty equivalent:

$$CE = \left(\mu - \frac{\sigma^2}{2t}\right).$$

This formula is equivalent to the mean variance criterion presented in the Chapter 9^3. However the expected utility criterion is more flexible, because it can cover situations where the risk tolerance index of the decision maker varies with his wealth or with other parameters that may change in relation with the risks incurred. For firms, this will lead to the notion of shareholder value function, which is presented in Chapter 12 of this book. The VNM utility function is the equivalent for individuals of the shareholder value function for corporations. We now present an application of the VNM utility function to insurance decisions.

APPLICATION: TO BUY OF NOT TO BUY INSURANCE?

Consider an individual or a corporation confronted with a risk of fire: With some probability p, a fire can occur, causing loss L. This decision maker can fully insure this risk by paying a premium P, but he can also retain the risk. In the first case, his utility is $u(W - P)$, where W denotes the policyholder's initial wealth. In the second case, his expected utility is

$$\mathcal{E}u = pu(W - L) + (1 - p)u(W).$$

In the absence of insurance, the certainty equivalent of the losses is defined implicitly by

$$u(W - CE) = pu(W - L) + (1 - p)u(W). \tag{8.1}$$

The rational decision is to buy insurance whenever $P < CE$, which can be interpreted as the maximum acceptable premium.

Numerical Example:

probability of fire	$p = 0.5\%$
loss in case of fire	$L = \$160,000$
individual's wealth	$W = \$250,000$
utility function	$u(x) = \sqrt{x}.$

We have by definition (8.1):

$$u(W - CE) = \sqrt{W - CE} = p\sqrt{W - L} + (1 - p)\sqrt{W}$$
$$= 0.005\sqrt{90,000} + 0.995\sqrt{250,000} = 499.$$

Thus,

$$CE = 250,000 - (499)^2 = 999.$$

The maximum premium that is acceptable for the customer is thus $CE = 999$.

Note that because of risk aversion (which is captured by the property that $u(\ell) = \sqrt{\ell}$ is concave), the actuarial premium $P = 0.005 \times (160,000) = 800$ is lower than CE. Therefore, any insurance premium P in the interval [800, 999] will be "viable" for the insurer, in the sense that it will attract the customer and simultaneously cover the expected losses of the insurer.

8.3 MARKETS FOR EXCHANGING RISKS

With the development of financial markets, the risks specialists of large corporations now have access to several market solutions for exchanging their risks, particularly the large ones. This section starts by a description of some of these market solutions and then relates their functioning to the theoretical model of risk exchange developed by Arrow and Borch.

8.3.1 The Practice

A first example of a market solution for exchanging risk is the Catastrophe Risk Exchange (CATEX) created in New York in 1996 (*see* Box 8.3). Others are derivative products like catastrophe options and catastrophe bonds traded in the Chicago Board of Trade (CBOT).

The CBOT has a long history in the derivatives industry. It was created in 1848 to provide an effective mechanism for buying and selling physical agricultural commodities. In 1992, just after Hurricane Andrew, the insurance and re-insurance industry was looking for new ways of managing and covering catastrophe risks. Several organizations, including the CBOT created new products such as cat options and cat bonds. These products allowed significant expansion of the capacity of the re-insurance market.

BOX 8.3 ■ CATEX

Catastrophe Risk Exchange (CATEX) is a technology solution provider who has been authorized (and is regulated) by the New York Insurance Department as a re-insurance intermediary since 1996.

CATEX provides insurance and re-insurance firms with an instrument to manage more efficiently their portfolio of risks by offering an Internet-based transaction system to exchange catastrophe risks. CATEX is a sort of electronic marketplace on which insurance companies can list risks that they are eager to cede or to swap against other risks. In the first case, the format is a classical re-insurance treaty, in the second, it is a re-insurance swap transaction.

The standard unit of risk is $ 1 million. As an example, an insurance company will increase the diversification on its portfolio by exchanging 15 units of Florida windstorm risk against 20 units of California earthquake risk.

Beside an enhanced management of catastrophe risks, CATEX also reduces transaction costs through its standardized technology solution that improves the administration of re-insurance treaties. This is a significant added value to the market, as reduced costs of administration may develop the number of transactions and create a more efficient market.

CATEX is not the only organization providing this type of services: the Bermuda Commodity Exchange has been developed with the same objective.

In 1995, CBOT proposed a new contract based on an index for insured loss developed by the Property Claims Service (PCS). These cat options are available for nine regions and states in the United States: National, East, Southeast, Northeast, Midwest, West Florida, Texas, and California.

BOX 8.4 ■ Catastrophe Bonds

They allow the securitization of liabilities linked to catastrophe risks:

- A special purpose vehicle (SPV) provides re-insurance to the insurer (excess loss over some threshold ℓ^*).
- SPV issues a bond (called a catastrophe bond). The payment promised by this bond is indexed on the losses ℓ of the insurer.[4]

  - If the losses ℓ of the insurer are smaller than some predetermined threshold ℓ^*: SPV repays the full value of the bonds B.
  - If $\ell > \ell^*$: the SPV only pays $\ell - \ell^*$ to the insurer and $B - (\ell - L^*)$ to bondholders.

In this way, re-insurance risk is fully transferred to bondholders.

Insurance and re-insurance companies can buy the cash settled options to complement traditional re-insurance treaties; PCS options are traded on catastrophes trigger to protect insurers against catastrophe above a certain level.

8.3.2 The Theory

The actuary Karl Borch and the economist Kenneth Arrow have investigated the theoretical question of how risks should be shared within a community of individuals. This is an interesting application of the expected utility framework. Consider, for example, two individuals, indexed $i = 1, 2$ and characterized by VNM utility functions $u_1(\cdot)$ and $u_2(\cdot)$. To simplify notation, suppose that there are only two states of the world $\{1, 2\}$, with probabilities p_1, p_2.

Individuals' wealths are W_1 and W_2, but individual 1 loses L_1 in state 1 and individual 2 loses L_2 in state 2.

Suppose now that risks can be traded on an exchange at prices P_1, P_2. This means that individual i can receive θ_s \$ in state s in exchange for an unconditional payment $P_s \theta_s$ \$ (in both states).

For an insurance position θ_1, θ_2, individual i obtains the following expected utility:

$$U_i = p_1 u_i \left(W_{i1}^0 + \theta_1 - P_1 \theta_1 - P_2 \theta_2 \right) + p_2 u_i \left(W_{i2}^0 + \theta_2 - P_1 \theta_1 - P_2 \theta_2 \right),$$

where W_{i1}^0 and W_{i2}^0 are the "before trade" wealths given in Table 8.1. The optimal insurance position θ_1, θ_2 is obtained by maximizing U_i. It is characterized by the first-order conditions (zero derivatives):

$$\frac{\partial U_i}{\partial \theta_1} = p_1 u_i'(W_{i1})[1 - P_1] - p_2 u_i'(W_{i2})P_1 = 0,$$

and

$$\frac{\partial U_i}{\partial \theta_2} = -p_1 u_i'(W_{i1})P_2 + p_2 u_i'(W_{i2})[1 - P_2] = 0,$$

where W_{i1} and W_{i2} represent the "after-trade" wealths of individual i:

$$W_{is} = W_{is}^0 + \theta_s - P_1 \theta_1 - P_2 \theta_2.$$

Solving for P_1 and P_2, we obtain:

$$P_1 = \frac{p_1 u_i'(W_{i1})}{p_1 u_i'(W_{i1}) + p_2 u_i'(W_{i2})} \quad \text{for all } i,$$

TABLE 8.1. *Before Trade Wealths*

States \\ Wealths	Individual 1	Individual 2
State 1	$W_1 - L_1$	W_2
State 2	W_1	$W_2 - L_2$

and similarly,

$$P_2 = \frac{p_2 u_i'(W_{i2})}{p_1 u_i'(W_{i1}) + p_2 u_i'(W_{i2})} \quad \text{for all } i,$$

Thus, the optimal position taken by each individual on the risk exchange is such that the marginal rate of substitution between incomes in the two states is equal to the ratio of prices:

$$\frac{p_1 u_i'(W_{i1})}{p_2 u_i'(W_{i2})} = \frac{P_1}{P_2} \qquad \text{for} \quad i = 1, 2, \tag{8.2}$$

where W_{is} denotes the after-trade wealth of individual i in state s. The intuition for this can be established by contradiction: if $\frac{P_1}{P_2}$ was, for example, strictly less than this marginal rate of substitution, individual i could increase his expected utility by buying a little more of insurance against risk 1 and a little less of insurance against risk 2.

Equation (8.2) implies a very important property: after-trade wealths of risk-averse individuals are necessarily **co-monotonic**—that is, they move in the same way in the different states. If, for example, $W_{11} > W_{12}$ (individual 1's after trade wealth is higher in state 1) then by concavity of u_1 we have that $u_1'(W_{11}) < u_1'(W_{12})$ (marginal utility is higher in state 2), and therefore, by the above property:

$$\frac{u_1'(W_{11})}{u_1'(W_{12})} = \frac{p_2 P_1}{p_1 P_2} < 1.$$

Now the analogous inequality is also valid for individual 2:

$$\frac{u_2'(W_{21})}{u_2'(W_{22})} = \frac{p_2 P_1}{p_1 P_2} < 1.$$

This implies (by concavity of u_2) that $W_{21} > W_{22}$: individual 2's after-trade wealth is also higher in state 2.

8.3.3 Diversifiable Risk

Consider first the case where the possible losses of the two individuals are equal. This means $L_1 = L_2 = L$, so that there is no aggregate risk. Total wealth is constant across states:

$$W_{11} + W_{21} = W_{12} + W_{22} = W_1 + W_2 - L.$$

The co-monotonicity property established above implies that after-trade wealths of individuals must be constant across states: if, say, W_{11} was strictly less than W_{12}, this would be true also for individual 2 and by aggregation $W_{11} + W_{21} < W_{12} + W_{22}$. This would contradict the property that total wealth is constant across states.

After-trade incomes of individual 1 are thus

$$W_{11} = W_1 - L + \theta_1 - \theta_1 P_1 + \theta_2 P_2 \qquad \text{in state 1,}$$

TABLE 8.2. *After Trade Wealths When Risks Are Diversifiable*

States \ Wealths	Individual 1	Individual 2
State 1	$W_1 - p_1 L$	$W_2 - p_2 L$
State 2	$W_1 - p_1 L$	$W_2 - p_2 L$

and

$$W_{12} = W_1 - \theta_2 - \theta_1 P_1 + \theta_2 P_2 \qquad \text{in state 2.}$$

Equality of these two incomes implies that

$$\theta_1 + \theta_2 = L.$$

Moreover, buying one unit of each contract gives \$1 for sure, which implies that

$$P_1 + P_2 = 1.$$

Now, using that $W_{11} = W_{12}$, equation (8.2) gives

$$\frac{P_1}{P_2} = \frac{p_1}{p_2}.$$

Thus, the ratio of prices $\frac{P_1}{P_2}$ is equal to the ratio of probabilities $\frac{p_1}{p_2}$. Because $P_1 + P_2 = p_1 + p_2 = 1$, it must be that $P_1 = p_1$ and $P_2 = p_2$. We see that in this case (the case of fully diversifiable risks) market prices of risks are just equal to their probabilities. Moreover, using all these properties, we can compute after-trade wealths:

$$W_{11} = W_{12} = W_1 - p_1 L,$$

and similarly,

$$W_{21} = W_{22} = W_2 - p_2 L.$$

This arrangement can be obtained by an insurance mutuality where individual risks are pooled. Each individual is completely insured, in exchange for the payment of an actuarial premium, $p_1 L$ for individual 1, and $p_2 L$ for individual 2 (note that the mutuality principle does not imply that premiums are necessarily equal across individuals: if $p_1 \neq p_2$, then premiums are different).

8.3.4 Aggregate Risks

In more general cases, perfect diversification cannot be attained: some aggregate risk remains. Assume, for example, that the loss L_1 of individual 1 in state 1 is smaller than the loss L_2 of individual 2 in state 2. Thus, aggregate wealth is smaller in state 2 (which we interpret as a recession) than in state 1 (which we interpret as a boom).

In this case, the co-monotonicity property implies that after-trade wealths of both individuals are also smaller in state 2 than in state 1:

$$W_{11} > W_{12} \quad \text{and} \quad W_{21} > W_{22}.$$

Then prices of risks are not equal to their probabilities:

$$\frac{P_1}{P_2} = \frac{p_1}{p_2} \frac{u_i'(W_{i1})}{u_i'(W_{i2})} < \frac{p_1}{p_2}.$$

Because $P_1 + P_2 = p_1 + p_2 = 1$, this implies that $P_1 < p_1$ and $P_2 > p_2$.

The market price of risk 1, which is also equal to the risk adjusted probability of state 1, is lower than the historical probability p_1 of state 1 (the reverse is true for state 2).

Property 8.1. *When there is some aggregate risk, the risk neutral probability measure[5] (P_1, P_2) gives more weight to unfavorable events (like a recession) and less weight to favorable events (like a boom) than the "historical" probability measure (p_1, p_2). In other words, the risk neutral measure is pessimistic.*

Finally, optimal risk sharing implies that every individual bears some fraction of aggregate risk: no one is perfectly insured. More precisely, the fraction of risk borne by each individual has to be proportional to the risk tolerance of the individual. To get simple formulas, we consider the case where utility functions are exponential:

$$u_i(x) = t_i \left[1 - \exp -\frac{x}{t_i} \right],$$

where $t_i > 0$ is the risk tolerance factor of individual i. Marginal utilities are given by $u_i'(x) = \exp -\frac{x}{t_i}$.

In this case, after-trade wealths W_{is} can be computed explicitly, because marginal rates of substitution are easy to compute

$$\frac{u_i'(W_{i1})}{u_i'(W_{i2})} = \exp \left[\frac{W_{i2} - W_{i1}}{t_i} \right].$$

These marginal rates of substitution must be equal across individuals. Thus, we must have:

$$\frac{W_{11} - W_{12}}{t_1} = \frac{W_{21} - W_{22}}{t_2}.$$

This means that the loss incurred by individual i in case of a recession (state 2) is proportional to t_i. Because the total loss $(W_{11} + W_{21}) - (W_{12} + W_{22})$ is equal to $L_2 - L_1$, we see that

$$W_{11} - W_{12} = \frac{t_1}{t_1 + t_2}(L_2 - L_1),$$

$$\text{and} \quad W_{21} - W_{22} = \frac{t_2}{t_1 + t_2}(L_2 - L_1).$$

TABLE 8.3. *Aggregate Risks, After Trade Wealths*

States / Incomes	Individual 1	Individual 2
State 1	$W_1 - \frac{t_1 L_1}{t_1 + t_2}$	$W_2 - \frac{t_2 L_1}{t_1 + t_2}$
State 2	$W_1 - \frac{t_1 L_2}{t_1 + t_2}$	$W_2 - \frac{t_2 L_2}{t_1 + t_2}$

Property 8.2. *Optimal risk sharing implies that aggregate risk is allocated to each individual in proportion to his risk tolerance.*

The efficient allocation of risk can be obtained through a co-insurance arrangement, whereby individual 1 transfers a fraction $\frac{t_2}{t_1 + t_2}$ of his risk to individual 2 and accepts a fraction $\frac{t_1}{t_1 + t_2}$ of individual 2's risk:

$$\begin{cases} W_{11} = W_1 - \frac{t_1 L_1}{t_1 + t_2} \\ W_{12} = W_1 - \frac{t_1 L_2}{t_1 + t_2} \end{cases}$$

Note that after-trade wealths of all individuals are lower in state 2 than in state 1 (this is because $L_2 > L_1$); aggregate risk is borne by all. However, if $t_1 < t_2$, individual 1 is less risk-tolerant than individual 2 and thus bears less risk.

Rule 8.1. *Optimal Risk Sharing*

The expected utility criterion gives a useful methodology for deciding how to use market instruments for sharing risks among firms or individuals. Two very different cases have to be distinguished: diversifiable risks and aggregate risks.

A risk is diversifiable if it does not impact the total resources of the community. This type of risk can be completely eliminated by mutualization: each individual fully transfers his own risk to the exchange, and prices of risks only reflect their actuarial values (no risk premium). For this type of risk, the risk neutral measure coincides with the historical probability measure.

By contrast, an aggregate risk (like the risk of a recession) has a non-predictible impact on the total resources of the community. This type of risk has to be shared by all the members of the community in proportion to their risk tolerance. Individuals or firms with an exposure that is larger than their risk tolerance (relative to the total risk tolerance of the community) are net sellers of the risk on the exchange, whereas individuals or firms with an exposure that is lower than their risk tolerance are net buyers of the risk.

8.4 THE LIMITS OF THE EQUILIBRIUM APPROACH

8.4.1 The Case of Incomplete Markets

When financial markets are complete, risks are optimally allocated, and RNV works. A sophisticated investor who knows the economic fundamentals can, in principle, compute the risk adjusted probability measure: multiplying historical probabilities by marginal utilities of consumption and scaling them to get a probability measure. But, of course, it is much simpler to deduce the risk-adjusted measure from observed assets prices: this is the RNV methodology, which is equivalent to, but much simpler than, the equilibrium approach.

Everything breaks down when markets are not complete: risk allocation is not necessarily optimal and risk premiums cannot be deduced from the mere observation of asset prices. They depend in a complicated way on economic fundamentals. Chapter 9 explores the only case where risk premiums are easy to compute, even when markets are incomplete: if the joint distribution of all asset returns is Normal, the Capital Asset Pricing Model (CAPM) is indeed valid, and risk premiums are proportional to one simple factor: the regression coefficient of the asset return on the market return (the beta of the asset). Unfortunately, outside this Normal world, there is no simple way to compute risk premiums.

Of course, it could be argued that markets are "approximately" complete, in which case the RNV approach would be "approximately" valid. Unfortunately, there is a lot of indirect empirical evidence suggesting that financial markets are far from being complete. For example, market completeness would imply optimal risk sharing, and thus co-monotonicity of after-trade incomes. Recent crises tend to exhibit a different pattern, whereby some investors make a lot of money, whereas the majority of others loses: co-monotonicity is violated. More generally, many economists consider that financial markets sometimes magnify real shocks instead of dampening them, which is also a clear symptom of market incompleteness.

8.4.2 Knightian Uncertainty and the Ellsberg Paradox

The expected utility criterion has an important drawback: it does not fit very well the observed behavior of individuals who are uncertain about the (historical) probability distributions of risks.

The psychologist Ellsberg is famous for organizing the following experiment: individuals are asked to select between two urns containing black and white balls and then to draw one ball from the urn they have selected. The first urn contains the same numbers of black and white balls. The content of the second urn is uncertain. In the first experiment, individuals are told that they will receive a prize if they pick up a black ball. In the second experiment, it is the reverse: they receive a prize if they pick up a white ball. Asked to select one urn in each experiment, a great majority of individuals select the first urn (the one with a 50% chance to win) in both cases.

This seems natural but happens to be totally incompatible with the expected utility framework. Indeed, in this framework, each individual is supposed to form an expectation, p, of the frequency of black balls in the second urn. An individual who behaves like an expected utility maximizer will always select different urns in the two experiments (independently of his VNM utility function). If $p > 1/2$, he should select the first urn in the first experiment and the second urn in the second experiment. If $p < 1/2$, the converse is true. When $p = 1/2$, he should be strictly indifferent. None of these cases can explain the observed behavior of the majority of individuals. This observed behavior can only be explained by uncertainty aversion: most individuals prefer a situation where the distribution or risks is known to a situation where the distribution of risks is uncertain.

To capture the intuition behind Ellsberg's results, assume, for example, that individuals hesitate between three scenarios:

Scenario 1: The second urn also contains the same numbers of black balls and white balls.

Scenario 2: The second urn contains more black balls.

Scenario 3: The second urn contains more white balls.

Suppose now that the individual always considers the **worst-case scenario:** he aims at maximizing the **minimum** of the probabilities of gain in the three scenarios. It is clear then that he will select the first urn (which guarantees a probability of gain of 50%) in both experiments. This is because, in both experiments, there is a scenario that gives a strictly smaller probability of gain with the second urn.

8.4.3 When Markets Stop Functioning

The subprime crisis has also shown that some well-established markets can just stop functioning in some circumstances. This is the case in the example of the Asset-Backed Commercial Paper (ABCP) market that was a vital source of short-term financing for many firms and that completely dried up in the middle of the subprime crisis. One explanation often provided by economists is **adverse selection:** buyers had less information than sellers about the quality of the paper being sold. The following simple model, adapted from Akerlof's famous paper ("The Market for "Lemons": Quality Uncertainty and The Market Mechanism" *Quarterly Journal of Economics* 84(3), 488–500), illustrates how adverse selection can provoke the interruption of markets.

Consider a financial market where banks have the possibility to sell some of their assets to investors. The quality q of each asset, measured by the expected present value of its future cash flows, is known to the seller (the bank) but not to the buyers (the investors). Buyers only know the statistical distribution of the quality of asset being securitized. We are going to show that such markets are fragile: When adverse selection becomes too strong, these markets can stop functioning.

The maximum price P that buyers are ready to pay for each of these assets (that they cannot distinguish) is indeed the **average** quality of the assets on the markets:

$$P = \mathcal{E}(q|q \text{ is on the market}).$$

Suppose now that banks have access to a new investment opportunity, characterized by an expected present value of $(1 + R)$ per unit of investment. If they can securitize one of their assets at price P and reinvest the proceeds into this new opportunity, they obtain an expected present value of $P(1 + R)$, to be compared with q if they keep their original asset. Thus, banks are ready to sell their assets for a price below their quality (this is the economic justification of securitization), but there is a lower limit; the minimum price at which a bank accepts to securitize an asset of quality q is:

$$P_{\min}(q) = \frac{q}{1 + R} < q.$$

If q was observable by buyers, then the market price would fully reflect it:

$$P = q,$$

and all gains from trade would be exploited:

$$P = q > P_{\min}(q) = \frac{q}{1+R} \text{ for all } q.$$

However, when q is not observable by buyers, the sellers might refuse to securitize some of their assets. This happens when

$$q > P(1+R).$$

By contrast, the banks are always willing to securitize their low-quality assets, such that:

$$q \le P(1+R).$$

This is the essence of the adverse selection phenomenon: a (securitization) market always attracts the lowest quality sellers (banks). In general, trade is not efficient: the good quality assets are retained, and the banks that hold them cannot refinance. Sometimes the market can even stop altogether. To see this, assume that the statistical distribution of asset qualities is uniform on some interval $[q_0, q_1]$. When $q_1 - q_0$ is small (mild adverse selection), all assets are securitized (efficient trading) at price $P = \frac{1}{2}(q_0 + q_1)$. This happens if and only if $P \ge \frac{q_1}{1+R}$, which is equivalent to $q_1 \le q_0 \frac{1+R}{1-R}$.

In the opposite case:

$$q_1 > q_0 \frac{1+R}{1-R},$$

only the assets with quality in the interval $\left[q_0, P(1+R)\right]$ are put on the market, and the securitization price P is equal to the average quality of the assets on the market:

$$P = \frac{1}{2}\left[q_0 + P(1+R)\right],$$

which allows to determine the equilibrium price:

$$P = \frac{q_0}{1-R},$$

and the volume of trade

$$V = P(1+R) - q_0 = \frac{2q_0 R}{1-R}.$$

Suppose now that the minimum quality of assets suddenly deteriorates: q_0 becomes zero. Then the volume of trade also becomes equal to zero: the market stops functioning altogether. The presence of very low-quality assets that cannot be distinguished from the others is enough to precipitate the complete halt of securitization markets.

9 Risk Management in a Normal World

Risk managers and financial modelers often assume that distributions of risks are jointly normal, even when normality is rejected by the data! There are two main reasons for this:

- The return on any portfolio of risks that have a (jointly) normal distribution also has a normal distribution, whose mean and variance can be computed by simple formulas: linear for the mean, quadratic for the variance.
- The distribution of any (scalar) normal random variable is completely determined by its mean μ and its variance σ^2. In fact, it is equivalent to a simple transformation $\mu + \sigma \tilde{y}$ of a normal random variable with mean 0 and variance 1 (such a random variable $\tilde{y}$ is called a standard normal).

In particular, the expected utility of a (scalar) normal random variable of mean μ and variance σ^2 only depends[1] on μ and σ:

$$\mathcal{E}u(\tilde{x}) = \mathcal{E}u(\mu + \sigma \tilde{y}) = \frac{1}{\sqrt{2\pi}} \int u(\mu + \sigma y) \exp\left(-\frac{y^2}{2}\right) dy.$$

This chapter explores the beauties of the Normal world: the mean–variance criterion can be used safely [Section (9.1)], portfolio choice is easy [Section (9.2)], the diversification principle works well [Section (9.3)] and portfolio efficiency can be measured by the Sharpe ratio [Section (9.4)]. More importantly, in a Normal world, risk premiums are easy to compute even when markets are incomplete. They are given by the Capital Asset Pricing Model (CAPM), which is presented in Section 9.5. Normality assumptions also imply that hedging decisions on futures markets obey simple rules [Section (9.6)] as well as the allocation of economic capital between several divisions of a bank [Section (9.7)]. Unfortunately, the real world is not Normal. This is why the chapter concludes by showing the dangers of persisting to view the world as Normal, in spite of contrary empirical evidence [Section (9.8)].

9.1 THE MEAN–VARIANCE CRITERION

When risks are (jointly) normal, the trade-off between risk and return on a portfolio of assets can entirely be captured by two numbers: the expectation (or mean) $\mathcal{E}(\tilde{R})$ of the gross return $\tilde{R}$ of the portfolio and its variance $\text{var}(\tilde{R})$. Indeed the expected utility of the investor equals[2]

$$\mathcal{E}u(\tilde{R}) = \int u\left(\mathcal{E}(\tilde{R}) + y\sqrt{\text{var}(\tilde{R})}\right) dN(y) = V\left(\mathcal{E}(\tilde{R}), \text{var}(\tilde{R})\right),$$

where V is an increasing function of $\mathcal{E}(\tilde{R})$ (if u is increasing) and a decreasing function of $\mathrm{var}(\tilde{R})$ (if u is concave). In the case where u is exponential $\left(u(x) = t\left[1 - \exp -\frac{x}{t}\right]\right)$, the certainty equivalent of the portfolio is exactly:

$$CE = \mathcal{E}(\tilde{R}) - \frac{1}{2t}\mathrm{var}(\tilde{R}). \qquad (9.1)$$

t is a strictly positive coefficient that characterizes the **risk tolerance** of the investor. The greater t, the larger the level of risk the investor is willing to take for a given increase in the expected return. When the investor has an exponential von Neumann Morgenstern (VNM) utility:

$$u(x) = t\left[1 - \exp -\frac{x}{t}\right],$$

his risk tolerance t is constant:

$$-\frac{u''(x)}{u'(x)} \equiv t.$$

For more general utilities, risk tolerance depends on the investor's wealth, but the mean variance criterion is still valid.

This mean variance criterion is one of the most commonly used risk management tools in finance. It allows each investor to evaluate his investment decisions in a consistent fashion. It relies on two assumptions:

- Risk can be accurately measured by the variance of the return.
- All investors prefer projects with a higher expected return (measured by the mean or average return) and a lower risk. Thus, there is a risk–return trade-off.

In a normal world, the first assumption is true and the second assumption holds as soon as an investor's utility function is increasing (monotonicity) and concave (risk-aversion).

Individual investors may have different preferences: They may be ready to take on more or less risk for a given increase in the mean return. In economists' terminology, investors may be more or less risk-averse. These differences in behavior are captured here by the parameter t, characteristic of each investor, and called the **risk tolerance index** of the investor. Formally, t can be defined as half the increase in the variance of the investment's return that the investor accepts in exchange for an increase of 1% in the expected return. The lower t, the more risk-averse the investor. This parameter t differs across investors but should remain constant across all risky choices by the same investor to preserve consistency of his choices. We now present different applications of this mean–variance criterion.

9.2 PORTFOLIO CHOICE

Consider some investor who wants to allocate his wealth between two assets: a riskless asset (say a Treasury Bond with a maturity equal to the investor's time horizon)[3] that provides a sure return r_F (the risk-free rate) and a risky asset (e.g., a Stock Index Fund) that provides a stochastic return $\tilde{r}$. Typically, the expectation of $\tilde{r}$ is higher than r_F (i.e., on average, the risky asset has a higher return), but the probability that $\tilde{r} < r_F$ is not negligible. This means that an investment in the risky asset may, in some cases, end up being less profitable than an investment in the Treasury Bond. Let us denote by θ the fraction of his wealth that the investor puts in the risky asset. The net return obtained by the investor on his portfolio is thus

$$\tilde{R} = (1 - \theta)r_F + \theta\tilde{r}. \tag{9.2}$$

If the investor uses a mean–variance criterion with risk tolerance t, he aims at maximizing:

$$U = \mathcal{E}[\tilde{R}] - \frac{1}{2t} \text{var}[\tilde{R}].$$

Replacing $\tilde{R}$ by its value given by (9.2), we can write U as a function of θ:

$$U(\theta) = (1 - \theta)r_F + \theta\mathcal{E}(\tilde{r}) - \frac{\theta^2}{2t} \text{var}(\tilde{r}). \tag{9.3}$$

This is a quadratic function of θ, which is represented in Figure 9.1. U reaches its maximum when

$$U'(\theta) = 0.$$

Now we have:

$$U'(\theta) = -r_F + \mathcal{E}(\tilde{r}) - \frac{\theta}{t} \text{var}(\tilde{r}).$$

Thus:

$$\theta^* = t \cdot \frac{[\mathcal{E}(\tilde{r}) - r_F]}{\text{var}(\tilde{r})}.$$

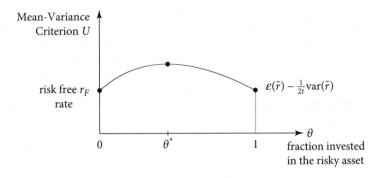

Figure 9.1 Influence of portfolio composition θ on the Mean-Variance Criterion U. θ^* is the optimal choice.

Rule 9.1. *Investment in a Single Risky Asset*
The fraction θ^* of the investor's wealth that should be invested in the risky asset is

$$\theta^* = t \times \frac{\mathcal{E}[\tilde{r}] - r_F}{var\,[\tilde{r}]}, \tag{9.4}$$

where

$$t = risk\ tolerance\ of\ the\ investor$$

$$\mathcal{E}[\tilde{r}] = expected\ return\ on\ the\ risky\ asset$$

$$r_F = return\ on\ the\ riskless\ asset$$

$$var\,[\tilde{r}] = variance\ of\ the\ risky\ asset's\ return.$$

The optimal portfolio is thus characterized by θ^*—that is, the fraction of wealth invested in the risky asset. Formula (9.4) shows that this fraction θ^* is:

- an increasing function of t, the risk tolerance index of the investor;
- an increasing function of the expected excess return $\mathcal{E}(\tilde{r}) - r_F$ on the risky asset;
- a decreasing function of var $(\tilde{r})$, the variance of the return on the risky asset.

Numerical Example:
As an illustration, consider the following numerical example: risk tolerance index $t = 2$, risk-free rate $r_F = 2\%$ expected return on the risky asset $\mathcal{E}(\tilde{r}) = 6\%$, variance var $(\tilde{r}) = 20\%$

$$\theta^* = t\frac{[\mathcal{E}(\tilde{r}) - r_F]}{var\,(\tilde{r})} = 2 \times \frac{[6-2]}{20} = 0.4.$$

The model suggests that the investor should invest 40% of his portfolio in the stock index and 60% in Treasury bonds.

9.3 THE DIVERSIFICATION PRINCIPLE

If there are n risky assets with independent returns $\tilde{r}_i (i = 1, \ldots, n)$ the mean–variance approach recommends that the investor should allocate his wealth according to the same rule:

$$\theta_i = t \times \frac{\mathcal{E}[\tilde{r}_i] - r_F}{var\,[\tilde{r}_i]}.$$

However, when returns are not independent (but still Normal), the formula is more complicated. Correlations have to be taken into account (*see* Appendix 1 for details). For example, when there are two risky assets ($n = 2$) with equal variance and the same expected return, the fraction of wealth invested in each of them should be:

$$\theta = t \times \frac{\mathcal{E}(\tilde{r}) - r_F}{var\,[\tilde{r}]}\left[\frac{1}{1+\rho}\right],$$

TABLE 9.1. *The Impact of Correlation on Portfolio Choice*

Assets' correlation	$\rho = -0.5$	$\rho = -0.2$	$\rho = 0$	$\rho = 0.2$	$\rho = 0.5$
Fraction to be invested in each risky asset	$\theta = 0.80^4$	$\theta = 0.50$	$\theta = 0.40$	$\theta = 0.34$	$\theta = 0.26$

where $\rho = \text{cor}\,(\tilde{r}_1, \tilde{r}_2)$ denotes the correlation between the returns of the two assets. The value $\rho = 0$ corresponds to the case of independent assets described above. When ρ is negative, diversification decreases the risk on the portfolio; thus, the investor can invest more in each asset. When ρ is positive, the opposite is true.

The diversification principle is the scientific version of the well-known proverb: "Do not put all your eggs in the same basket." It is more precise that the proverb, as it shows that correlation matters. Indeed, investors should try to allocate their wealth into different assets with **negative** correlation: If one of these assets loses, it is likely that the others will gain.

By contrast, allocating one's wealth to assets that are positively correlated does not reduce risk.

To illustrate the importance of the diversification effect, consider the same numerical example as in Section 9.2: risk tolerance index $t = 2$, risk-free rate $r_F = 2\%$, expected return on each risky asset $\mathcal{E}(\tilde{r}) = 6\%$, variance var $(\tilde{r}) = 20\%$. Table 9.1 represents the fraction θ for different values of the correlation ρ between the risky assets.

We see that the impact of correlation on optimal financing decision is non-linear: a decrease in ρ from 0.5 to 0.2 has only a minor impact, whereas a decrease from -0.2 to -0.5 leads to a large increase in the fraction invested in risky assets.

The case of several risky assets is treated in more detail in Appendix 2.

9.4 EFFICIENT PORTFOLIOS AND THE SHARPE RATIO

Consider now a set of risky securities (like the stocks included in the S&P 500 index in the New York Stock Exchange) and plot their expected returns and standard deviations in a graph as well as those of all the portfolios that can be obtained by combining these securities. Markowitz was the first to characterize the shape of the region obtained in the (standard deviation, expected return) plane.[5] It is represented by the shaded area in Figure 9.2.

If these portfolios are combined with the risk-free asset (corresponding to F in Figure 9.2), we see that all mean variance efficient portfolios lie on the line FP.

This means that all these portfolios (such as the one represented by E in Figure 9.2) can be obtained by investing some fraction θ of the investor's wealth in a fixed portfolio P (itself mean–variance efficient) and the remaining fraction $1 - \theta$ in the risk-free asset. The excess return $\mathcal{E}(\tilde{r}) - r_F$ and the standard deviation $\sqrt{\text{var}\,(\tilde{r})}$ are both proportional[6] to θ. Because $\tilde{r} = \theta\tilde{r}_p + (1 - \theta)r_F$ (where $\tilde{r}_p$ is the return on portfolio p) we have: $\mathcal{E}(\tilde{r}) - r_F = \theta(\mathcal{E}(\tilde{r}_p) - r_F)$ and $\sqrt{\text{var}\,(\tilde{r})} = \theta\sqrt{\text{var}\,(\tilde{p})}$.

Thus,

$$\frac{\mathcal{E}(\tilde{r}) - r_F}{\sqrt{\text{var}\,(\tilde{r})}} = \frac{\mathcal{E}(\tilde{r}_p) - r_F}{\sqrt{\text{var}\,(\tilde{r})}}$$

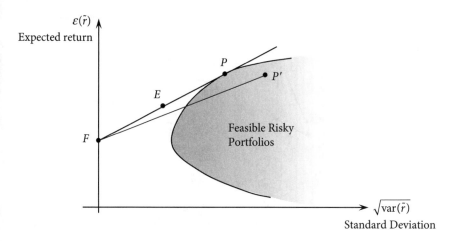

Figure 9.2 Feasible portfolios (the shaded area).

is invariant across all mean–variance efficient portfolios. This means that these efficient portfolios can be easily detected by computing their Sharpe ratio, defined as

$$SR = \frac{\mathcal{E}(\tilde{r}) - r_F}{\sqrt{\text{var}(\tilde{r})}}$$

—namely, the ratio of the expected excess return of the portfolio over its standard deviation.

A mean–variance efficient portfolio is indeed characterized by the property that its Sharpe ratio is equal to the maximum possible Sharpe ratio among feasible portfolios.

Consider, for example, Figure 9.2: portfolio P' is inefficient because its Sharpe ratio (represented by the slope of the line FP') is lower than that of portfolio P.

If all investors adopt mean–variance criteria, all the portfolios selected by these investors are mean–variance-efficient. This implies that the market portfolio is itself mean–variance efficient. Thus, the maximum Sharpe ratio is equal to the Sharpe ratio of the market portfolio

$$SR^M = \frac{\mathcal{E}(\tilde{r}^M) - r_F}{\sqrt{\text{var}(\tilde{r}^M)}}.$$

As we already saw, the set of efficient portfolios forms a line in the (standard deviation, expected return) plane. It is called the **market line**. This is because any efficient portfolio can be obtained by combining the riskless asset and the market portfolio. Inefficient portfolios are below the market line. The slope of the market line is equal to SR^M.

Figure 9.3 illustrates this property.

Numerical Example: *Riskless rate $r_F = 2\%$, expected market return $\mathcal{E}(\tilde{r}^M) = 6\%$, variance on market return var $(\tilde{r}^M) = 20\%$. The Sharpe Ratio of the market portfolio*

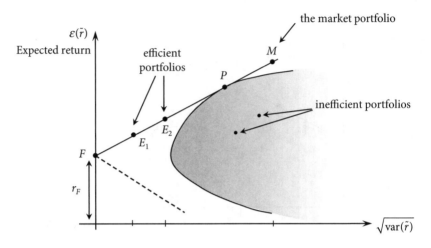

Figure 9.3 The market portfolio *M* and the market line *FM*.

is thus:

$$SR^M = \frac{\mathcal{E}(\tilde{r}^M) - r_F}{\sqrt{\text{var}\,(\tilde{r}^M)}} = \frac{0.06 - 0.02}{\sqrt{0.2}} \sim 8.94\%.$$

The Sharpe Ratio is the slope of the market line *FM* in Figure 9.3. In this figure, we have assumed that the market portfolio *M* corresponded to an aggregate risk tolerance index $t_M = 5$. t_M is the weighted sum of all investors' risk tolerance indices, where the weights reflect the wealth of each investor.

For example, an investor with risk tolerance $t_1 = 1$ will select portfolio E_1 (corresponding to $\theta_1 = \frac{1}{5} = 20\%$), whereas an investor with risk tolerance $t_2 = 2$ will select portfolio E_2 (corresponding to $\theta_2 = \frac{2}{5} = 40\%$).

9.5 THE CAPITAL ASSET PRICING MODEL (CAPM)

The CAPM, elaborated by Markovitz, Shiller, and Sharpe, is the most spectacular offspring of the Normal world. It enables investors and risk professionals to compute risk premiums, even if markets are incomplete, through a very simple formula that does not require detailed information on economic fundamentals. As explained in Appendix 2, it relies on the observation that in a Normal world, all investors should hold portfolios that are mean–variance-efficient. Such portfolios can be obtained by combining the risk-free asset and the market portfolio (this result is known as the two-fund principle) in different proportions, depending on the investor's risk tolerance. Thus, the market portfolio itself must be mean–variance-efficient, which implies that the risk premium on any risky asset *k* (defined as the difference between the expected return $\mathcal{E}(\tilde{r}_k)$ on this asset and the risk-free return r_F) should be proportional to the regression coefficient of $\tilde{r}_k$ on the market return $\tilde{r}_M$:

$$\beta_k = \frac{\text{cov}(\tilde{r}_k, \tilde{r}_M)}{\text{var}(\tilde{r}_M)}.$$

The CAPM formula above (*see* Appendix 2 for details) means that at the equilibrium of financial markets, the excess return on each asset only depends on its correlation with the market return. Thus, the risk premium on asset k—namely, its excess return $\mathcal{E}(\tilde{r}_k) - r_F$—only depends on β_k, which measures systematic risk and not on the variance $(\tilde{r}_k)$. This is because the model assumes that investors can perfectly diversify their portfolios and therefore can eliminate the idiosyncratic risk component.

Alas, the very elegant CAPM formula has been consistently rejected by the vast majority of empirical studies. The most convincing statistical analyses of the determinants of risk premiums show indeed that one factor (the market return) is not sufficient to explain the variability of risk premiums. More factors are needed, implicitly showing again that Normal hypothesis is of very limited relevance for studying financial markets.

9.6 FUTURES CONTRACTS AND HEDGING

Futures contracts are a fundamental instrument for corporate risk management. The mean–variance framework constitutes a first approach for determining optimal hedging decisions through future contracts.

Consider, for example, an entrepreneur who wants to hedge his earnings by using a futures contract. This may be because some fraction of the company's revenue is paid in U.S., dollars although the company is incorporated in Europe. Then, the entrepreneur can use a dollar–euro futures contract to cover some fraction of the exchange rate risk. Mathematically, let $\tilde{y}$ denote the company's (gross) earnings, $\tilde{s}$ the (spot) exchange rate dollar–euro (the price of \$1 in euros), F the future price of the U.S. dollars in euros, and x the futures position taken by the entrepreneur—that is, the number of contracts bought by the firm (or sold if $x < 0$). The net earnings of the company are:

$$\tilde{W} = \tilde{y} + x(\tilde{s} - F). \tag{9.5}$$

Assuming the entrepreneur uses a mean–variance criterion with risk tolerance index t:

$$U = \mathcal{E}(\tilde{W}) - \frac{1}{2t}\,\text{var}(\tilde{W}), \tag{9.6}$$

the optimal future position is obtained by replacing $\tilde{W}$ by its expression given in (9.5):

$$U = \mathcal{E}(\tilde{y}) + x(\mathcal{E}(\tilde{s}) - F) - \frac{1}{2t}\left[\text{var}(\tilde{y}) + 2x\,\text{cov}(\tilde{y}, \tilde{s}) + x^2\,\text{var}(\tilde{s})\right], \tag{9.7}$$

BOX 9.1 ■ Futures Contracts

A futures contract is a commitment by two parties to exchange some product (which can be a commodity, a currency, or a financial asset) at a future date (the delivery date) for a prespecified price F (the futures price). The futures position x of an economic agent represents the number of contracts bought (if $x > 0$) or minus the number of contracts sold (if $x < 0$). At the expiration date, the profit or loss incurred by the agent on his futures position x is the product of x by $(\tilde{s} - F)$, where $\tilde{s}$ denotes the spot price of the product underlying the contract. When the contract is signed, $\tilde{s}$ is of course unknown, hence it is modeled as a random variable. Because there are always a buyer and a seller in a futures contract, one of them ultimately incurs a loss, exactly matching the gain of his counterparty. This is why the exchanges that organize the trading of futures contracts require participants to post cash deposits or collateral to guarantee that they will be able to fulfill their obligations at the delivery date; these deposits are called margins. By contrast, forward contracts, which are the over-the-counter equivalent of futures contracts, often function without margin requirements and are thus exposed to the default risk of the counterparties.

---

and maximizing U with respect to x. The maximum is obtained when the derivative of U with respect to x is zero. Now:

$$U'(x) = \mathcal{E}(\tilde{s}) - F - \frac{1}{2t}\left[2 \operatorname{cov}(\tilde{y}, \tilde{s}) + 2x \operatorname{var}(\tilde{s})\right].$$

By solving $U'(x^*) = 0$, we obtain:

$$x^* = -\frac{\operatorname{cov}(\tilde{y}, \tilde{s})}{\operatorname{var}(\tilde{s})} + t \cdot \frac{\mathcal{E}(\tilde{s}) - F}{\operatorname{var}(\tilde{s})}. \tag{9.8}$$

Proposition 9.1 Hedging on futures markets. *The optimal futures position of a mean–variance entrepreneur who wants to hedge random earnings $\tilde{y}$ through a futures contract written on an underlying product with spot price $\tilde{s}$ is*

$$x^* = -\frac{\operatorname{cov}(\tilde{y}, \tilde{s})}{\operatorname{var}(\tilde{s})} + t\frac{\mathcal{E}(\tilde{s}) - F}{\operatorname{var}(\tilde{r})}.$$

The optimal futures position is thus the sum of two terms:

- A hedging position $-\frac{\operatorname{cov}(\tilde{y}, \tilde{s})}{\operatorname{var}(\tilde{s})}$ that does not depend on the risk tolerance of the entrepreneur but only on the **joint distribution** of the gross earnings $\tilde{y}$ and the price $\tilde{s}$ of the security underlying the hedging instrument.
- A speculative position $t\frac{\mathcal{E}(\tilde{s}) - F}{\operatorname{var}(\tilde{s})}$, which is an increasing function of t (the risk tolerance index of the investor), of the excess expected return $\mathcal{E}(\tilde{s}) - F$ of the hedging instrument and a decreasing function of the variance of the return on the hedging instrument $\operatorname{var}(\tilde{s})$ (when $\mathcal{E}(\tilde{s}) - F > 0$).

Comparing with formula (9.4) of Section 9.2, we see that the speculative position has the same expression as the optimal investment in a financial instrument for a mean–variance investor.

The optimal futures position takes a simpler expression when the gross earnings of the company are written as

$$\tilde{y} = \beta\tilde{s} + \tilde{z}, \tag{9.9}$$

where $\beta = \frac{\text{cov}(\tilde{y},\tilde{s})}{\text{var}(\tilde{s})}$ is the regression coefficient of $\tilde{y}$ on $\tilde{s}$, and $\tilde{z}$ is a random shock. This regression coefficient measures the company's exposure to exchange risk. By construction of β, $\tilde{z}$ is uncorrelated to $\tilde{s}$. In this case, formula (9.8) can be written:

$$x^* = -\beta + t\frac{\mathcal{E}(\tilde{s}) - F}{\text{var}(\tilde{s})}. \tag{9.10}$$

Numerical Example: *Consider a company that expects 100 million earnings in dollars and 600 million earnings in* €. *Thus:*

$$\tilde{y} = 100\tilde{s} + 600 + \tilde{z}$$

(expressed in € *millions), where $\tilde{z}$ is a random shock on the company's earnings in euros. We assume that $\mathcal{E}(\tilde{z}) = 0$ and that $\tilde{z}$ is uncorrelated with the exchange rate $\tilde{s}$. The company's exposure to currency risk is thus (in millions of dollars):*

$$\beta = 100.$$

To fix ideas, assume that $\mathcal{E}(\tilde{s}) = 0.80$, $F = 0.76$ and var $(\tilde{s}) = 0.02$ (thus, $\frac{\mathcal{E}(\tilde{s})-F}{\text{var}(\tilde{s})} = 2$).

The following table represents the optimal number of hedging contracts as a function of the risk tolerance index of the firm.

Risk tolerance index	$t = 0$	$t = 1$	$t = 2$	$t = 10$
Hedging position x^* (in millions of dollars)	-100	-98	-96	-80

We see that with a zero tolerance index ($t = 0$) the firm chooses to hedge its currency risk fully ($x^* = -100$). However, because hedging is costly for the firm (this is because $\mathcal{E}(\tilde{s}) > F$), partial hedging is more likely.

9.7 CAPITAL ALLOCATION AND RAROC

9.7.1 Optimal Diversification Between Risky Activities

Although it is often rejected by the data, the normality assumption is usually maintained, because it gives simple decision rules. For example, suppose that we can decompose the total portfolio A of assets of a firm (say, a bank) into two activities $i = 1, 2$. For each activity i, we denote by A_i the assets invested (thus, $A = A_1 + A_2$), $\theta_i = \frac{A_i}{A}$ the corresponding proportion of total assets, and $\tilde{R}_i$ the net (random) return on this activity at horizon T. The return on assets is thus:

$$ROA = \theta_1\tilde{R}_1 + \theta_2\tilde{R}_2,$$

a weighted sum of the returns on the different activities. We denote by μ_i the expectation of $\tilde{R}_i$, σ_i^2, the variance of $\tilde{R}_i$, and ρ the correlation of $\tilde{R}_1$ and $\tilde{R}_2$. If the distribution of these returns is jointly normal, the distribution of the *ROA* is also normal and we have:

$$\mu \equiv \mathcal{E}(ROA) = \theta_1\mu_1 + \theta_2\mu_2, \tag{9.11}$$

$$\sigma^2 \equiv \text{var}(ROA) = \theta_1^2\sigma_1^2 + \theta_2^2\sigma_2^2 + 2\rho\theta_1\theta_2\sigma_1\sigma_2. \tag{9.12}$$

Assume for simplicity that mean returns are equal: $\mu_1 = \mu_2 = \mu$. Then an optimal diversification can be obtained by choosing proportions θ_1 and $\theta_2 = 1 - \theta_1$ that minimize the variance of the ROA. Replacing θ_2 by its value $1 - \theta_1$ in formula (9.12) and rearranging terms, we obtain:

$$\sigma^2 = \theta_1^2\sigma_1^2 + (1 - 2\theta_1 + \theta_1^2)\sigma_2^2 + 2\rho\sigma_1\sigma_2\theta_1(1 - \theta_1)$$
$$= \theta_1^2(\sigma_1^2 + \sigma_2^2 - 2\rho\sigma_1\sigma_2) - 2\theta_1(\sigma_2^2 - \rho\sigma_1\sigma_2) + \sigma_2^2.$$

The derivative of σ^2 with respect to θ_1 is easy to compute:

$$\frac{d\sigma^2}{d\theta_1} = 2\theta_1(\sigma_1^2 + \sigma_2^2 - 2\rho\sigma_1\sigma_2) - 2(\sigma_2^2 - \rho\sigma_1\sigma_2).$$

The proportion θ_1 that minimizes σ^2 (and thus the short-term VaR) is

$$\theta_1^* = \frac{\sigma_2^2 - \rho\sigma_1\sigma_2}{\sigma_1^2 + \sigma_2^2 - 2\rho\sigma_1\sigma_2}.$$

This formula can be rewritten as:

$$\theta_1^* = \frac{1}{2}\left[1 + \frac{\sigma_2^2 - \sigma_1^2}{\sigma_1^2 + \sigma_2^2 - 2\rho\sigma_1\sigma_2}\right].$$

Note that θ_1^* is always equal to $\frac{1}{2}$ when $\sigma_1^2 = \sigma_2^2$: When the two assets have the same (mean and) variance, optimal diversification is obtained (independently of assets' correlation ρ) by a completely balanced portfolio $\theta_1^* = \theta_2^* = 1/2$. However when asset 2 is more risky ($\sigma_2 > \sigma_1$), asset 1 should have a higher share than asset 2 ($\theta_1^* > \frac{1}{2} > \theta_2^*$). Moreover, θ_1^* is then increasing in the correlation ρ, as illustrated by the following example.

Numerical Example: *(Weekly) volatilities* $\sigma_1 = 2\%$ $\sigma_2 = 4\%$

$$\theta_1^* = \frac{16 - 8\rho}{20 - 16\rho} = \frac{4 - 2\rho}{5 - 4\rho}$$

The optimal allocation of assets is thus highly non-linear with respect to assets' correlation ρ as suggested by the following table:

Assets correlation ρ	−0.5	−0.2	0	0.2	0.5
Optimal proportion θ_1^*	0.71	0.76	0.8	0.86	1

9.7.2 Internal Capital Allocation

The Normality assumption can also be used to allocate capital to new risky activities or to reallocate existing capital between the different activities of the firm. Consider indeed the portfolio model of Section 9.7.1 and investigate the possibility of investing an additional amount into activity 1 (i.e., increasing A_1). Computations are simpler if the planned increase is marginal—that is, small with respect to the volume of assets already in place. We make this assumption, and consider that the objective of the bank is to keep the probability of failure below some level $1 - \alpha$. As shown in Section 6.2, the initial amount of capital needed to attain this objective is given by $E = (A_1 + A_2)\sigma N^{-1}(\alpha)$. Suppose now that A_1 is increased by a small amount.

The required capital E decreases if and only if the product of $(A_1 + A_2)^2$ by σ^2 increases. Using formula (9.12), we see that

$$(A_1 + A_2)^2 \sigma^2 = A_1^2 \sigma_1^2 + A_2^2 \sigma_2^2 + 2\rho A_1 A_2 \sigma_1 \sigma_2.$$

The derivative of the right-hand side of this formula with respect to A_1 (keeping A_2 fixed) is:

$$2A_1 \sigma_1^2 + 2\rho A_2 \sigma_1 \sigma_2 = 2A \left(\theta_1 \sigma_1^2 + \theta_2 \rho \sigma_1 \sigma_2 \right),$$

which is proportional to

$$\mathrm{cov}\,(\tilde{R}_1, ROA) = \theta_1 \sigma_1^2 + \theta_2 \rho \sigma_1 \sigma_2.$$

This shows that increasing activity 1 will lead to a decrease in economic capital if and only if:

$$\mathrm{cov}\,(\tilde{R}_1, ROA) < 0.$$

This is in line with the mean–variance methodology. This implies, for example, that between two assets (or activities) with the same mean return and the same variance, the one that has the smallest correlation with the existing portfolio of assets is more profitable for the firm, when the cost of capital is taken into account. In particular, finding new activities that are negatively correlated with existing assets is a good idea, as it improves diversification.

9.7.3 The *RAROC* Criterion

The risk-adjusted return on capital (or *RAROC*) is a criterion elaborated by Bankers Trust for assessing the "true" economic value created by a firm (or an investment) by taking into account the cost of capital. The formula is:

$$RAROC = \mathcal{E}(ROA) - WACC,$$

where

$$WACC = r_E \frac{E}{A} + r_D \frac{D}{A}$$

is the weighted average cost of capital (WACC), r_E is the return on equity demanded by shareholders, and r_D is the return on debt demanded by bondholders or banks. The capital ratio $\frac{E}{A}$ is determined by the value at risk computed above. Therefore:

$$RAROC = \mu - r_E(\sigma N^{-1}(\alpha) - \mu) - r_D(1 - \sigma N^{-1}(\alpha) + \mu)$$

or

$$RAROC = (\mu - r_D) - (r_E - r_D)(\sigma N^{-1}(\alpha) - \mu).$$

Numerical Example *Consider, for example, an asset with expected return $\mu = 10\%$ and (annual volatility) $\sigma = 20\%$. The return on equity demanded by shareholders is $r_E = 8\%$ and the interest rate on debt is $r_D = 4\%$. For a 99% safety level α (implying $N^{-1}(\alpha) = 2.33$) the risk-adjusted return on capital is:*

$$RAROC = (10 - 4) - (8 - 4)\left(\frac{20 \times 2.33 - 10}{100}\right) \sim 5.5\%.$$

9.8 THE DANGERS OF VIEWING THE WORLD AS "NORMAL"

After explaining the simplicity and elegance of risk management in a "Normal" world, this section illustrates by two simple examples the dangers of using these methods in the real world, which is unfortunately not "Normal."

9.8.1 Portfolio Choice in a Non-Normal World

Consider the set-up of Section 9.2.1 (portfolio choice with one risky asset), but assume that the return $\tilde{R}$ is not normal but only conditionally normal. More precisely:

- During "tranquil" times (99% of the time) $\tilde{R}$ is normal with mean μ and standard deviation σ. In this case, the conditional means is μ and the conditional variance σ^2.
- During "crisis" times (which only occur with probability $p = 1\%$), $\tilde{R}$ is also normal with the same mean μ but standard deviation doubles: it becomes 2σ. In this case, the conditional means is still μ but the conditional variance becomes $4\sigma^2$.

Thus, the departure from non-normality is minimal: it results from the (small) probability of a crisis.[7] We must compute the unconditional mean and variance of the return $\tilde{R}$. They are equal to the expectations of the conditional means and variances. Because the conditional mean of $\tilde{R}$ is μ whether there is a crisis or not, the unconditional mean of $\tilde{R}$ is also equal to μ. The unconditional variance v increases but only by a small amount:

$$v = \mathcal{E}(R^2) - \mu^2 = p(\mu^2 + 4\sigma^2) + (1 - p)(\mu^2 + \sigma^2) - \mu^2$$
$$= \sigma^2(1 + 3p).$$

Based on the (incorrect) normality assumption, an investor with risk tolerance t would select to invest a fraction

$$\theta_{\text{NORMAL}} = t \times \frac{\mu - r_F}{\sigma^2(1 + 3p)}$$

of his wealth in the risky asset. This is immediately deduced from Rule 9.1 in Section 9.2. Because $p = 1\%$, we see that under the normality assumption the impact of the possibility of a crisis on portfolio choice is very small—roughly, a reduction of the risky investment by 3%.

Consider by contrast a (Knightian) investor who recognizes the non-normality of $\tilde{R}$ and who is uncertain about the actual probability of a crisis. If this investor exhibits strong uncertainty aversion, he will select the portfolio that maximizes his expected utility in the worst-case scenario—that is, when the variance of $\tilde{R}$ is $4\sigma^2$:

$$\theta_{\text{KNIGHTIAN}} = t \times \frac{\mu - r_F}{4\sigma^2} = \frac{1+p}{4}\theta_{\text{NORMAL}}.$$

The contrast between the behaviors of a "Normal" and a "Knightian" investor is illustrated by Figures 9.4 and 9.5 below. We take $p = 1\%$ and $\sigma^2 = 20\%$.

The "Normal" investor replaces mixture of normals by a normal with variance $4p\sigma^2 + (1 - p)\sigma^2 = 20.6\%$. By contrast, the "Knightian" investor only considers the worst-case scenario in which the variance is 80%.

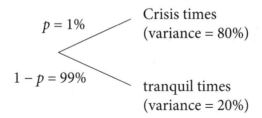

Figure 9.4

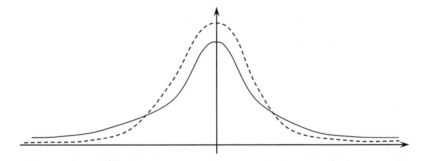

Figure 9.5 Densities of a normal distribution (dotted line) and a Cauchy distribution (solid line).

Thus, the more prudent Knightian investor, who recognizes the non-normality of returns and is uncertain about the actual probability of a crisis, will basically take four times less risk than the "normal" investor.

Numerical Example: *Like in Section 9.2, we assume $t = 2$, $\mu = 6\%$, $r_F = 4\%$, $\sigma^2 = 20\%$. Benchmark portfolio (no crisis) $\theta = 40\%$.*
An investor employing the normal approximation will select $\theta_{NORMAL} = \frac{40}{103} \sim$ 38.8%, whereas a Knightian investor will only invest $\theta_{KNIGHTIAN} = 10\%$ of his wealth in the stock index. Should a crisis occur, the 99% VaR of the "normal" investor's port-folio becomes $38.8\%(2\sigma)N^{-1}(99\%) \approx 0.4 \times 2 \times \sqrt{0.2} \times 2.33 = 8.35\%$. By contrast, the 99% VaR of the "Knightian" investor's portfolio is four times smaller ($\sim 2.1\%$).

9.8.2 Mutualization in a Non-Normal World

Consider an insurance company who wants to mutualize two i.i.d. risks, $\tilde{x}_1$ and $\tilde{x}_2$, that follow Cauchy distributions with mean zero and dispersion parameter σ. As we saw in Section 5.5 (Box 5.5), the density of such a distribution is

$$f_\sigma(x) = \frac{\sigma}{\pi(\sigma^2 + x^2)}.$$

In fact, this distribution is very similar to that of a normal distribution of mean 0 and standard deviation σ, except that it has heavy-tails (and infinite variance).
Like for the normal, the VaR at any level α is proportional to σ:

$$\mathrm{VaR}_\alpha(f_\sigma) = \sigma \mathrm{VaR}_\alpha(f_1).$$

This is because the distribution function satisfies

$$F_\sigma(x) = F_1\left(\frac{x}{\sigma}\right).$$

However, mutualization of risks does not work in a Cauchy world. This is because if $\tilde{x}_1$ and $\tilde{x}_2$ are independent and follow Cauchy distributions with parameter σ, $\tilde{x}_1 + \tilde{x}_2$ follows a Cauchy distribution of parameter 2σ. Thus, the economic capital needed to cover both risks at level α is exactly twice the economic capital needed to cover each of them separately:

$$\mathrm{VaR}_\alpha(\tilde{x}_1 + \tilde{x}_2) = \mathrm{VaR}_\alpha(\tilde{x}_1) + \mathrm{VaR}_\alpha(\tilde{x}_2).$$

There is absolutely no gain from diversification.

9.8.3 The Metallgesellschaft Debacle

The Facts

Metallgesellschaft AG (MG in the sequel) is a German conglomerate (owned largely by Deutsche Bank, Dresdner Bank, Daimler-Benz, Allianz, and the Kuwait Invest-ment Group). Its subsidiary, MGRM, was in charge of refining and marketing oil products in the United States.

In 1991, MGRM hired the star trader Arthur Benson. In 1992 to 1993, MGRM committed to sell oil forward contracts for a total of 160 million barrels and duration of 10 years.

MGRM decided to hedge this position by buying 55 million contracts on the NYMEX (future exchange) and entered into over-the-counter (OTC) swap positions for 105 million barrels to obtain a complete hedge.

In December 1993, it was revealed that MGRM had lost $1.5 billion on oil derivatives. Ultimately, MG was bought by GEA Group Aktiengesellschaft.

What Went Wrong

MGRM had decided to exploit scale economies by buying only short-term futures contracts (which are very liquid) and rolling them over 10 years.

Then oil prices went temporarily down: MGRM lost money on its futures positions. But these losses were (in principle) compensated by gains on their forward positions.

However, MGRM did not have enough cash to satisfy margin calls. It had to unwind its futures contracts. Then oil prices went up again, resulting in big losses on their naked forward position.

Analysis

Notation: 3 dates ($t = 0, 1, 2$) spot price of oil $\tilde{S}_t$ future price F forward price P (signed at $t = 0$, for delivery at $t = 1$).

If MGRM had bought long-term futures, its net position would have led to a sure gain $P - F$ at $t = 2$, as shown by the following table:

Cash flows \ Dates	$t = 1$	$t = 2$
Forward position	0	$P - \tilde{S}_2$
Futures position	0	$\tilde{S}_2 - F$

But MGRM bought short-term futures and therefore was confronted with the risk of roll-over losses.

If it had had enough cash to hold on to its position, the losses would have been limited:

Cash flows \ Dates	$t = 1$	$t = 2$
Forward position	0	$P - \tilde{S}_2$
Futures position	$\tilde{F}_2 - F_1$	$\tilde{S}_2 - \tilde{F}_2$

Notation: F_1 future price for delivery at $t = 1$ (known at $t = 0$)
           $\tilde{F}_2$ future price for delivery at $t = 2$ (known at $t = 1$).

Thus, the oil prices fall at $t = 1$ would have resulted in a loss at $t = 1$ (because $\tilde{F}_2 < F_1$) but a gain at $t = 2$ (because $\tilde{S}_2 > \tilde{F}_2$).

The aggregate losses would not have been dramatic. What happened in reality is that there was not enough cash to pay margin calls therefore the futures positions were cancelled.

Then the increase in spot price at $t = 2$ resulted in a big loss on naked forward positions $P - \tilde{S}_2$.

Three lessons can be learned from this case:

- There is a need for a dynamic approach to RM.
- The timing of cash flows is fundamental.
- Liquidity is equally important as solvency.

9.8.4 The Long-Term Capital Markets[8] Story

The Facts

The Hedge Fund LTCM was founded in 1993 by two famous financial economists (and would be Nobel Laureates), Robert Merton and Myron Scholes, and a star Wall Street trader, John Meriwether (formally head of the bond arbitrage group at Salomon Brothers). The objective of the fund was to exploit arbitrage opportunities on international bond markets.

In the beginning, the strategy worked well. LTCM clients earned huge returns: 43% in 1995, 41% in 1996. In 1997, the return was "only" 17%, but LTCM decided to buy back $2.7 billion of its shares, providing comfortable return to its shareholders.

In January 1998, the fund had capital of $4.7 billion and total assets of $125 billion, hence a leverage of $\frac{125}{4.7} \sim 27$. Moreover, the fund had derivatives positions in excess of $1.250 billion in notional value. The managers of the fund had decided to target annual volatility of the same magniture as that of the S & P 500 index. This annual volatility of 20% corresponded to a daily dollar volatility of roughly $\frac{4700 \times 0.20}{\sqrt{360}} \sim \$50$ million.

On August 17, 1998, Russia defaulted on its domestic debt. This started a period of dramatic market movements. On August 21, LTCM lost $551 million—that is, more than 10 times the target daily volatility of the fund.

By early September, the fund's investors had lost half their equity and the fund was close to bankruptcy. On September 23, the New York Fed organized a private bail-out of the fund by 14 leading banks and investment houses. They invested $3.65 billion in the fund and obtained 90% of the fund's equity.

What Went Wrong

The enormous profits made by LTCM in 1994 through 1996 drew the attention of the financial sector. This had three adverse consequences for LTCM:

- it created a large number of imitators (on August 21, when LTCM lost $551 million, Citicorp's equity fell by more than $2 billion on similar positions);
- it put pressure on LTCM to keep pursuing high profits; and

- it made markets less liquid for LTCM.

The impact of imitations was huge, because LTCM could not fully exploit arbitrage opportunities as before. Suppose that LTCM has detected an underpriced security and bought it. When imitators did the same, the price of the security rose, eliminating the arbitrage opportunity that LTCM had first identified. Another consequence of imitation was that the fund faced poor market conditions when it had to move out of positions, because it did not do so alone. For example, Salomon provoked big losses to LTCM when it closed its bond arbitrage department and thus liquidated its positions in the summer of 1998.

LTCM's arbitrage models, although very sophisticated, did not account for the possibility of liquidity shortages, like the one provoked by a massive withdrawal of funds by the large international banks that were hurt by the Russian default, generating contagion on other financial markets.

Moreover, LTCM had adopted marked-to-market valuation for its derivatives positions. This was meant to convey accurate information to its investors. However, as spreads widened, LTCM incurred temporary losses on these derivatives positions, although the long-term position was safe. This is why it ran out of cash, illustrating once more that appropriate cash management is crucial for long-term use of hedging instruments.

Three lessons can be drawn from LTCM case:

- Imitation destroys arbitrage opportunities.
- Liquidity management is a necessary complement of risk management.
- VaR calculations are generally sufficient to detect excessive risk taking, but model risk has to be taken into account.

Numerical Example:
In this section, a mean variance portfolio model is calibrated in an attempt to approximate the strategy followed by LTCM.

Over the period of 1990 to 1997, the average yearly returns on corporate bonds were 7.28%, compared to 5.75% for Treasury bonds and 5.36% for Treasury bills (taken as the riskless asset). The yearly volatility of returns were $\sigma_1 = 5.47\%$ for corporates, $\sigma_2 = 6.58\%$ for Treasury bonds and the correlation between them was $\rho = 96.54\%$.

We can use the formula derived in Appendix 1, which gives the optimal positions (θ_1, θ_2) in risky assets as a function of the investor's risk tolerance index t, the vector of excess returns (μ_1, μ_2) and the matrix Σ of variance–covariances of returns. For $t = 2$, we find (*see* Appendix 1 for details) that the optimal investment for $1 equity is $20 in corporate bonds, with short positions of $16 in Treasury bills and $3 in the riskless asset. Leverage is thus 20, still less than the actual leverage of LTCM in January 1998 (which was 27).

The yearly volatility of the portfolio is:

$$\sigma = \sqrt{\theta_1^2\sigma_1^2 + \theta_2^2\sigma_2^2 + 2\rho\theta_1\theta_2\sigma_1\sigma_2} \sim 27.7\%.$$

If the correlation ρ drops to 0.8, like what happened after the announcement of the Russian default, the volatility more than doubles:

$$\sigma' = \sqrt{\theta_1^2\sigma_1^2 + \theta_2^2\sigma_2^2 - 2\rho'\theta_1\theta_2\sigma_1\sigma_2} \simeq 65.8\%.$$

APPENDIX 1: PORTFOLIO CHOICE WITH SEVERAL RISKY ASSETS

Consider a situation where n different risky assets are available to the investor. These assets are indexed by $k = 1,\ldots,n$. We denote by μ the n-vector of excess expected returns (i.e., $\mu_k = \mathcal{E}(\tilde{r}_k) - r_F$ for all k) and V the $n \times n$ matrix of variance–covariance of the returns (i.e. $v_{kl} = \text{cov}(\tilde{r}_k,\tilde{r}_l)$ for all $k,l = 1,\ldots,n$). We assume that V is non-singular, which means that its inverse V^{-1} is well-defined.[9]

A portfolio is represented by a n-vector $\theta = \begin{pmatrix} \theta_1 \\ \vdots \\ \theta_n \end{pmatrix}$, where θ_k represents the fraction of the investor's wealth that is invested in risky asset k. By difference, $1 - \sum_{k=1}^{n} \theta_k$ is the fraction invested in the riskless asset. The optimal portfolio for an investor who uses the mean–variance criterion defined by formula (9.1) is the n-vector θ^* that maximizes:

$$U(\theta_1,\ldots,\theta_n) = \left(1 - \sum_{k=1}^{n}\theta_k\right)r_F + \sum_{k=1}^{n}\theta_k\mathcal{E}(\tilde{r}_k) - \frac{1}{2t}\text{var}\left(\sum_{k=1}^{n}\theta_k\tilde{r}_k\right)$$

$$= r_F + \sum_{k=1}^{n}\theta_k\mu_k - \frac{1}{2t}\sum_{k=1}^{n}\sum_{l=1}^{n}v_{kl}\theta_k\theta_l.$$

Using vector notations, this is also equal to:

$$U(\theta) = r_F + \theta \cdot \mu - \frac{1}{2t}\theta^t(V\theta),$$

where $\theta^t = (\theta_1,\ldots,\theta_n)$ is the transposed (row vector) of column vector θ. The optimal portfolio θ^* is characterized by:

$$\frac{\partial U}{\partial \theta_k}(\theta^*) = \mu_k - \frac{1}{t}\sum_{l=1}^{n}v_{km}\theta_m^* = 0 \text{ for all } k,$$

or in vector notation:

$$\mu = \frac{1}{t}V\theta^*.$$

Because V is non-singular, the optimal portfolio is uniquely defined by:

$$\theta^* = tV^{-1}\mu. \tag{9.13}$$

Notice that (9.13) is just the multidimensional extension of (9.4).

As an illustration, consider the numerical example presented in the LTCM case study above. Data concerning the United States for the period on 1990 to 1997, for a horizon of 1 year:

- Average return on Treasury bills (riskless asset) $r = 5.36\%$
- Average return on Corporate bonds $\mathcal{E}(\tilde{r}_1) = 7.28\%$
- Average return on Treasury bonds $\mathcal{E}(\tilde{r}_2) = 5.75\%$
- Volatilities: $\sigma_1 = 6.58\%$ (T-bonds), $\sigma_2 = 5.47\%$ (corporates) with a correlation between corporate return and T-bonds returns of $\rho = 96.54\%$.

To calibrate the model, one uses a benchmark investor who holds simultaneously some stocks and some T-bills over a 1-year horizon. The risk tolerance index t of this investor is determined by using his indifference between investing in stocks (with 1 year expected return 10% and a yearly volatility of $\sigma = 20\%$) and in T-Bills (with 1 year return 2%). The mean–variance criterion gives $0.1 - \frac{1}{2t}[0.2]^2$ for stocks and 0.02 for T-bills. Equality implies that $2t = \frac{0.04}{0.08}$ or $t = 0.25$.

We can now compute the optimal portfolio of corporate bonds, treasury bonds, and the risky asset for an equity value of $1, and the risk tolerance index determined above.

Excess returns are $\mu_1 = (7.28 - 5.36)\% = 1.92\%$ for corporate bonds, and $\mu_2 = (5.75 - 5.36)\% = 0.39\%$ for T-Bonds. The variance–covariance matrix is

$$V = \begin{pmatrix} \sigma_1^2 & \rho\sigma_1\sigma_2 \\ \rho\sigma_1\sigma_2 & \sigma_2^2 \end{pmatrix} = 10^{-4} \begin{pmatrix} (5.47)^2 & 0.9654(5.47)(6.58) \\ 0.9654(5.47)(6.58) & (6.58)^2 \end{pmatrix}.$$

Its inverse is:

$$\Sigma^{-1} = 10^4 \begin{pmatrix} 0.49 & -0.39 \\ -0.39 & 0.34 \end{pmatrix}$$

The optimal portfolio for $1 equity is

$$\begin{pmatrix} \theta_1 \\ \theta_2 \end{pmatrix} = t\Sigma^{-1}\mu = (0.25)10^4 \begin{pmatrix} 0.49 & -0.39 \\ -0.39 & 0.34 \end{pmatrix} \begin{pmatrix} 1.92\% \\ 0.39\% \end{pmatrix} \simeq \begin{pmatrix} 20 \\ -16 \end{pmatrix}.$$

The optimal investment for $1 of the investor's own money (what can be called equity) is thus $20 of corporate bonds, with short positions of $16 in T-bills and $3 in T-bonds. Leverage is thus huge:

$$\lambda = \frac{\text{Debt}}{\text{Equity}} = 19.$$

APPENDIX 2: DERIVING THE CAPM FORMULA

The CAPM, elaborated by Markovitz, Lintner, and Sharpe, is a very convenient tool for evaluating the risk premia of risky assets. It is obtained by determining the expected returns of risky assets in an equilibrium situation. Consider a group of I mean–variance investors (indexed by $i = 1, \ldots, I$) characterized by risk tolerance indices t^i and wealths W^i, $i = 1, \cdots, I$. The portfolios optimally chosen by these investors are thus given by formula (9.13):

$$\theta^i = t^i V^{-1}\mu \qquad \text{for all } i,$$

when V is the variance–covariance matrix and μ the n-vector of excess expected returns.

The demand for asset k—that is, total wealth invested in asset k—is thus:

$$\bar{W}_k = \sum_{i=1}^{I} \theta_k^i W^i = \left(\sum_{i=1}^{I} t^i W^i \right) (V^{-1}\mu)_k \text{ for all } k. \qquad (9.14)$$

At the equilibrium of financial markets, this vector is equal to the total supply of financial assets. Dividing by total market capitalization $\bar{W} = \sum_{k=1}^{n} \bar{W}_k$ we obtain $\theta_k^M = \frac{\bar{W}_k}{\bar{W}}$, which represents the fraction of total capitalization invested in asset k. The vector $\theta^M = (\theta_1^M, \ldots, \theta_n^M)$ is called the market portfolio. By formula (9.14), this market portfolio satisfies:

$$\theta^M = t^M V^{-1}\mu, \qquad (9.15)$$

where $t^M = \frac{\sum_{i=1}^{I} t^i W^i}{\bar{W}}$ represents the average risk tolerance indices of all investors (weighted by their wealths), which is called the market risk tolerance index.

The return on this market portfolio is denoted $\tilde{r}^M$. We have by definition:

$$\tilde{r}^M = \sum_{k=1}^{n} \theta_k^M \tilde{r}_k.$$

Thus, we can compute the vector of excess expected returns at the equilibrium of financial markets by inverting relation (9.14):

$$\mu = \frac{1}{t^M} V \theta^M,$$

or for each asset k:

$$\mu_k = \mathcal{E}(\tilde{r}_k) - r_F = \frac{1}{t^M} \sum_m v_{km} \bar{W}_m. \qquad (9.16)$$

Note that the sum in the right-hand side of (9.16) is just the covariance between the return $\tilde{r}_k$ on asset k and the return $\tilde{r}^M$ on the market portfolio. Thus, formula (9.16) implies that:

$$\mathcal{E}(\tilde{r}_k) = r_F + \frac{\text{cov}(\tilde{r}_k, \tilde{r}^M)}{t^M}. \qquad (9.17)$$

The problem with this formula is that the parameter t^M (the market risk tolerance index) is not directly observable. However, formula (9.17) is satisfied for each asset k, and is linear in $\tilde{r}_k$. Thus, it is also satisfied at the level of the market portfolio:

$$\mathcal{E}(\tilde{r}^M) = \sum_{k=1}^{n} \theta_k^M \mathcal{E}(\tilde{r}_k) = r_F + \frac{\text{cov}\left(\sum_{k=1}^{n} \theta_k^M \tilde{r}_k, \tilde{r}^M \right)}{t^M}$$

$$= r_F + \frac{\text{var}(\tilde{r}^M)}{t^M}.$$

Thus,

$$t^M = \frac{\mathcal{E}(\tilde{r}^M) - r_F}{\mathrm{var}\,(\tilde{r}^M)}. \tag{9.18}$$

Formula (9.17) can then be rewritten as:

$$\mathcal{E}(\tilde{r}_k) - r_F = \beta_k \left[E(\tilde{r}_M) - r_F \right], \tag{9.19}$$

where

$$\beta_k = \frac{\mathrm{cov}\,(\tilde{r}_k, \tilde{r}^M)}{\mathrm{var}\,(\tilde{r}^M)},$$

is the regression coefficient of $\tilde{r}_k$ on $\tilde{r}^M$.

This formula has important implications for the measurement of risks. Indeed, one can always decompose the excess return on asset n in two components: one that is correlated with the market return $\tilde{r}^M$ and one that is uncorrelated to it:

$$\tilde{r}_k - r_F = \beta_k \left[\tilde{r}^M - r_F \right] + \tilde{u}_k.$$

More specifically, the CAPM formula is:

$$\mathcal{E}(\tilde{r}_k) - r_F = \beta_k \left[\mathcal{E}(\tilde{r}_M) - r_F \right].$$

The first component is called the **systematic risk** component (as it varies with the market return $\tilde{r}^M$). The second component $\tilde{u}_k$ is called the **idiosyncratic risk** component as it is specific to asset k and uncorrelated with the market return $\tilde{r}^M$.

Because $\tilde{r}_M$ and the regression's residual $\tilde{u}_k$ are uncorrelated (by construction), the variance of $\tilde{r}_k$ is just the sum of the variances of these two components:

$$\mathrm{var}\,(\tilde{r}_k) = \beta_k^2 \,\mathrm{var}\,(\tilde{r}^M) + \mathrm{var}\,(\tilde{u}_k).$$

■

PART FOUR

Risk Management and Shareholder Value

Part IV is the core of the book. It starts by showing the inadequacy of standard methods for assessing shareholder value (Chapter 10): Market imperfections have to be introduced into these assessments. Chapter 11 models these market imperfections and shows that they lead to a non-linear relation between the "fundamentals" of a firm (measured by several indicators such as profitability, solvency, or liquidity) and its market capitalization. We call this non-linear relation the "shareholder value function."

Chapter 12 shows that this shareholder value function provides simple answers to some of the key questions of risk management.

10 Why Market Imperfections Matter for Shareholder Value

Managers of corporations are supposed to act for the best interests of shareholders[1] and thus to maximize shareholder value, defined as the total value of the shares of the company. When these shares are publicly traded, their market capitalization gives a good measure of shareholder value, provided that stock prices correspond to the "fundamental" value of companies, a property called stock market efficiency.[2] It is thus natural to consider that risk management decisions (like all strategic decisions made by the managers of the firm) should aim at maximizing shareholder value, or its observable proxy—namely, market capitalization. This chapter starts by a summary of the methods used by practitioners for evaluating stock prices.

These methods are all based on simple linear or even multiplicative formulas: for example, shareholder value is estimated by multiplying some indicator of the firm's profitability (typically earnings or dividends) by a coefficient (the "multiple") that is supposed to reflect other parameters, like the sector of activity of the firm, current macro-economic variables, or soft information about the firm's prospects. However, we argue that these methods are inadequate for guiding the risk management decisions of the firm. Section 10.2 argues that the relation between the firm's "fundamentals" and its shareholder value is likely to be **non-linear**. Moreover, Section 10.3 shows that incentive problems generate financial frictions.

10.1 STANDARDS METHODS FOR ASSESSING SHAREHOLDER VALUE

Financial analysts have essentially developed four types of methods for assessing the value of a stock:

- dividend-based methods;
- cash flow-based methods;
- rules of thumb based on financial ratios; and finally
- methods based on economic value creation.

This section briefly discusses these four types of methods (for more detail, the reader is referred to a corporate finance text book such as Brealey-Myers [2000] *Principles of Corporate Finance*, 6th edition, McGraw-Hill).

10.1.1 Dividend-Based Methods

Using the risk neutral valuation method presented in Chapter 7, one can find the (theoretical) value of a stock S_0 (after current dividends δ_0 have been paid) as the risk neutral (expected) present value of all future dividends per share.

Because dividends are difficult to forecast far in the future, it is easier to use another method and to try instead to forecast the stock price at the end of next period. Indeed, if stock markets are efficient, one can also write:

$$S_0 = \frac{\delta + \mathcal{E}(S_1)}{1+r}, \tag{10.1}$$

where $\mathcal{E}$ denotes the risk neutral expectation, δ is the next dividend per share (to be paid at $t = 1$), S_1 is the stock price at $t = 1$, and r denotes the (1 year) risk-free rate. A classical way to assess S_1 is to postulate that the expected stock price grows at some rate g, smaller than r:

$$\mathcal{E}(S_1) = S_0(1+g).$$

Then formula (10.1) can be transformed as follows:

$$S_0(1+r) = \delta + \mathcal{E}(S_1) = \delta + S_0(1+g),$$

which gives, after simplification, the Gordon-Shapiro formula:

$$S_0 = \frac{\delta}{r-g}. \tag{10.2}$$

Thus, the benchmark price S_0 of a stock, often used by financial analysts in their recommendations to investors (buy the stock if the market price is below S_0, sell it in the opposite case), can be computed as a multiple of the next dividend per share δ. The coefficient $\frac{S_0}{\delta}$ (which is also the inverse of the dividend yield $\frac{\delta}{S_0}$—that is, dividends per share divided by stock price) increases with the expected growth opportunities of the firm (represented by g) and decreases with the interest rate r.

The Gordon-Shapiro formula may explain why managers are very careful to fulfill the expectations of shareholders concerning dividends distribution: the stock price is very sensitive to the announcements of dividend distributions. As a result, dividends are typically very stable over time and do not fully reflect fluctuations in the firm profitability. This is why other methods have been developed for valuing firms: They are based on cash flows rather than dividends.

10.1.2 Cash Flow-Based Methods

The value of a firm equity can also be computed as the difference between the value of its assets and the value of its debt, as shown in the balance sheet below:

	E Equity
A Assets	
	D Debt

This is the method used by accountants to evaluate the book value of equity. However, accountants typically use backward-looking methods for valuating assets (i.e., acquisition prices), and nominal values for valuing debt (i.e. neglecting the probability of default). Financial analysts recommend instead to use cash flow forecasts to evaluate assets and liabilities:

$$\text{Value of Assets} = RNV \text{ (all future free cash flows)},$$

where free cash flows equal operating cash flows minus taxes and capital expenditures. Similarly,

$$\text{Value of Debt} = RNV \text{ (all future payments to debt holders)}.$$

When debt is publicly traded (bonds), its value can be measured easily by looking at its market price. The theoretical benchmark S_0 for the stock price is then given by:

$$S_0 = \frac{\text{Value of Assets} - \text{Value of Debt}}{\text{Number of Shares}}.$$

Like dividends-based methods, cash flow-based methods are difficult to implement because they require forecasts of cash flows far away in the future. This is why financial analysts have developed rules of thumb that are based on simple financial indicators and on comparisons with similar firms in each industry.

10.1.3 Rules of Thumb

These methods are very pragmatic and require a lot of expertise. They rely on the observation that within the same industry, shareholder values of different firms are roughly proportional to some indicators such as: revenues, net earnings or book values of equity.

As an illustration, private equity firms have developed valuation methods that are specific to each industry sector.

However, it is important to note that financial analysts often correct these industry averages by taking into account the specific situation of the firm under consideration: level of debt, liquidity ratio, volatility of earnings…

The most important concept introduced in this book—namely the shareholder value function—is a (pragmatic) way to systematize the relation between the indicators used by financial analysts (revenues, net earnings, debt, liquidity, volatility of earnings, book value of equity) and shareholder value (or its proxy—that is, market capitalization) combined with the risk mapping that produces stochastic scenarios or Monte Carlo simulations for these different indications. The shareholder value function will allow one to forecast the impact of all the risks confronting the firm on shareholder value, and thus to optimize risk management.

10.1.4 Methods Based on Economic Value Creation

These methods were initially developed by financial institutions, following the success of risk-adjusted measures on the return on capital. The idea is to subtract from the free cash flow a term that reflects the cost of financial capital. Consider, for simplicity, a firm that maintains a constant level of working capital (so that its capital expenditures exactly cover the physical depreciation of working capital). Thus, the free cash flow during a given period equals earnings (EBITDA) minus taxes minus depreciation. The firm generates a positive economic surplus if this free cash flow exceeds the total required remuneration by debtholders and shareholders. Thus, it is natural to define the economic value added by the firm as the free cash flow minus the total cost of capital (interest expenses on debt plus equity multiplied by the return on equity required by shareholders). Provided that capital is appropriately measured, the discounted sum of economic value added (where the discount factor is equal to the weighted average cost of capital) is equal to shareholder value, defined by the cash flow-based methods presented above.

10.2 WHY THE SHAREHOLDER VALUE FUNCTION IS LIKELY TO BE NON-LINEAR: A SIMPLE EXAMPLE

Consider a firm that is valued by financial analysts according to a simple multiplier formula:

$$SV = (PER) \times (Earnings). \tag{10.3}$$

Expected earnings are $\bar{x} = 100$ and the price earnings ratio of the industry is 15, leading to expected shareholder value $\overline{SV} = 1500$. When true earnings x are announced, shareholder value is adjusted accordingly. A typical feature of financial analysts' reaction to the earnings announcement is that it may be asymmetric: financial analysts often react more to bad news ($x < 100$) than to good news ($x > 100$), as illustrated by Figure 10.1. The slope of the shareholder value function is higher below $\bar{x} = 100$ than above $\bar{x}$.

To fix ideas, suppose that the slope of SV is 14 above $\bar{x}$ and 15 below it and that earnings are Bernoulli (*see* Figure 10.2).

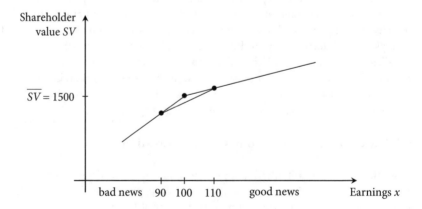

Figure 10.1 Earnings announcements and shareholder value.

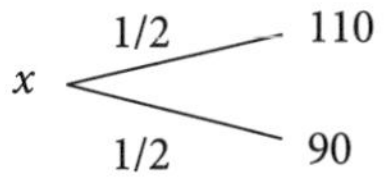

$$x \left\langle \begin{array}{l} \overset{1/2}{} 110 \\ \\ \overset{1/2}{} 90 \end{array} \right.$$

Figure 10.2

If the risk on earnings can be transferred to outsiders (without any cost) so that net earnings are equal to 100 with certainty, shareholder value increases:

$$\Delta(SV) = 1500 - \left[\frac{1}{2} \times 15 \times 90 + \frac{1}{2} \times 14 \times 110 \right]$$

$$= \frac{1}{2} \times 15 \times 10 - \frac{1}{2} \times 14 \times 10 = 5.$$

This is because shareholder value's reaction to downside risk (15) is higher than its reaction to upside risk (14). As we already showed, this can be explained by different kinds of financial frictions. If the PER used by financial analysts was constant and independent of the level of earnings (this is consistent with the Modigliani Miller Theorem), then the shareholder value function would be linear. In this case, risk transfers would be at best irrelevant (if costless) or more likely would reduce shareholder value (if costly). However, empirical evidence (*see* Section 15.3) shows that the PER is not constant and that the shareholder value function is likely to be concave.

10.3 INCENTIVE PROBLEMS GENERATE FINANCIAL FRICTIONS

Introducing conflicts of interest among managers, shareholders, and debtholders leads to a natural explanation of why the shareholders value function is likely to be non-linear. We explain this in a very simple set-up adapted from Holmström and Tirole's influential article ("Financial Intermediation, Loanable Funds and the Real Sector" *Quarterly Journal of Economics* (1994), 112(3), 663–691). It models a small firm,[3] owned and managed by the same individual. This firm needs outside funds for financing a risky investment I. This investment returns a cash flow R if it succeeds but nothing in case of failure. The risk-free rate is normalized to zero. The main difference with the Bernoulli model that we have used several times in the book is that the probability of success of the investment is not given *a priori* but is **endogenous**. It depends on the technology chosen by the entrepreneur (the owner-manager of the firm) among two available technologies. One technology is efficient and has a high probability of success p. However, another, more risky technology exists that has a lower probability of success $p - \Delta p$ (with $\Delta p > 0$) but gives a private benefit B to the entrepreneur. This second technology is inefficient (this means that $B < R\Delta p$), but the entrepreneur may find it in his interest to select it then when the firm is too much indebted. Indeed, if the nominal debt D of the firm is too high, then the entrepreneur will deliberately select the inefficient technology. This happens when the total expected payoff of the entrepreneur is lower for the efficient technology than for the more risky technology:

$$p(R - D) < (p - \Delta p)(R - D) + B.$$

This is equivalent to

$$D > D^* \equiv R - \frac{B}{\Delta p}.$$

Anticipating this, outside financiers will never lend more than pD^*, the maximum expected payoff[4] they can extract from the entrepreneur while preserving his incentives to select the efficient technology: the firm is credit-constrained.

Indeed the maximum borrowing capacity of the firm—namely, pD^*—may be insufficient to finance the project at full capacity. More precisely, if the cash reserves m of the firm (which corresponds to its self-financing capacity) are less than

$$m^* = I - pD^* = I - p\left(R - \frac{B}{\Delta p}\right),$$

the project can only be partially financed. By contrast, if $m > m^*$, then the entrepreneur can borrow pD^*, invest I and pay himself a dividend $m - m^*$ with his excess cash. The existence of two regimes implies that the shareholder value function is non-linear (and concave). More precisely,

$$\begin{cases} SV(m) = m + pR - I \text{ if } m \geq m^* \\ \qquad = \frac{m}{m^*}[m^* + pR - I] \text{ if } m < m^*. \end{cases}$$

In the lower regime ($m < m^*$), the firm is credit-constrained and does not pay any dividends to its owner: cash is more valuable inside the firm than outside.

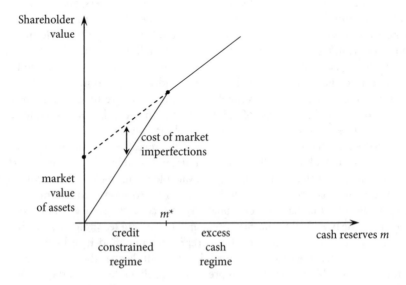

Figure 10.3 Shareholder value and the cost of market imperfections.

In the upper regime ($m > m^*$), the firm has enough cash to invest at full capacity and pay an immediate dividend. In that regime, the shareholder value function coincides with the sum of cash reserves and the market value of the firm's assets. However in the first regime ($m < m^*$), the firm is credit-constrained and market imperfections have a cost, as shown in Figure 10.3.

The next chapter presents a more elaborate model, in continuous time, where the shareholder value function has the same pattern: concave and linear above the target cash level m^*.

11 The Shareholder Value Function

The choice of investments and the way to finance them are crucial determinants of corporate value. But appropriate liquidity management is probably as important as investment selection and financing decisions. Even a very profitable firm can be jeopardized by liquidity problems:

- Too little cash can provoke financial distress and liquidation of productive assets.
- By contrast, holding too much cash reduces profitability.

In this chapter, we temporarily leave investment and financing decisions on the side and focus on the impact of liquidity shocks on shareholder value. This focus allows one to concentrate on cash reserves m as the crucial variable. In this chapter, the level m of cash reserves summarizes all relevant information for shareholders. In real-life situations, other variables are equally important, such as leverage, investment opportunities, expected profitability, and volatility of cash flows. By taking these variables as given, we can present our core methodology in a simple fashion. We derive the shareholder value function, which gives shareholder value as a function of the level of cash reserves. We then deduce from it precise guidelines for insurance and hedging decisions.

11.1 A TARGET LEVEL OF CASH

All else being fixed (particularly the value of productive assets and the level of debt), the variations in the level m of cash reserves held by a firm impact one-for-one on the book value of its equity E. Consider the simplified balance sheet:

Productive assets (A)	Equity (E)
Cash reserves (m)	Debt (D)

If A and D are fixed, then the book value of equity equals:

$$E = m + A - D.$$

Thus, one more dollar of cash reserves increases book value by exactly one dollar.

By contrast, if we consider instead the market value of equity (which we call shareholder value and denote by SV), then the relation changes. Indeed, it is generally the case that one more dollar of cash reserves in the firm increases shareholder value by **more** than one dollar, especially if the level of cash reserves is low. The reason is that additional cash reserves decrease the probability that the firm will have to depend on external funds to finance its future investments or operating costs. Because external funds are more costly than internal funds, cash reserves are valuable.

However, accumulating cash reserves is also costly, because their remuneration rate is less than the opportunity cost of funds for investors—that is, the cost of capital.[1] Indeed, both debtholders and shareholders demand a higher remuneration than the risk-free rate, as a compensation for the risk they take by investing in the firm. The cost of capital, which is a weighted sum of the expected returns demanded by debtholders and shareholders, is thus also above the risk-free rate. Therefore,[2] shareholder value SV ultimately decreases when the firm holds a lot of cash. It is maximized when all the cash in excess of a certain threshold m^* is distributed to the shareholders in the form of dividends or shares repurchase. In the next section and in the appendix, we develop a formal model where the function $SV(m)$ and the threshold m^* can be computed almost explicitly, as a function of the characteristics of the firm.

11.2 A MODEL FOR OPTIMIZING LIQUIDITY MANAGEMENT

In this section, we construct the model that constitutes the conceptual basis for our analysis. Like all models, it relies on simplifying assumptions that may seem extreme (fixed size of productive assets, fixed financial structure, no taxes,...). However, these assumptions can be relaxed. Our model is sufficiently robust to be able to incorporate different extensions without changing the fundamental conclusions.

11.2.1 The Basic Assumptions

We consider a firm characterized by the following balance sheet:

Productive assets (A)	Equity (E)
Cash reserves (m)	Debt (D)

For the moment, we assume a perfectly stationary environment. The size of productive assets A is fixed: there are no re-investments nor depreciation. Similarly, the volume of outstanding debt, D is also fixed. Moreover, to eliminate calendar effects, we assume that this debt is perpetual and pays a constant coupon c (per unit of time) until the firm fails. Earnings before interest are denoted y_t. The change in cash reserves is equal to earnings minus net interest expenses minus dividends:

$$\Delta m_t = y_t - (c - r_0 m_t)\Delta t - \delta_t, \tag{11.1}$$

where Δt denotes the length of each period. $c\Delta t$ denote thus the interests paid during each period, whereas $r_0 m_t \Delta t$ represents the interests received on cash reserves.[3] Finally, $\delta_t \geq 0$ denotes the dividend paid to shareholders during period t. We assume that recapitalizations ($\delta_t < 0$) are too costly to be undertaken.[4]

Earnings y_t are random and may sometimes be negative. They are independently and identically distributed across periods. Expected earnings per unit of time are denoted μ, and their (constant) volatility is denoted σ. Therefore, period t earnings y_t can be decomposed as[5]

$$y_t = \mu \Delta t + \sigma \Delta Z_t, \tag{11.2}$$

where $\mu \Delta t$ represents expected earnings during each period and ΔZ_t is a random shock of mean zero and variance Δt. Although most of our analysis is valid for an arbitrary period length Δt, the analysis becomes simpler when Δt tends to zero, because we can apply the powerful tools of stochastic differential calculus.

In this case, the dynamics of cash reserves is given by a stochastic differential equation:

$$dm_t = (\mu - c + r_0 m_t)dt + \sigma\, dZ_t - dC_t, \tag{11.3}$$

where Z_t is a standard Brownian notion and dC_t represents the dividends process. Therefore C_t denotes the process of **cumulated** dividends (hence the notation C_t).

Because the size of productive assets and the financial structure of the firm are constant, the only decision to be made by the managers is when to distribute dividends and when to retain earnings. Accumulating cash reserves is costly because their remuneration rate r is less than the opportunity cost of cash for investors—that is, the cost of capital—that we denote by ρ.

However, cash reserves are needed to limit the risk of liquidation of the firm because of the fact that (in our model) the firm does not have the possibility to issue more securities if it needs cash.[6] We assume that the only thing the firm can do when it runs out of cash is to draw on a credit line from its bank. The maximum overdraft allowed by the bank is denote $m_0 < 0$. For simplicity, the interest rate charged on the overdraft is also equal to r.

At the first date τ where $m_t < m_0$ (the firm's overdraft exceeds the maximum allowed by the bank), the firm is liquidated. In this case, shareholders lose their stake and the management (and the workers) lose their jobs. Finally, the bank and other debtholders share the liquidation value ℓ of the productive assets.

11.2.2 Shareholder Value

In our simple, stationary model, all the relevant information about the future of the firm is summarized by the level of cash reserves m_t. In a more general (non-stationary) model, it would depend also on the availability of profitable investments or acquisitions and on financial markets conditions—notably, the levels of interest rates and risk premiums. But here the only variable that matters is m_t. Therefore, the decision to distribute dividends or to retain earnings only depends on the current level of cash reserves m_t. It can be shown that the optimal dividend policy is to distribute dividends when m_t exceeds a certain threshold m^* and to retain earnings when $m_t < m^*$. The threshold m^* can be interpreted as the target level of cash for the firm. As we will see, there may be conflicts of interest among managers, small shareholders, and large shareholders about the optimal target level m^*. For the moment, we assume that m^* is determined so as to maximize total shareholder value $SV(m)$ (the market value of equity).

The properties of this function $SV(m)$ are described in Section 11.3. Appendix 2 contains an analytic derivation of the shareholder value function.

11.3 LIQUIDITY AND SHAREHOLDER VALUE

As shown in the theoretical model of the Appendix 2, shareholder value $SV(m)$ is an increasing function of the level of cash reserves. It is represented in Figure 11.1, in the case where the firm's outside funding possibilities are limited to a credit line with maximum overdraft $m_0 < 0$ and the costs of issuing more debt or more equity are high.

Several properties of the shareholder value function are worth commenting:

- Shareholder value $SV(m)$ is always less than $NPV(m)$, which represents the sum of cash reserves m and the expected net present value of future cash flows generated by the firm's assets. The difference between NPV and SV represents the cost of financial frictions.
- When the size of the maximum overdraft authorized by the bank increases (m_0 moves to the left), shareholder value also increases (as represented by the dotted line on Figure 11.1) and the cost of financial frictions decrease. Indeed, the higher the authorized overdraft, the easier the access to external finance and thus the lower the probability of financial distress.

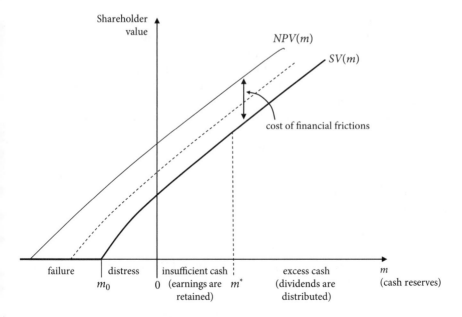

Figure 11.1 The shareholder value function.

- When $m \geq m^*$ (excess cash region), the cost of financial frictions attains its minimum, representing the opportunity cost for shareholders of holding cash reserves m^*. In this excess cash region, the marginal value of cash for shareholders is less than one if the additional cash remains in the firm and equal to one of they use it outside. This is why dividends are distributed.
- When $0 \leq m < m^*$, the firm does not have enough cash reserves. This implies that shareholders prefer to retain earnings (and thus do not receive any dividends) until a sufficient amount of cash has been accumulated.
- When $m_0 < m < 0$, the firm is in a situation of financial distress. The firm does not have any cash left to finance its operating costs. It is obliged to draw on the credit line provided by the bank. In this regime, the firm has a high probability of being liquidated. The marginal value of cash for shareholders is very high.
- Finally, if m falls below the maximum overdraft m_0, then the bank stops supporting the firm, which is obliged to default. In that regime, the marginal value of cash for shareholders is zero. This is because shareholders are protected by limited liability: marginal losses are not borne by them but by creditors. This remark has important consequences for risk management decisions, as we shall see in Chapter 12.

Thus, liquidity management and risk management are partial substitutes. An appropriate risk management policy allows to decrease the amount of idle cash that the firm has to maintain as a precautionary buffer.

APPENDIX 1: STOCHASTIC DIFFERENTIAL CALCULUS

The basic rule of differential calculus is the chain rule for derivatives: if x_t is a differentiable function of t and if $y = f(x)$ is a differentiable mapping, then $y_t = f(x_t)$ is also a differentiable function of t such that $dy_t = f'(x_t)dx_t$. When x_t is instead a diffusion process, the formula is more complex.

The rules of differential calculus have to be modified to deal with diffusion processes. Consider, for example, a stochastic process x_t (which can be a stock price, a level of earnings, an interest rate,...) that follows a diffusion equation:

$$dx_t = \mu(x_t)dt + \sigma(x_t)dZ_t,$$

where Z_t is a Brownian motion. This equation means that the change dx_t of x_t over an infinitesimal time interval $[t, t + dt]$, has an expectation $\mu(x_t)dt$ and a variance $\sigma^2(x_t)dt$. If x_t is transformed into y_t by a non-linear function $f(\cdot)$:

$$y_t = f(x_t),$$

the stochastic differential of y_t is not $f'(x_t)dx_t$ (like in traditional differential calculus) but contains an additional term:

$$dy_t = f'(x_t)dx_t + \frac{1}{2}f''(x_t)\sigma^2(x_t)dt.$$

This is the well-known Ito formula. Because $\mathcal{E}(dx_t) = \mu(x_t)dt$, this formula implies that

$$\mathcal{E}(dy_t) = \left[f'(x_t)\mu(x_t) + \frac{1}{2}f''(x_t)\sigma^2(x_t) \right] dt.$$

This formula has important consequences for the pricing of financial derivatives. Consider, for example, the case where y_t represents the expected discounted value at date t of a flow payments $\alpha(x_s)ds$ until some future date τ:

$$y_t \equiv f(x_t) = \mathcal{E}\left[\int_t^\tau e^{-r(s-t)}\alpha(x_s)ds \,\middle|\, x_t \right].$$

The vertical bar in the expectation indicates that it is computed conditionally on the current value of the state variable x_t.

If we actualize y_t at instantaneous rate r and add the present value of all payments between 0 and t, we obtain:

$$e^{-rt}y_t + \int_0^t e^{-rs}\alpha(x_s)ds = \mathcal{E}\left[\int_0^\tau e^{-rs}\alpha(x_s)ds \,\middle|\, x_t \right]$$

This is the conditional expectation at date t (given x_t) of the present value of all payments between 0 and τ. By the law of iterated expectations[7] this term has itself a constant expectation:

$$\mathcal{E}\left[e^{-rt}y_t + \int_0^t e^{-rs}\alpha(x_s)ds \right] \equiv \mathcal{E}\left[\int_0^\tau e^{-rs}\alpha(x_s)ds \right] \equiv \text{constant.}$$

If we differentiate this expectation with respect to t, we obtain:

$$\mathcal{E}\left[d(e^{-rt}y_t) \right] + e^{-rt}\alpha(x_t)dt = 0,$$

or

$$-re^{-rt}y_t dt + e^{-rt}\mathcal{E}(dy_t) + e^{-rt}\alpha(x_t)dt = 0.$$

Using Ito's lemma and symplifying by e^{-rt}, we obtain for all x_t:

$$ry_t = f'(x_t)\mu(x_t) + \frac{1}{2}f''(x_t)\sigma^2(x_t) + \alpha(x_t).$$

Because $y_t = f(x_t)$ and because this equality is satisfied for all x_t, we see that for all x:

$$rf(x) = f'(x)\mu(x) + \frac{1}{2}f''(x)\sigma^2(x) + \alpha(x).$$

Thus, the function f satisfies a second order ordinary differential equation (ODE). When this ODE can be solved analytically, it provides an explicit formula for y_t. We use this formula in Appendix 2.

APPENDIX 2: DERIVATION OF THE SHAREHOLDER VALUE FUNCTION

At each date t, shareholder value SV_t equals the expected present value (under the risk neutral probability measure) of future dividends up to the liquidation date τ:

$$SV_t = \mathcal{E}\left[\int_t^\tau e^{-r(s-t)} dC_s\right].$$

Given the stationarity of the model, SV_t only depends on the current level of cash reserves m_t. Thus, there exists a function $SV(\cdot)$ such that at each date t, $SV_t = SV(m_t)$. The function $SV(\cdot)$, which we call the shareholder value function, is the solution of a differential equation:

$$rSV(m) = (\mu - c + r_0 m)SV'(m) + \frac{\sigma^2}{2}SV''(m) \qquad (11.4)$$

for all m in the interval (m_0, m^*).

Recall that r_0, and the interest on reserves is smaller than r when $m > 0$ (the bank keeps a positive margin $r - r_0$) but larger than r when $m < 0$ (because the bank charges a risk premium on overdrafts). Because we want to get an explicit formula, we are going to assume[8] that $r_0 = m_0 = 0$. With these simplifying assumptions, it is easy to show that equation (11.4) has two elementary solutions of the form $m \to e^{\theta m}$. The parameter θ must satisfy the quadratic equation:

$$r = (\mu - c)\theta + \frac{\sigma^2}{2}\theta^2.$$

This equation has a negative solution θ_1 and a positive solution θ_2, as shown by Figure 11.2.

Then all the solutions of second-order equation (11.4) can be represented as linear combinations of these two elementary solutions:

$$SV(m) = \lambda_1 e^{\theta_1 m} + \lambda_2 e^{\theta_2 m}.$$

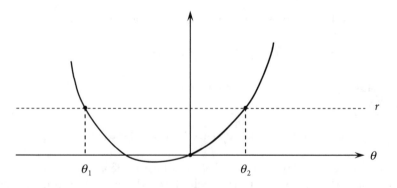

Figure 11.2 The two characteristic exponents θ_1 and θ_2.

λ_1 and λ_2 are determined by two boundary conditions:

- When $m = 0$, the firm is bankrupt

$$SV(0) = 0 = \lambda_1 + \lambda_2.$$

- When $m = m^*$ (target cash level), the marginal value of cash is one:

$$SV'(m) = \lambda_1 \theta_1 e^{\theta_1 m^*} + \lambda_2 \theta_2 e^{\theta_2 m^*} = 1.$$

Solving for λ_1 and λ_2 gives the unique solution of (11.4) for a given target cash level m^*:

$$SV(m) = \frac{e^{\theta_2 m} - e^{\theta_1 m}}{\theta_2 e^{\theta_2 m^*} - \theta_1 e^{\theta_1 m^*}}. \tag{11.5}$$

Finally the optimal value of m^* is obtained by maximizing this function with respect to m^*. This amounts to minimizing its denominator. This gives the first-order condition:

$$\theta_2^2 e^{\theta_2 m^*} - \theta_1^2 e^{\theta_1 m^*} = 0,$$

and finally:

$$m^* = \frac{1}{\theta_2 - \theta_1} \log \frac{\theta_1^2}{\theta_2^2}.$$

12 Risk Management and the Shareholder Value Function

Equipped with the shareholder value function, we are now in position to provide a simple and natural answer to some of the key decisions of risk management that were identified in Chapter 1. This chapter successively examines four of them:

- Decision 1: How much risk to take (Section 12.1)
- Decision 2: Which risks to insure (Section 12.2)
- Decision 3: How much liquidity to hoard (Section 12.3)
- Decision 4: How much hedging to perform (Section 12.4)

Needless to say, our model of shareholder value function is way too simple to be directly applicable in practice. The last part of the book (what to do in practice) gives indications on how our approach can be adapted in practice to provide solutions to the above questions.

12.1 DECISION 1: HOW MUCH RISK TO TAKE

Consider a firm that is characterized by the shareholder value function $SV(\cdot)$ and a current level of cash reserves m. This firm has to decide whether or not it must accept a new risk, represented by a random variable $\tilde{x}$, which can take positive (gains) as well as negative (losses) values. For simplicity, we assume that the time lag after which this risk will materialize is very small. This has two consequences: there is no discounting and the firm does have the time to modify its cash management policy to accomodate this new risk.[1] Then the answer is simple: the new risk $\tilde{x}$ should be accepted if and only if it increases shareholder value—that is, if

$$\mathcal{E}V(m+\tilde{x}) > V(m). \tag{12.1}$$

Considering the typical shape of the shareholder value function given in Figure 12.1, we see that the answer depends a lot on m, the current level of cash reserves. We examine below three particular cases.

Case 1: m is so large that $m+\tilde{x} \geq m^*$ with probability 1. Then in the relevant range, the marginal value of cash for shareholders is always one and (12.1) is equivalent to:

$$\mathcal{E}(\tilde{x}) > 0. \tag{12.2}$$

In other words, when the firm has an excess of cash and the downside risk (maximum loss) is limited, then the firm is risk neutral. Its decision to accept the risk or not should therefore be based entirely on the expected value criterion.

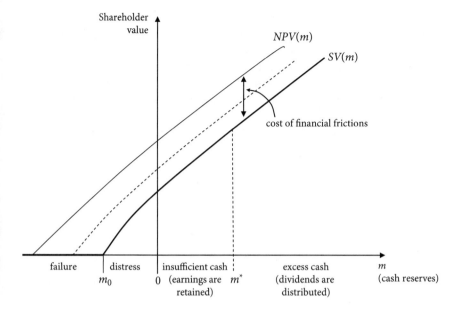

Figure 12.1 The shareholder value function.

Case 2: $m = m^*$ and $m + \tilde{x} \geq 0$ with probability 1. Then the gains ($\tilde{x} > 0$) have a marginal value of 1 for shareholders, whereas losses ($\tilde{x} < 0$) have a higher weight (because $V'(m^* + \tilde{x}) > 1$). Then the firm is risk-averse and should refuse risks that do not provide a sufficient net expected profit.

Case 3: m close to m_0. Then the firm is close to default and is ready to accept almost any risk with a sufficient upside ($\tilde{x} > 0$). The cost of losses will be very low because $V(m + \tilde{x}) = 0$ as soon as $m + \tilde{x} \leq 0$.

Thus, we see that the risk tolerance of the firm depends a lot on the level of cash reserves and the type of risk. One way to formalize this idea is to define the notion of shareholder risk measure:

$$\rho(\tilde{x}, m) = SV(m) - \mathcal{E}SV(m + \tilde{x}).$$

This number measures the decrease in shareholder value that occurs if the risk $\tilde{x}$ is accepted by a firm that is characterized by a shareholder value function SV and a level of cash reserves m.

Contrary to abstract risk measures introduced in Chapter 5, shareholder risk measures are context-dependent: they depend on the characteristics of the firm (through the function SV) and on the current level m of its cash reserves. A new risk, $\tilde{x}$, should be accepted by the firm if and only if

$$\rho(\tilde{x}, m) \leq 0.$$

12.2 DECISION 2: WHICH RISKS TO INSURE

Another application of the shareholder value function is to guide the insurance decisions of a corporation. We extend the model of Chapter 11 by considering a firm that is confronted with the risk of a loss L with some probability p. The firm can buy coverage $c \leq L$ from an insurance company for a premium $\pi = (1+\lambda)pc$ (where $\lambda > 0$ denotes the loading factor). For simplicity, we assume that insurance contracts have a short duration (so that we can neglect actualization and uncertainty of shareholders about future cash reserves m). Shareholders have thus to trade off the reduction π in their dividend for a reduction c on their risk of loss.

The level of cash reserves at the end of the period of interest is thus:

$$A = m - (L - c) \quad \text{if an accident occurs}$$

$$\text{(this event has probability } p),$$

or:

$$N = m - \pi \quad \text{if no accident occurs}$$

$$\text{(this event has probability } 1 - p).$$

The optimal level of coverage, c, for shareholders is the value c^* that maximizes the expectation of the shareholder value function:

$$\mathcal{E}SV(c) = pSV(m - L + c) + (1 - p)SV\left(m - \frac{(1+\lambda)pc}{1-\lambda}\right).$$

The derivative of this function is:

$$(\mathcal{E}SV)'(c) = pSV'(A) - p(1+\lambda)SV'(N).$$

To fix ideas, we assume that in the absence of an accident, the level of cash is always sufficient to distribute dividends, so that $SV'(N) = 1$. With this simplifying assumption, we have:

$$(\mathcal{E}SV)'(c) = p\{SV'(A) - (1+\lambda)\}$$

and the derivative of the expected shareholder value function vanishes when A is such that

$$SV'(A) = (1+\lambda) \equiv \gamma > 1.$$

γ is called the marginal cost of insurance.

To find the optimal coverage for shareholders as a function of L, we need to plot the function $SV'(m)$, which represents the marginal value of cash for shareholders.

We see that this marginal value decreases for $m > m_0$ (recall that m_0 is the maximum overdraft authorized to the firm by its bank). It is very high in the financial distress region ($m_0 < m < 0$) and equal to one in the excess cash region. Note that there is a unique m_1 such that $SV'(m_1) = \gamma$—that is, where the marginal value of cash equals the marginal cost of insurance. This level of cash m_1 can be interpreted as the (after insurance) target level of cash.

Thanks to Figure 12.2 we are now in a position to characterize optimal coverage decisions for shareholders. Indeed, equalling A (the level of cash in case of accident)

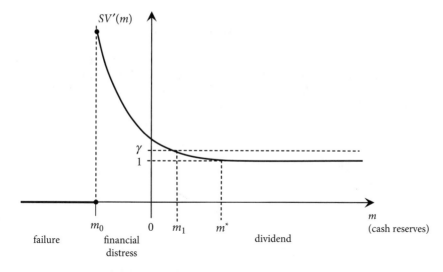

Figure 12.2 The marginal value of cash for shareholders.

with m_1 (the target level of cash after insurance), we find

$$m - L + c = m_1.$$

Thus, when the firm decides to buy coverage, it chooses the level $c^* = L - m + m_1$ such that the marginal value of cash for shareholders is just equal to the marginal cost of insurance. However, shareholders might also decide to buy no coverage at all ($c = 0$). This can only occur when

$$(\mathcal{E}SV)'(0) \leq 0,$$

which happens either when $m - L$ is lower than the failure threshold m_0 (the loss is so large that it provokes the failure of the firm) or when $m - L$ is higher than the dividend threshold m^* (the loss is so small that it does not prevent the distribution of dividends).

In conclusion to this section, we see that the insurance policy that maximizes shareholder value is remarkably simple:

- Select the same deductible $d = m - m_1$ for all risks of a size below $L_{max} = m - m_0$, the maximum loss that does not immediately precipitate the failure of the firm.
- This deductible is higher when the firm has more cash and when insurance is more expensive.
- Risks of size above L_{max} are simply not insured, because shareholders are protected by limited liability. As we will see, this may create problems from a social welfare viewpoint.

In terms of the global retention policy of the firm (when all risks are taken into account) small risks should be self-insured (deductible policy) but also large risks should be retained (because of limited liability).

BOX 12.1 ■ Insurance Demand by Firms

Insurance reduces the probability or the severity of large losses, but involves loadings and therefore constitutes a negative *RNV* operation. This implies that insurance destroys shareholder value both for financially distressed firms (because of limited liability) and for cash-rich firms (that are almost risk-neutral).

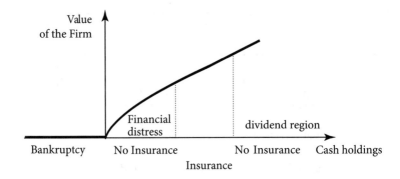

Figure 12.3

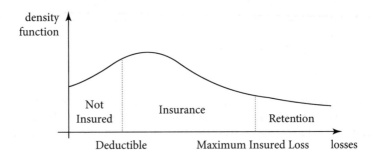

Figure 12.4

12.3 DECISION 3: HOW MUCH LIQUIDITY TO KEEP IN RESERVES

The model of Chapter 11 allows us to determine a target level of cash reserves for a firm. For simplicity, we consider the simple case where $m_0 = 0$ (no credit line) and $r_0 = 0$ (cash is not remunerated). In that case, we have an explicit formula for the target level of cash reserves:

$$m^* = \frac{1}{\theta_2 - \theta_1} \ln \frac{\theta_1^2}{\theta_2^2},$$

and for the shareholder value function:

$$SV(m) = \frac{e^{\theta_2 m} - e^{\theta_1 m}}{\theta_2 e^{\theta_2 m^*} - \theta_1 e^{\theta_1 m^*}},$$

where θ_2 and θ_1 are (respectively) the positive and negative roots of the quadratic equation

$$r = (\mu - c)x + \frac{\sigma^2}{2}x^2.$$

If one plots m^* as a function of net profitability $\mu - c$ and volatility σ, then one finds the shape represented in Figures 12.5 and 12.6.

The target level of cash m^* depends in particular of the net profitability of the firm. Surprisingly, this relation is not monotonic. Figure 12.5 illustrates this feature.

This comes from the fact that low profitability firms do not need a lot of cash (because they are likely to be liquidated). Similarly, high-profitability firms do not need such cash either (because they are unlikely to be financially distressed). It is the firms in the middle that need more cash reserves!

The figure 12.6 below illustrates that the target level of cash m^* increases with the volatility σ of cash flows: more risky technologies impose more cash holdings (which are costly). However, m^* never exceeds the expected net present value.

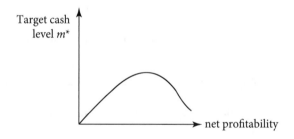

Figure 12.5 Target level of cash is an inverse U-shaped function of the firm's profitability.

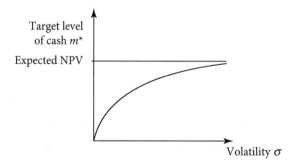

Figure 12.6 Target level of cash m^* is an increasing function of the volatility σ of the firm's cash flows.

The cost of financial frictions increases with the level of cash m^* that needs to be kept as reserves. Risk management decisions (like hedging or insurance) that reduce the level of m^* also reduce the cost of financial frictions and thus increase the net value of the firm.

12.4 DECISION 4: HOW MUCH HEDGING TO PERFORM

Hedging decisions reduce the volatility of cash flows and therefore the cost of financial frictions. This is because when σ decreases, the firm needs to hold less cash reserves.

We suppose in this section that the firm can reduce the volatility of its earnings from σ to $\sigma_0 = \sigma - \Delta\sigma$ by setting up a risk management unit and actively hedging some of its risks by using financial instruments like futures, forwards, swaps, and options.[2] Classical examples of risks that can be hedged in this way are currency risk (for firms that buy foreign goods as inputs or sell some of their output in foreign currency) or price risks (either input prices or output prices).

We will not go deep into the fine-tuning of hedging policy by the firm. We just consider instead the basic question: Is the expected gain of hedging for shareholders higher than the fixed cost of setting up the risk management unit? To answer this question, we will rely on the model of Section 11.2, where we have seen that the cost of financial frictions was roughly proportional to the target level of cash m^*, and Section 12.3 where we have seen that m^* was an increasing and concave function of σ. Figure 12.7 represents the value of m^* as a function of σ, with and without hedging.

The gains from hedging are more important for firms with "average" profitability (*see* Figure 12.8).

- Low-profitability firms don't gain much from hedging (because they are likely to be liquidated).
- Highly profitable firms don't gain much from hedging either (because they are unlikely to become financially distressed).

Finally, liquid firms hedge less than financially distressed firms. In particular, when the firm has enough cash to distribute dividends, any risk transfer with

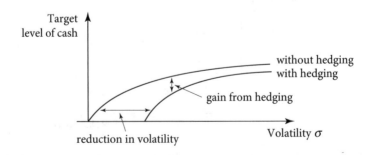

Figure 12.7

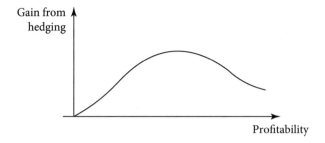

Figure 12.8

a negative EPV (under the risk neutral probability) should be banned by (small) shareholders. In principle, the Board of Directors should be in a position to enforce such decisions.

PART FIVE

What To Do in Practice

Risk management is a well-established activity. It uses a wide range of sophisticated methods that have been elaborated slowly through a patient trial-and-error process. However, it is fair to say that these methods, and more generally the panorama of risk management, have changed dramatically over the last 20 years. A completely new methodology has emerged. Instead of managing each risk on an individual basis, risk managers now tend to adopt an integrated approach, called enterprise risk management (ERM).

Chapter 3 has presented two important building blocks of ERM: **risk mapping**, which identifies, quantifies, and models the entire set of risks that threaten the entreprise, and **risk allocation**, which determines which risks are retained inside the entreprise (self-insurance) and which instruments (insurance, re-insurance, derivatives, securitization) are used to transfer to outsiders the risks that are not retained.

Many books have recently been published that explain this notion of ERM and show how it can be implemented within large corporations. However, something important is missing from the picture: What are we trying to do exactly? What is the precise aim and purpose of risk management? How should we organize the governance around risk management, first with the Board of Directors but also between the head office and operating entities?

The chief risk officer (CRO) of a large corporation is typically in a position to provide top management with a complete assessment of the risks that can impact the key accounting and financial variables of the corporation (such as earnings, economic value added, liquidity ratio, leverage and cost of capital,...). However, the precise implications for risk allocation decisions are not clear. Which of these variables are the best indicators of the firm performance? Which should be targeted by ERM? In other words, where should ERM go?

The objective of the last part of this book is to try and answer these questions and explain where ERM should go. We provide the missing link between the powerful methodology of risk mapping and the sophisticated instruments of risk allocation. This missing link is our notion of **shareholder value function** (SVF), which was already presented in Chapters 11 and 12.

Roughly speaking, a shareholder value function consists of two things:

- A list of fundamental variables that summarize the firm's accounting and financial situation: earnings, cash reserves, assets in place and investment opportunities, leverage, and cost of capital (or credit ratings).
- A function that maps these variables into shareholder value. In other words, the SVF is a way to systematize the assessment that financial analysts perform when they try to predict the way stock markets will react to any

new information about the relevant accounting and financial variables identified above.

The SVF bridges the gap between the two building blocks of ERM: using the quantified modeling of risks provided by risk mapping methods, the CRO is able to assess the impact of these risks on shareholder value and, therefore, recommend to the CEO an appropriate risk allocation strategy.

13 The Different Steps of the Implementation

This chapter recaps the different steps of our methodology and shows how they can be implemented in a consistent fashion. Our methodology essentially follows the usual three steps of risk management described in Chapter 3 (risk mapping, loss control, and risk allocation), but we add a fundamental, indispensable first step: estimating the shareholder value function (SVF).

13.1 ESTIMATING THE SHAREHOLDER VALUE FUNCTION

As we already mentioned, the SVF consists of two things:

- A list of fundamental variables that summarize the firm's accounting and financial situation: earnings, cash reserves, assets in place and investment opportunities, leverage, and cost of capital (or credit ratings).
- A function that maps these variables into shareholder value. In other words, the SVF is a way to systematize the assessment that financial analysts perform when they try to predict the way stock markets will react to any new information about the relevant accounting and financial variables identified above.

We have already seen a simple example of SVF, derived from a theoretical model. For simplicity, this SVF is only function of one variable: liquid reserves. In practice, however, other variables matter. The estimation of the SVF is therefore a very delicate exercise, based on past observations, statistical analysis, and probably a good amount of pragmatism.

As an illustration, consider a firm with expected earnings x, productive asset value A and liquid reserves m. Suppose that at each period there is a constant probability λ that the firm is forced to stop its activity (e.g., because of the loss of some key people), in which case the assets are liquidated for a value A. Note that we neglect liquidation costs, but they could easily be introduced. Note also that λ is computed under the risk-neutral probability measure to take risk premia into account. In the absence of financial frictions, the total value of the firm is just equal to the value of liquid reserves m plus the continuation value V_0 of its assets, corresponding to the expected present value of future earnings until liquidation plus asset liquidation value. If earnings x and liquidation value A are stationary (a constant growth rate could be introduced without difficulty), this continuation value satisfies:

$$V_0 = \frac{1}{1+r}[\lambda A + (1-\lambda)(x+V_0)],$$

which gives:

$$V_0 = \frac{\lambda A + (1 - \lambda)x}{r + \lambda}.$$

Incorporating the value m of cash reserves, we obtain the full value of the firm:

$$V = m + \frac{\lambda A + (1 - \lambda)x}{r + \lambda}.$$

We see that this value depends on the three variables identified above (cash reserves m, asset value A, and earnings x), as well as one exogenous factor (the interest rate r) and one unobservable parameter (the probability of liquidation λ).

The SVF depends on the same intrinsic variables (m, A, x), the same exogenous factor r and unobservable parameter λ, but in a more complex fashion, because of the potential financial frictions that can destroy shareholder value. As we saw several times, these financial frictions introduce non-linearities and transform SVF into a concave function of (m, A, x), thus justifying the need for risk management.

A possible strategy for estimating SVF would be:

- to identify a small set of relevant variables (in our example, cash reserves m, asset value A, and earnings x);
- to identify a small set of relevant exogenous factors (in our example, the interest rate r) and unobservable parameters (in our example, the probability of having to liquidate the firm);
- to specify a particular functional form for the SVF:

$$SV = \varphi(\theta, m, A, x, r)$$

where θ is a vector of parameters to be estimated (it includes λ), through a non-linear regression of shareholder value over past observations of the firm's financial variables (m, A, x) and of the exogenous factor r.

Alternative estimation strategies are possible:

- Calibrate the vector θ of parameters to obtain "reasonable" predictions of the reactions of shareholder value to small shocks on the variables (m, A, x) and factor r, as anticipated by the managers.
- Use a fully non-parametric method that does not presume any prespecified functional form but simply smooths out the histogram of past observations of shareholder value SV_t of the firm's financial variables (m_t, A_t, x_t) and the exogenous factor r_t.

13.2 A UNIFYING METRIC FOR RISK MAPPING: THE RISK VALUE MAPPING

We have now estimated (either parametrically or non-parametrically) the shareholder value function $SV(X, Y)$, where X is a vector of variables that characterize the firm (such as cash reserves m, earnings x, or asset value A) and Y is a vector of exogenous factors (such as the interest rate r). Note that unobservable parameters (such as the probability λ of having to liquidate) can either be viewed as deterministic (in which case there is no risk about them) or as stochastic (in which case they are potentially insurable). We now see how this estimated shareholder value function SVF can help us connect the two fundamental steps of risk management: risk mapping and risk allocation.

As we have seen in Chapter 3, the powerful methods of risk mapping allow the CRO of a modern corporation to construct a complete picture of the risks that can have an impact on the firm and to quantify them through scenarios and histograms. The difficulty is that these risks (which we represent by a vector Z) typically have different impacts on the many financial variables characterizing the firm (such as cash reserves m, earnings x, or asset value A). Therefore, CEOs don't know *a priori* which of these variables they should consider in priority, knowing that it is generally impossible to hedge all of them simultaneously.

The SVF solves this problem by providing a unifying metric. The CRO just needs to estimate the expectation of shareholder value at the future date T that constitutes the planning horizon of the firm (say, the end of they year) **conditionally** on current information and on the future value of the risk vector Z at horizon T:

$$V(z) = \mathcal{E}(SV(X_T, Y_T)|Z_t = z].$$

To take a concrete example, consider a firm that manages an international of hotels and Z represents the risk of a hurricane in the Caribbean. $V(Z)$ captures the impact of such an event on shareholder value. This function is called the **risk-value mapping**.

As a simple illustration, consider the case where shareholder value only depends on liquid reserves m that is, we take $X = m$ as the only state variable and interest rates that is, we take $Y = r$ as the only exogenous factor. Risk mapping has identified only two risks: interest rate r and exchange rate \$/, denoted $s(Z = (r,s))$. Liquid reserves at the horizon date T are given by

$$m_T = m_0 + \theta s_T + \varepsilon_T, \tag{13.1}$$

where m_0 denotes current liquid reserves, θ is the exposure of the firm to exchange rate risk, and ε_T is a zero-mean random variable that is independent of risk vector $Z_T = (r_T, s_T)$. Denote the shareholder value function by $SV(m,r)$. Now the risk-value mapping is defined by

$$V(r,s) \equiv \mathcal{E}\left[SV(m_0 + \theta s + \varepsilon_T, r)\right],$$

where the expectation is taken over the non-hedgeable risk ε_T. The risk-value mapping is thus a function that maps the future realization of the risk (r,s) into the expected shareholder value at the horizon date ε_T.

13.3 THE NEW INSTRUMENTS OF RISK MANAGEMENT

This section briefly presents some of the new instruments used by the risks specialists of large corporations.

13.3.1 Insurance-Linked Securities

Insurance-linked securities (ILS) such as Cat bonds or insurance securitization vehicles are a way to increase capacity on a risk by using financial market techniques. The principle of an ILS is simple even if, in practical terms, it requires a good quantity of legal work and documentation; the idea is to issue bonds that will not be fully reimbursed in case of an external event (typically a catastrophe). For example, an insurance company may issue a bond to cover itself against the risk an earthquake in California: in case of an earthquake with predetermined characteristics (in terms of magnitude and localization) during the 10-year period of the bond's life, the insurance company only has to repay the interests on the bond (not the principal) to the investors.

Insurance-linked securities have their origin in the hard market for catastrophe cover that followed Hurricane Andrew in 1992. At this time, re-insurance capacity for catastrophe covers—that is, reinsurance contracts protecting the insurance company against the damage caused by a natural event—were expensive and too limited to satisfy market needs.[1]

An important element of an ILS is the definition of the event that triggers the coverage. There is no need to point out that it should be well-defined to avoid any potential disputes between investors and the entity issuing the bonds. There are three types of triggers:

- an indemnity trigger, based on the amount of losses of the entity issuing the bond;
- an index trigger that uses indexes developed to measure the importance of losses resulting from a given event; and
- a parametric trigger that uses, for example, Richter or Mercalli scales to measure the magnitude of an earthquake.

Figure 13.1 shows the typical structure of a Cat bond.

After a slow start in the 1990s, the ILS market is now growing exponentially, as shown in Figure 13.2.

BOX 13.1 ■ Examples of Securitization of Insurance-Related Risks

Swiss Re, one of the world's largest re-insurers has already a good experience in the securitization of insurance-related risks. In July 2002, it organized the issuance of $255 million of catastrophe-linked securities through a Cayman-based special purpose vehicle called Pioneer 2002 Ltd. These securities were split into six tranches, each linked to specific catastrophe indices (such as North Atlantic Hurricane or Japanese Earthquake) and with different ratings and different spreads to the 3-month LIBOR.

Similarly, in December 2003, Swiss Re organized a $400 million issuance of securities linked with extreme mortality induces to cover some of its life insurance risk.

AXA, the French insurer, securitized a portfolio of motor insurance receivables (called SPARC) at the end of 2005.

① The Sponsor enters into a financial contract with a Special Purpose Vehicle (SPV)

② The SPV hedges the financial contract by issuing Notes to investors in capital markets

③ Proceeds from the securities offering are invested in high quality securities and held in a collateral trust

④ Investment returns are swapped to a LIBOR-based rate by the Swap Counterparty

⑤ In some transactions, principal and interest on the Notes may be guaranteed by a Note Guarantor

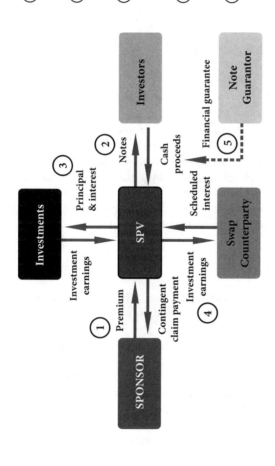

Source: Swiss Re

Figure 13.1 Typical Cat Bond Structure. Source: Swiss Re.

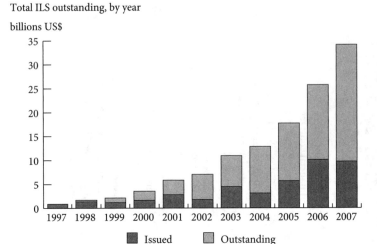

Figure 13.2 Total ILS outstanding, by year billions US$. (Source: Swiss-Re report, 2008).

13.3.2 Captives

A captive is basically an insurance or re-insurance vehicle owned by a corporation that can use it for the management of its own risk and is supposed not to be active in the insurance or re-insurance market. This definition is somewhat too simplistic, as some captives are owned by a group of companies and others may be active in a small market activity (e.g., providing capacity to a market pool). Medium-size companies or companies that do not wish to invest capital in this activity may also rent a captive, generally to a captive management organization.

The Importance of Captives

The first captives were created in the late 1960s. Since then, the growth in the number of captives has been steady, and there are now (as of May 2006) more than 4000 captives around the world.[2]

U.S. corporations have been the first to develop this vehicle and still represent around half of existing captives, which is roughly consistent with their global market share. Most multinational corporations own one or several captives. Amid non-U.S. corporations, the penetration of captives (as of 2010) is stronger in European multinationals than in Asian ones.

Historically, captives have been located in places providing good financial conditions. Roughly speaking, these conditions are:

1. a low taxation of profits
2. ability to create technical reserves to fund future risks
3. good infrastructure, like tax and legal advisers

As a result and even if this reason is no more dominant, most captives are domiciled "off-shore." In terms of nationality, captives should be analyzed from a dual point of view: location of the parent company and domiciliation of the captive itself. The preferred location remains Bermuda with around one-third of captives, followed by the Cayman Islands. European companies' favorite locations are Guernesey, Luxembourg, and recently Ireland, which founded its development on the possibility to create insurance vehicles and not only re-insurance ones as in the initial model. With the sophistication of risks management techniques and 20 years of high activity in mergers and acquisitions, many companies now own several captives vehicles. This may provide some additional flexibility but is likely to ultimately require some consolidation efforts.

How Do You Use a Captive?

Captive insurance or re-insurance companies are a very powerful tool for risk management, and very sophisticated schemes have been developed over the years. Without getting into too many details, captives are typically used for:

1. reducing the cost of insurance by exploiting arbitrage opportunities between different insurance or re-insurance markets;
2. managing more efficiently some risks (such as high- and medium-frequency risk and also the risks associated with international activities); and
3. creating capacity in low-frequency/high-severity risks or in areas in which professional insurance or re-insurance markets do not provide enough capacity.

Let us illustrate this through some simplified examples.

Example 1: A corporation wants to insure its property risks. The direct market (i.e., insurance companies) are ready to cover it for a rate of $1\,^0/_{00}$ on the amount insured.

If professional re-insurers propose a lower rate of $0.8\,^0/_{00}$, then the corporation can ask its insurance company to cede a share of the risk to its captive (e.g., 40%).

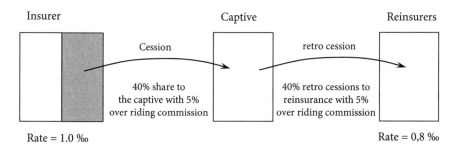

Insurer		Captive		Reinsurers
	Cession		retro cession	
	40% share to the captive with 5% over riding commission		40% retro cessions to reinsurance with 5% over riding commission	

Rate = 1.0 ‰   Rate = 0,8 ‰

Figure 13.3

Then the captive will retrocede the same share of the risk to re-insurers. The profit of the operation is $40\%(0,95\% \times 1^0/_{00} - 0,95 \times 0,8^0/_{00}) = 7,6\%$. It should be noted that this operation is not risk-free as the captive is exposed to a counterparty risk in case of failure of re-insurers.

Example 2: A company with two subsidiaries in two different countries wants to retain a fraction R of its risks at the group level, while allowing its subsidiaries to retain different fractions (R_1 and R_2) of their risks at the local level to account for their local specificities.

Note: R, R_1, R_2 optimal risks retention, for the group and subsidiaries 1 and 2.

The idea is to cede to a captive vehicle the part of the risk between R_1 (or R_2) and R, the optimal group retention.

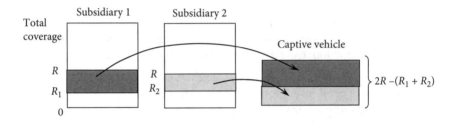

Figure 13.4

Example 3: A company wants to create capacity for a risk that is not easily transferred to an insurance market—for example, effect of the Severe Acute Respiratory Syndrome (SARS) on tourism.

It is possible to transfer some cash to a captive vehicle and to adjust jointly the level of cover and outside protections like re-insurance cover or future market positions. The cash will be used to cover future losses. One of the advantages of this operation is that the company pays insurance premiums, which are often tax deductible.

13.3.3 Finite Risk Insurance

Finite risk insurance is a contract between a corporation (or a cedant) and an insurer (or a re-insurer) that bundles risk transfer and risk financing. The main characteristics of this instrument are:

1. a multiyear contract term;
2. the insurers (or re-insurer) bears a limited part of the risk;
3. investment income is part of the pricing; and
4. it is a mechanism to share results between the corporation and the carrier.

An Example

A car manufacturer X wants to transfer and finance the risk of recall of its products through a 3 year finite contract with some insurers.

- The contract is characterized by several limits:
  - the limit per event (a recall) is $20 million,
  - the deductible is $2 million per event to be paid by the corporation,
  - the limit per year is $80 million,
  - the total limit for the 3 year duration of contract is $175 million.

- The premium paid for company X is divided into a premium and a fund that is placed on an account (called the experience account) producing interests at a predetermined rate.
- At the end of the 3-year period, company X will recover 97% of the experience account if it is positive.
- From the point of view of the insurer, the risks assumed are underwriting risk, credit risk (X may default on paying its share of claims), and interest rate risk.

Use of Finite Risk Insurance

Finite risks contracts are sophisticated tools mainly used to:

- create capacity where traditional solutions are too expensive or do not provide enough capacity;
- increase company retention of risks through a multiyear program;
- build a special purpose vehicle (SPV) to finance special risks.

Two types of finite contracts co-exist: prospective covers that are related to future events or underwriting years and retrospective covers where the instrument is used for past events or prior underwriting years. In this latter category, the insurer is still covering some underwriting risks because of the difficulties to estimate some past claims incurred but not settled.

Future of the Finite Risk Contract

The finite risk contract is a powerful instrument for providing coverage and capacity for risks that have to be managed over a long period of time and also for creating capacity for unusual or specific covers.

The evolution of accounting and fiscal regulations will be key for development of finite risk contracts as they will determine the interest of these instruments for corporations in the future. We may anticipate periodic attempts by tax authorities to discourage the use of these techniques, as they are viewed as mainly motivated by tax reduction motives. However, risk professionals are likely to develop alternative ways to manage their risks efficiently.

14 Learning from an Example

This chapter presents an example illustrating how the methodology presented in this book can be applied in practice. For this, we use a fictitious pharmaceutical company, (that we call Med Corp) with a commercial profile and a financial structure close to the actual ones of the leaders of the pharmaceutical industry. The breakdown of revenue by geographical zone is represented in Figure 14.1 and Figure 14.2 gives main products as percentage of revenue.

BOX 14.1 ■ The Financial Profile of Med Corp

→ Revenue: $27 billion: breakdown by zone (see Figure 14.1)

Europe:	45%
United States:	35%
Other:	20%

→ Main products as a % of total revenues (see Figure 14.2)

Product #1:	8%
Product #2:	7.6%
Product #3:	6%
Top 5 products:	32.8%
Top 10 products:	52.7 %

→ Simplified P&L

	in $ billion	in %
Revenue:	27	100
Expenses:	18	66.7
- R&D:	4	14.8
- Cost of sales:	6	22.2
- General expenses:	6	22.2
- Other:	2	7.4
Margin:	9	33.3
Cost of financing:	1	3.7
Net earnings:	8	29.6

→ Simplified balance sheet (book values)

$A = 73$	$E = 46$
$C = 13$	$D = 40$

(in $ billion)

→ Shareholder value (market value) $SV =$ $100 billion.

→ Price earning ratio

$$\left(\frac{\text{Market value}}{\text{Net earnings}} \right) = \frac{100}{8} = 12.5.$$

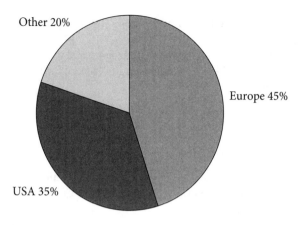

Figure 14.1 Revenue by zone

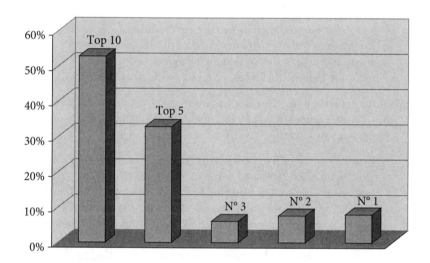

Figure 14.2 Main products as a percentage of revenue

14.1 PRESENTATION OF MED CORP

Focused on a business standpoint, a quick analysis of Med Corp leads to following comments:

- Like most leaders in the pharmaceutical industry, Med Corp's activity is mainly located in the most developed markets—United States and Europe—but the importance of emerging markets is likely to grow.
- Revenues are concentrated on a few blockbuster products: the top 10 products represent more than half of Med Corp's revenues.

- Med Corp has a good level of net margin ratio (margin/revenues), at 33% of revenues.
- Shareholders value ($100 billion) is high compared to revenue ($\times 3.7$) and is more than twice the book value of equity ($46 billion).
- Price earning ratio is 12.5.

14.2 RISK ANALYSIS

14.2.1 Internal Risks

We now analyze the main risk exposures of Med Corp, which can be done even if we do not have all the relevant information on Med Corp. From shareholders' points of view, the main risks are:

- On a short-term basis, not being able to protect the revenue stream and the reputation of Med Corp. Therefore, it is necessary to focus on risks that may have a negative impact on revenue:

  - a large liability claim on one of the top products;
  - a damage to one of the main centers of production;
  - a withdrawal of authorization for a product; and
  - a dispute around intellectual property or the patent of a drug.

- On a long-term basis, the main risk is not to stay among the leaders of an industry that concentrates at a fast rate. A successful implementation of this strategy supposes:

  - to attract and retain the key talents in research and development (R&D), who will be able to develop new products;
  - to manage efficiently the portfolio of products through R&D and acquisitions. The optimum situation is to have a good balance between blockbuster products and less mature products that have a strong potential of future sales;
  - to manage carefully the company's external growth through an appropriate mergers and acquisitions strategy;[1] and
  - to increase the activity in emerging markets.

14.2.2 External Risks

The risks analysis for Med Corp can also benefit from the study of the impact of major liability claims on other large pharmaceutical firms. For example, in December 2004, Merck, a large U.S. drug manufacturer had a problem with Vioxx, one of its most important products. After a warning from the Food and Drug Administration ([the FDA], the agency that controls the safety of drugs in the United States), the shareholder value of the firm was reduced by nearly 50% in a few weeks, as illustrated by Figure 14.3:

MERCK & CO INC
as of 15–Dec–2006

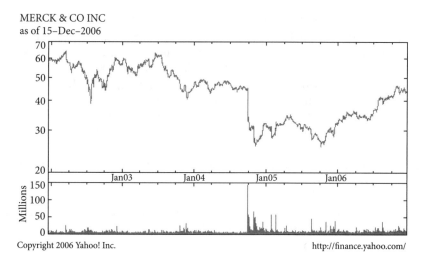

Copyright 2006 Yahoo! Inc.   http://finance.yahoo.com/

Figure 14.3 Stock price for Merch & co inc

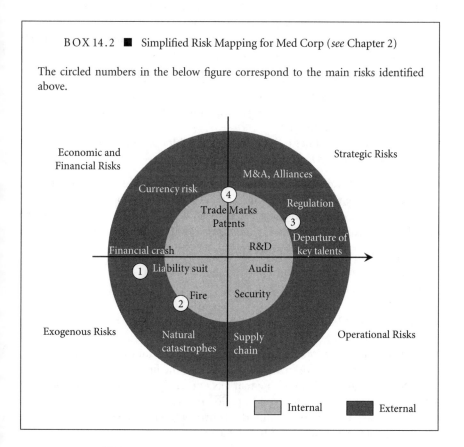

BOX 14.2 ■ Simplified Risk Mapping for Med Corp (*see* Chapter 2)

The circled numbers in the below figure correspond to the main risks identified above.

The management of Med Corp can use this type of information to estimate the impact of a similar FDA warning on one of its top products. For financial analysts and investors in Med Corp or in other drug manufacturers, this risk is one important source of volatility of the share prices in this industry.

Following the methodology developed in Chapter 2, Box 14.2 presents a simplified version of the risk mapping for Med Corp.

Within this tool, Med Corp can communicate its risk management policy to all stakeholders: employees, shareholders, management, analysts, and regulators.

14.3 SHAREHOLDER VALUE AND RISK MANAGEMENT FOR MED CORP

This section uses the example of Med Corp for illustrating the impact of risk management on shareholder value, as explained in Chapter 12.

14.3.1 Empirical Evidence of the Importance of Risk Management

First, Med Corp—and more specifically its board and the top executive—should learn from what has happened to other corporations.

We already mentioned several examples where an appropriate risk management policy would have reduced the impact of adverse events:

- The recall of Vioxx by Merck after a warning from the Food and Drug Administration (Section 14.1);
- The management of Greenpeace allegations in the case of the oil platform Brent Spar (Section 1.1);
- Insufficient use of basic risk measures like Value at Risk (VaR) in the Orange County default (Section 8.5).

These cases illustrate how shareholders' value is affected by unwanted events, even more so when risk management is inexistent or inappropriate.

As an example of a possible scenario that can destroy some value for Med Corp shareholders, we study the possible consequences of a liability claim:

- impact on revenue;
- cost of claims paid to third parties; and
- increase in the financing cost.

14.3.2 Shareholders, Value in the Pharmaceutical Sector

One of the main missions for the board of Directors and the CEO of a public company is to increase the shareholders' value of the firm. To achieve this objective, they have to understand how markets and analysts form their opinion (*see* Chapter 10 for several examples of valuation methods).

The first step is often to benchmark the firm with its competitors to determine the key characteristics of the industry leaders.

Figure 14.4 illustrates the shareholder value of several large pharmaceutical companies in 2006.

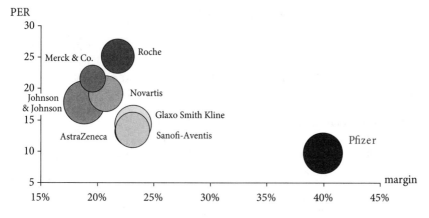

Figure 14.4 Shareholder value pharmaceutical industry (2000)

Price earning ratios (PERs) serve as a function of margin rates in the pharma industry (2006 figures). Size of the bubble is proportional to revenues.

PER is the ratio between price of the stock and earning per share or, in other terms, the ratio between the total market capitalization and the earning. The fluctuation of the PER are:

- positively correlated to the growth ratio of the earnings, and
- negatively correlated to the interest rate and risque.

In our example, if an unwanted event like a large product liability claim occurs, the financial market will most probably reduce their expectation on the future earning of Med Corp and the PER will drop.

Consequently, Med Corp shareholders will be affected by two factors: the cost of the claims that reduces the earnings and the reduction of the PER, which affects the market capitalization.

It is interesting to note that financial markets have different valuations for companies that, at first sight, seem to have similar financial characteristics. In Figure 14.4 several groups appear, going from strong to average and low performers.

In practice, financial analysts and investors have developed more sophisticated methods for the valuation of public companies. These methods take into account additional factors, for example:

- the quality of management;
- the quality of the portfolio of products and the duration of the patents associated with each of these products;
- the image of the firm in the public;
- the quality of the distribution network; and
- the exposure to currency fluctuations.

For the management of the firm, a challenge is to position the firm in the pack of leading firms. Risk management has a key role to play in this respect.

14.3.3 Impact of a Product Liability Claim

In concrete terms, assume that a series of claims affect Product #2, which represents 7.6% of Med Corp's revenue. If these claims occur at mid-year (therefore, the annual revenue on Product #2 is reduced by 50%), the first consequences are easy to compute (figures are in billion-dollars):

- Reduction in revenue: $7.6\% \times 27 \times 50\% = 1.027$
- Reduction in earnings:[2] $9/27 \times 1.027 = 0.342$
- Reduction in shareholder value:[3] $100/8 \times 0.342 = 4.275$

Note that this first reduction of roughly 4.3% in shareholder value only takes into account the drop in Med Corp revenues. Most probably, analysts and financial markets consider that a liability claim of this magnitude has a strong impact on the future profits of Med Corp and its ability to stay among the top players of pharmaceutical industry. Consequently, they may lower the PER of Med Corp, which will move it to a less performing group in the Figure 14.4.

Assume that the PER is reduced by 10% from $\frac{100}{8} = 12.5$ to 11.3; the reduction in the shareholder value is now

$$11.3 \times (8 - 0.342) = 86.5\%,$$

therefore a reduction of 13.5%.

The other elements to be assessed are the cost of the claims that will be paid to customers and how Med Corp will finance this liability to third parties. Considering the importance of Product #2 in the revenue, it is probably a blockbuster and, therefore, the number of claimants may be very high (especially in the United States because of the possibility of class action). Moreover, even if, at the end of all litigations, Med Corp is not held responsible by the courts, such a claim always generates very high litigation costs paid to lawyers and experts.

In our example, we assume the following figures (in billion-dollars):

- Cost of litigations: 0.3.
- Payments to third parties: 1.

If the cost of litigation is paid over 3 years, a simple computation shows that shareholder value will be reduced the first year by another 1.25 billion—that is, 1.25% of initial shareholder value. The estimate payment to third parties will increase the debt of Med Corp (total debt $= 10 + 1 = 41$).

Assume that the cost of litigation is $100 million each year and payments to third party (plaintiffs) are $200 million for the first and second year and $600 million for the third year.

Figure 14.5 also illustrates the financial aspects of risk management and risk transfer. Like banks or financial institutions, Med Corp is exposed to interest rate risks: the flow of funds chart presented above is similar to that generated by a portfolio of bonds or loans.

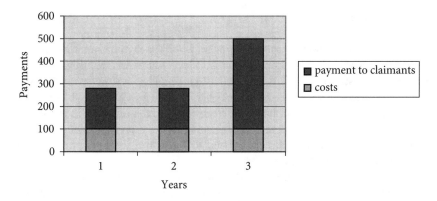

Figure 14.5

Then, if financial markets apply the same rate to Med Corp, the cost of financing will increase by 2.5% and a new reduction of shareholders' value will take place.

Finally, if financial markets consider that this claim may have a strong impact on the reputation of Med Corp and on its ability to tap financial markets in the future, they may downgrade its rating and thus increase the interest rate applicable to its debt. Med Corp will have to face a double problem: a need for a cash injection to settle the claims and a higher financing cost.

Let us give a numerical illustration: Before the claim, the cost of financing was $1/40 = 2.5\%$, which is quite low. If the downgrading leads to a 50-basis point increase, the total cost of financing will increase by $200 million with a reduction of shareholder value of 2500 million.

For simplicity, we assume that the PER, which is the ratio of the shareholder value to earnings, remains stable but calculus would be the same with a lower PER.

The previous section on the possible risk management policy for Med Corp gives us some tools that could efficiently reduce the impact of adverse events on Med Corp market value:

• Med Corp could have contracted a liability coverage that pays for litigation costs and reduces the amount of additional debt.
• Med Corp could have secured a contingent capital agreement to avoid an increase in its debt during a troubled period and consequently having the risk of being downgraded by banks and analysts.

14.4 A RISK TRANSFER POLICY FOR MED CORP

This section discusses what could be the best way for Med Corp to transfer the risks identified above, either to the insurance companies or to financial markets. To keep a simple approach, we will concentrate on two main risks: property (damages to the property belonging or leased by Med Corp and caused by exogenous factors) and product liability (possible claims arising from patients who have taken Med Corp drugs).

14.4.1 Property

In property, the main risk exposure appears when the firm has a lot of property value (i.e., important production centers,...) located in areas with high exposure to natural catastrophes. This is because insurance and re-insurance markets only provide limited capacity in certain zones like Japan, Florida, and California. The chief risk officer (CRO) will have to determine the retention level, the capacity, and the structure of the risk transfer. In some large corporations, the decisions concerning retentions are validated by the CEO and the executive committee and sometimes by the board of directors.

For selecting the retention level, the CRO has to consider the cash position of the firm (*see* Chapter 12) but also the state of the insurance market. He may benefit from a soft market (i.e., when some inexpensive capacity is available) to reduce the retention. In the example below, the retention level has been set at $100 million.

This retention can be structured with different instruments of coverage: deductible, captive, and also finite. Figure 14.6, 14.7, and 14.8 show several possible structures (figures are in million-dollars).

Structure 1 for Insured Retention

Figure 14.6 represents how claims will be paid depending on their size:

- A claim under $10 million will be paid by Med Corp.
- The (mezzanine) tranche between $10 million and $50 million is covered by the captive of Med Corp.
- The senior tranche (between $50 million and $100 million) is covered by a finite contract.
- Finally, the tranche above $100 million is transferred to insurance companies.

For example, if the value of a claim is $175 million, Med Corp will pay directly $10 million, the Med Corp captive will pay $40 million, the finite program will contribute for $50 million, and insurance markets will pay $75 million.

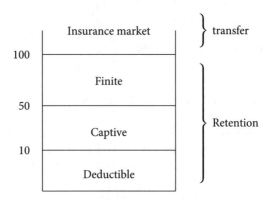

Figure 14.6 Structure 1 for insured retention

Structure 2 for Insured Retention
An alternative structure is shown in Figure 14.7:

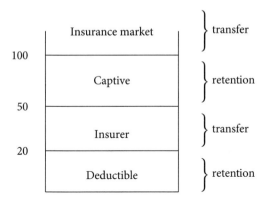

Figure 14.7 Structure 2 for insured retention

In structure 2, Med Corp chooses to participate in the first $20 million through a deductible, an insurer is covering the tranch of the claims between $20 million and $50 million, and its captive provides coverage for the claims between $50 million and $100 million. This structure is appropriate if Med Corp can find on the insurance market one or several insurers that are ready to offer good prices for covering the layer between $20 million and $50 million, which is appropriate when market conditions are soft.

Prices on insurance and re-insurance markets are cyclical, with a succession of hard markets with little capacity and high prices and soft markets with abundant capacity and low prices. When market conditions are very soft,[4] the low level of prices will most probably lead Med Corp to decrease its self-insured retention because it can sell the risk to insurance markets with a potential actuarial profit. This type of operation illustrates well that arbitrage opportunities exist in the real world. Some insurance programmes have a positive risk neutral valuation!

The evaluation of the capacity needed to cover property risks is easier than for product liability risks, even if it requires a good technicity and an efficient information system.

Property policies cover two main risks: the damage caused to property by exogenous causes like fire, earthquake, or flood and the business interruption, which is the loss of profit consecutive to property damage. For example, after a fire in a factory, the property program will indemnify Med Corp not only for the cost of the factory itself but also for the loss of profit whenever Med Corp is not able to provide customers with the products that were normally produced in this factory.

In terms of capacity, Med Corp may need something around $3 billion or $4 billion. With the first option on the SIR, the structure could be:

Structure of Med Corp Property Program

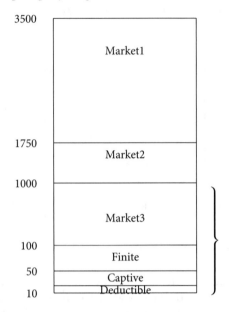

Figure 14.8 Med Corp property program

In the structure above, Med Corp's self-insured retention of $100 million is composed of a $10 million deductible, $40 million of insurance coverage in its captive, and $50 million in a finite that combines self-insurance and insurance coverage. After a threshold of $100 million, the risk is covered by insurance and re-insurance markets.[5]

In our example, and similarly to what is usually done in practice, the insurance coverage is divided into several layers mainly used to optimize market opportunities. This is because some insurers and some insurance markets tend to specialize in a specific type of coverage, which implies that the placement of coverages is easier when divided into several layers.

For example, some insurance markets will specialize in natural catastrophic covers, in high-severity/low-frequency covers in specific industries. From the point of view of the insurer, this practice allows diversification and a homogenous portfolio of risks and lowers the variance of the result.

14.4.2 Liability

The internal and external risks analysis presented above reveals the importance of product liability risks for a drug manufacturer. This results from:

- the severity of the risks, as claims can be very expensive.
- the duration of these claims: a very long period (7–10 years) of time is generally needed to settle the product liability claims.

- the special impact of this type of claims on public opinion and financial analysts.

Consequently, the CRO of Med Corp has to cope with very strict constraints when considering the transfer of product liability risks.

- The duration and severity of claims impose work with insurers and re-insurers that have a very strong financial capacity. This is to ensure their solvency at the time claims will have to be paid in the future. This explains why liability insurance and re-insurance markets are dominated by a few highly professional players. When markets are soft, there are some very aggressive and opportunistic players that should not be mixed with the solid and long-term-oriented insurers but may be used for lower layers of coverage and for smaller amounts.
- The nature of the U.S. judicial system imposes a specific analysis of the exposure of the firm on this market.

Similarly to for property insurance, several issues have to be addressed: the proportion of risks to be retained by the firm, the total capacity bought on the market, the structure of the program. We now examine them in turn.

Retention

Pharmaceutical companies are generally very profitable, and it is the case in the example of Med Corp so that they can afford a relatively high retention of risks around $100 million. Chapter 13 of this book explains how the SVF can be used to determine the optimum level of self-insured retention.

We have studied in Chapter 14 some of the modern instruments used for self-insurance. In Figures 14.9 and 14.10, we suggest two possible structures for the retention of Med Corp (figures are in million-dollars).

Structure 1 for Insured Retention

- Med Corp pays directly the first $50 million on each claim.
- Med Corp uses its captive to cover the next $50 million.

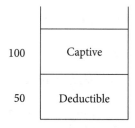

100   Captive

50   Deductible

Figure 14.9 Structure 1 for insured retention

Structure 2 for Insured Retention

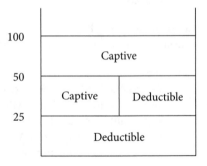

Figure 14.10 Structure 2 for insured retention

- Med Corp pays directly the first $25 million on each claim.
- Med Corp pays 50% of the claims between $25 million and $50 million.

The captive covers 50% of the claims between $25 million and $50 million and 100% of the claims between $50 million and $100 million.

Under the scheme described in structure 2, the captive of Med Corp covers a bigger part of the risk. This could be interesting in some cases—for example, when the cash situation and financial structure of some of Med Corp subsidiaries cannot allow them to bear a self-insured retention of $50 million. A similar example is presented in Figure 14.11.

Structure 3 for Insured Retention

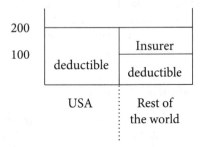

Figure 14.11 Structure 3 for insured retention

- For claims in the United States, the deductible or self-insured retention is now $200 million.
- For claims in the rest of world, the deductible is $100 million.

The self-insured retention can be structured between deductible and captive, as in structures 1 and 2 described above.

This structure illustrates the case of an increased SIR for U.S. claims. This could be explained by the fact that the U.S. judicial system is more favorable to victims and claimants. Consequently, insurance markets are only ready to provide coverage after a higher threshold than in Europe.

Total Capacity and Structure

This question is a difficult one—its answer depends on several factors like the type of drugs produced by Med Corp, the weight of their blockbuster products, and the exposure to the U.S. market. Therefore, total capacity brought by one given firm may vary, but generally drug manufacturers tend to buy a high capacity (say, around $1 billion in the case of Med Corp) and exclusively from carriers with strong solvency. This capacity is generally structured in several layers because insurers and re-insurers sometimes want to provide capacity only above a certain threshold.

In some cases, the retention level may be different for claims arising in the United States. This is because of some specificities of the U.S. legal system; the frequency and severity of liability claims is much higher than in the rest of the world so that insurers are reluctant to participate in layers of coverage that they consider too low. For Med Corp, it is also better to increase the self-insured retention on layers where the expected value of claims is not too volatile instead of transferring it to an insurer who will add its own expenses and loading to it. Two possible structures are suggested in Figures 14.12 and 14.13 (figures are in million-dollars).

Structure 1 for Med Corp Liability Program

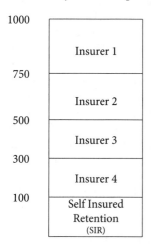

Figure 14.12 Structure 1 for liability program

This SIR can be organized around the different options described above. Note that each insurer can be replaced by a group of insurers and re-insurers

Structure 2 (With Different SIR in the United States)

Structure 2 illustrates the case of an increased deductible for U.S. claims. This is justified by the fact that the U.S. judicial system is often more favorable to victims. Consequently, insurance markets want to to provide higher incentives to Med Corp to avoid claims—hence, a higher deductible.

Note that insurer 4 could be the Med Corp captive.

For the moment, finites[6] are not widely used in casualty insurance because of the high duration of claims. This can be understood easily because at the end of

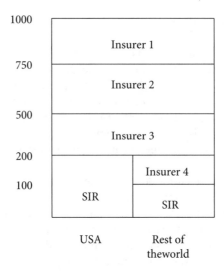

Figure 14.13 Structure 2 for liability program

the finite contracts (which are generally put in place for a period of 3 to 5 years), a good proportion of the large casualty claims are not completely settled, as their duration is closer to 8 years. So, it would be uneasy to close the finite contract and to share the profit between Med Corp and the insurance and re-insurance market. As we have seen, finites are more appropriate for property coverage. The demand of capacity for this risk may also lead big pharmaceutical companies to generate together some coverage that is specific to their industry. This can be done by creating some kind of insurance mutual or a risk transfer agreement. Such a solution was arranged very successfully by the oil industry which created OIL, an insurance company that quickly became a major player in the market. However, for liability risk, things are much more complicated because of the duration of claims.

This simplified example shows the type of decisions that can be taken by a risk manager of a large firm and it also illustrates several of the concepts presented in this book.

The main rules and lessons to be drawn from the case of Med Corp can be summarized as follows:

- **Understand the overall strategy underlining the risk management policy.** The risk management policy of a firm must be consistent with the global strategy chosen by the board and the CEO. For example, a company that operates on a very mature market should decide to be highly risk-averse to avoid bad surprises for shareholders and financial markets. The CRO must engage a discussion on this matter with the leadership of the firm. For this internal communication purpose, the tools presented in the Chapters 4 and 5 are particularly useful.
- **Adjust the risk management policy to the financial situation of the firm.** This is an important implication of the SVF methodology. The risk appetite

of the firm should not be set once and for all, but it must reflect the current financial situation of the firm. In particular, the level of self-insured retention must depend on the cash position of the firm. The methodology presented in Chapters 12 and 13 is well-suited to this purpose.

- **Know and test the new instruments of coverage offered on the market.** The risk management techniques are moving fast as both traditional players and financial markets constantly innovate and propose new instruments to manage and transfer risks. The risk manager should be aware of these innovations; he/she should analyze them carefully and, when needed, test them. As an illustration, many re-insurance companies have tested Cat bonds for the management of their own risks. The knowledge of these instruments puts them in a good position for offering these products to their clients.
- **Be aware of the market situation in terms of prices (soft vs. hard market) and use it whenever possible.** Insurance and re-insurance markets are characterized by alternating periods of high prices (hard market) and low prices (soft market). Risk managers should understand these insurance cycles to optimize their decisions in terms of the level of self-insured retention or the use of the company's captive.
- **Implement a robust loss prevention policy.** A very important part of the role of risk managers is to collaborate with all the different divisions of the firm to implement an efficient loss prevention policy. This policy aims at reducing the probability of occurrence of risks and enhancing the perception of risks carriers like insurance and re-insurance companies. This point is illustrated in Chapter 3.
- **Think out of the box in terms of which risks can occur.** The identification of risks, which is the first foundation of modern risk management methodology (*see* Chapter 3), should start by a robust risk mapping exercise. Risk managers should also be creative in their identification of risks: imagine new perils and access news scenarios in which several unwanted events may be correlated (*see* September 11th tragedy, for example). Finally, risk managers should never underestimate model risk. Even the best models rely on strong assumptions and have limited validity. As we have argued repeatedly in this book, this should be one of the main lessons to draw from the subprime crisis.

15 Conclusion: Some Simple Messages

This last chapter summarizes the main lessons to be drawn from this book through some simple messages; it focuses on the essential points to be remembered for understanding the objectives of risk management in a corporate environment. We also recall the main features of a successful risk management policy.

15.1 MESSAGE # 1: QUANTITATIVE MODELS ARE NEEDED BUT THEY MUST BE USED WITH PRECAUTION

In short, we believe that if managers and risks practitioners take the time to understand the basics of the economic and actuarial theories that form the academic background of risk theory, they will raise their level of performance. This does not imply a full knowledge of academic work but rather a good understanding on the basic principles underlying models, how and when to use them, and their limits. The leadership of corporations will have more and more pressure from all stakeholders to articulate their vision of risk and how they intend to manage.

This book can be a useful tool for facilitating this evolution. We have developed several models giving some ideas and methods on the best practices in risk management. The most important are the following:

- Ruin theory, because this powerful tool is key to understand the link between a risk and the amount of capital to cover it. The most popular risk metrics and tools like VaR or RAROC are directly drawn from Ruin Theory.
- Risk neutral valuation, because it is the first step to understanding the pricing of derivatives that are widely used in finance and have become a powerful tool of risk management.
- Utility functions, because they give a theoretical framework for decisions in uncertain environments. For the officers in charge of the management of risks, these functions are useful to understanding and formalizing the objectives of the firm's different stakeholders.

15.2 MESSAGE # 2: RISK MANAGEMENT CREATES VALUE FOR SHAREHOLDERS

They are several reasons why risk management may increase shareholder value.

- First, risk managers (inside or outside the firm) bring expertise in risk reduction (frequency or severity). Thus, risk management is not only about risk transfers.

194

- Second, when taxes and bankruptcy costs are taken into account, financial structure and risk management matter.
- Third, the financial situation of a firm has an impact on its future capacity to borrow and thus to finance new projects.
- Finally, the profitability of a firm depends on the performance of its managers, which may in turn depend on the incentives provided by the remuneration schemes of these managers and, indirectly, on the financial structure of the firm.

15.3 MESSAGE # 3: THINGS TO DO IN PRACTICE

15.3.1 Modern Risk Management Must Use a Risk Mapping Methodology

Several chapters of this book illustrate that the biggest and more devastating losses come from unpredicted risks: loss of the image of being a pure product for Perrier in the United States, lack of internal control for AIG.

It is important to keep in mind the main steps of a risk mapping methodology:

- Identification of risks.
- Quantification and modeling to obtain a statistical distribution of aggregate losses and correlation with external variables.
- Scenarios and simulations.

Moreover, risk mapping is the first necessary step to move from a silo approach to a firm wide and holistic risk management.

15.3.2 Loss Prevention and Protection Should be Considered as Key Priorities for the Management of Corporations

Corporations are exposed to new, larger, and sometimes unexpected risks. It is therefore very important to focus on the reduction of the severity and frequency of losses. This should not be limited to external perils like fire or natural catastrophes but to the entire spectrum of risks as identified by the risk mapping.

There are three main reasons to invest in loss prevention and protection:

- It has a direct impact on the result of the firm: direct losses, cost of transfer of risk to external markets.
- As many risks are correlated, reducing the frequency of unwanted events leads to reducing the risk of occurrence of a chain of events that may, in the end, damage the financial situation of the firm. Let us take an example of such a chain of undesirable events that can lead to a catastrophic scenario: fire in a small plant of a car manufacturer, delay in launching a new car, loss of market share to competitors, reduction of shareholder value.
- The emphasis of loss prevention and protection in a corporation reinforces the awareness and commitment of the management to the risk management policy.

15.3.3 Corporations Should Develop a Good Knowledge of Instruments and Tools of Risks Transfer to Exploit Possible Arbitrage Opportunities

Insurance and financial markets have developed many sophisticated instruments for risks transfer. All firms can find the vehicle that is the most adapted to their risk management policy. It is therefore key that top management and risk managers are well-aware of what instruments are available on the marketplace.

In particular, alternative risk transfer methods allow firms to optimize simultaneously their financing and their risk management. Large firms should investigate how they can use modern tools like captive insurance companies, finite risk insurance, and securitization.

15.4 MESSAGE # 4: KEY INGREDIENTS FOR A SUCCESSFUL RISK MANAGEMENT APPROACH

The implementation of enterprise risk management (ERM) in large and complex organizations is not easy or costless. ERM has to be adapted to the corporation culture and objectives. We consider that the main factors of success for a successful integration of risk management and corporate financing are:

- a clear governance concerning decisions about risks;
- a holistic approach and implementation across the silos of the organization;
- an efficient system of risks measurement; and
- the use of modern quantitative tools and financial instruments.

The first factor of success is to define a clear governance around the management of risks. This should encompass all stakeholders of a corporation (regulators, shareholders, management, employees, government agencies), as the views and interests of these stakeholders may sometimes be divergent.

A successful implementation requires a drastic change in the traditional silo approach of risk management, where only little coordination exists between the different sectors that are managing the risk of the corporation: treasurer, general manager, risk and insurance manager, compliance officer. The ERM methodology can only be implemented if a cross-sectors and cross-disciplines exercise is carried out by the corporation leadership. As mentioned before, the management of hazards and financial risks should be done jointly and consistently.

The process on risk management should also be based on good measurement tools for different risks; their sophistication may depend on the type of industry, but each corporation will have to develop and implement a consistent measure of their risks. This system is fundamental to define a common language and enhance the communication between all risk management stakeholders.

***

Integration between risk management and financing activities is the next frontier for modern corporations. If it is performed adequately, it can be simultaneously rewarding for shareholders, management, and employees.

■ NOTES

■ Introduction

1. Cited by the New York Times, 9 October 2008, Internet Edition.

■ Chapter 1

1. If losses exceed this amount, the firm becomes insolvent, and its creditors (banks or bondholders) are forced to cover the excess losses.

2. Illiquidity can provoke the default of an otherwise solvent firm. If there is some doubt about the future profitability of the firm or else if banks and investors are themselves liquidity constrained, the firm may not find liquidity on the market even though it is technically solvent.

3. For a good account of the subprime crisis, *see* Blundell-Wignall, A., P. Atkinson, and S.H. Lee: "The Current Financial Crisis: Causes and Policy Issues," Financial Market Trends OECD 2008.

4. The definition and analysis of credit default swaps are provided in Box 7.1.

5. Source: Associated Press, September 15, 2008.

6. MetalGesellschaft and LTCM are well-known cases of firms that incurred massive losses on derivatives markets, not because their strategies were intrinsically flawed but because they did not have enough liquidity to pursue them. These cases are analyzed in Chapter 9.

■ Chapter 2

1. Source: Swiss Re "Natural Catastrophes and Man-Made Disasters in 2007" Sigma 1, 2008.

■ Chapter 3

1. Note that some risks are too big to be borne by any economic agent alone. A collective scheme has to be designed. Classic examples are wars, large catastrophes, or pandemic illnesses, such as swine flu.

2. Recall that, in our acception of the term, risks can also be favorable (upside risks).

3. The notions of distribution function, variance–covariance matrix and copula are explained in Sections 4.3 and 5.3, respectively.

4. The concept of Value at Risk (VaR) is explained in Section 5.5.

5. Finites are presented in more detail in Chapter 15.

■ Chapter 4

1. The last section of this chapter explores the dangers of the stationarity assumption.

2. For the average cost, insurers study how the price of windshields has evolved in the past years and they forecast the price for the coming year. For the frequency, the estimation comes from the analysis of the results of their portfolio or, more broadly, the market statistics.

3. Section 4.8 discusses some of the dangers of the stationarity assumption.

4. In more general cases, $\tilde{x}$ could also incorporate gains. For simplicity we focus here on pure losses.

5. A formal definition of statistical independence is given in Chapter 5.

6. For more detail on CDOs, *see* Fender & Kiff (2004) "CDO rating methodology," BIS working paper n^0 163, and the interesting article by Coval, Jurek, & Stafford "The Economics of Structured Finance" (Harvard Business School, Working Paper 09-060, 2009).

7. In practice, loans portfolios comprise more than three loans. The numerical values that we give are just illustrative and are not realistic.

8. A formal definition of statistical independence is given in Chapter 5.

9. See Box 4.2.

10. Cited by R. Lowenstein "When Genious Failed: The Rise and Fall of LTCM," 2000, New York: Random House.

11. The predictability of financial assets prices is a different matter. It is related to the validity of the Efficient Markets Hypothesis, which we discuss in Chapter 7.

■ **Chapter 5**

1. Perfect independence is not necessary: the Law of Large Numbers still holds if the correlation between risks is not too strong (*see* Section 5.3 for the definition of the correlation).

2. The variance of a random variable is the expectation of the square of its deviation from the mean. This notion is developed below in Section 5.2.

3. This is the strong LLN. The weak LLN, which is easier to prove, states that for all $\varepsilon > 0$, the probability that $|\bar{X}_n - \mu| \geq \varepsilon$ converges to zero when n tends to infinity.

4. We will see later how to select s as a function of the risk tolerance of shareholders.

5. This notion is the basis of Ruin Theory, which is developed in Chapter 6.

6. This is also true for a wider class of distributions, called **elliptical** distributions. *See* Embrechts, P., Kluppelberg C., & T. Mikosch (1997), *Modelling of Extreme Events for Insurance and Finance*, Springer, Berlin, for detail.

7. Of course, in practice the number of loans is much larger than 2. The assumption $n = 2$ is only made to simplify exposition.

8. The original reference is Sklar, A. (1959) "Fonctions de répartition à n dimensions et leurs marges," ISUP, Paris University (in French). For a succinct presentation *see* Embrechts, P., Kluppelberg C., & Mikosch T. (1997), *Modelling of Extreme Events for Insurance and Finance*, Springer, Berlin.

9. As already noted, the case $C(x_1, x_2) = x_1 x_2$ corresponds to statistical independence between $\tilde{x}_1$ and $\tilde{x}_2$.

10. In the formula that defines the Gaussian copula, the function under the integral is precisely the density of a Normal distribution with zero mean, unit variance, and correlation ρ given in Box 5.3. This comes from the fact that when $\tilde{x}_1$ and $\tilde{x}_2$ are themselves standard normals, $F_1(x_1) = N(x_1)$ and $F_2(x_2) = N(x_2)$. Thus, in that case, the distribution function of $(\tilde{x}_1, \tilde{x}_2)$ is precisely $F(x_1, x_2) = C(N(x_1), N(x_2))$.

11. This table is taken from McNeil, A. (1999) "Extreme Value Theory for Risk Managers," reprint ETH, Zurich.

12. Whithehouse, M. "Slices of Risk," *The Wall Street Journal*, September 12, 2005.

13. This was the spirit of the treatment of market risk in the Basel 2 accord that determined capital requirements for banks, prior to the subprime crisis. Banks had to determine the VaR (typically at level $\alpha = 99\%$ for an horizon of 1 week) on their market portfolio, either by their own internal models or by using a standard model validated by the Basel committee. The capital requirement imposed by Basel 2 for market risks was equal to 3 times

the *VaR* (multiplication by 3 was a precaution intended to cover model risk). However, it revealed grossly insufficient.

14. Mandelbrot, B. (1963) "The Variation of Certain Speculative Prices," *Journal of Business*, 36: 394–419.

15. *See* Axtell, R. (2001) "Zipf Distribution of U.S. Firm Sizes," *Science*, September, 293, 5536: 1818–1820.

16. *See* Gabaix, X. (1999) "Zipf's Law and the growth of Cities," *American Economic Review*, 89(2): 129–132.

17. The probability of losses in excess of zero is not one because negative losses are always possible with a Normal distribution.

18. However, this does not work for certain types of risks. The next section shows that mutualization may actually **increase** risk when distributions are heavy-tailed!

19. This property is discussed in detail in Ibragimov and Walden (2006) "The Limits of Diversification When Losses May Be Large," HIER Discussion Paper, Harvard University.

20. A random vector $(\tilde{x}_1, \tilde{x}_2, \ldots, \tilde{x}_n)$ has an elliptical distribution if its joint density $f(x_1, \ldots, x_n)$ can be written as a transformation of the density of a joint Normal distribution. Such distributions are called elliptical because they are constant on the level sets of the mapping: $x \to {}^t(x - \mu) V^{-1}(x - \mu)$, (which are ellipsoids) where μ is the vector of means and V the variance–covariance matrix of this Normal distribution.

21. It is taken from Embrechts, P., Kluppelberg C., & Mikosch T. (1997), *Modelling Extremal Events for Insurance and Finance*, Springer, Berlin.

22. The variance–covariance matrix of $(\tilde{x}_1, \tilde{x}_2)$ is $V \begin{pmatrix} 1 & 0 \\ 0 & 1 \end{pmatrix}$. If $(\tilde{x}_1, \tilde{x}_2)$ was **jointly** normal, it would have a density (on **all** $\mathbf{R}^2$) given by $f(x) = \frac{1}{2} \exp - \frac{1}{2}(x_1^2 + x_2^2)$: *see* Box 5.5. As implied by definition 5.2, a bivariate Normal distribution cannot be concentrated on two lines.

23. It is also easy to construct counter examples with continuous random variables.

24. Note that tranching in CDOs is different from the model of tranching used here. In a CDO (*see* Box 5.1) the tranching formula is instead:

$$\begin{cases} x_i = 0 \text{ if } \tilde{x} < a_{i-1} \\ \quad = \tilde{x} - a_{i-1} \text{ if } a_{i-1} \leq \tilde{x} < a_i \ . \\ \quad = a_i - a_{i-1} \text{ if } x_i > a_i \end{cases}$$

25. Artzner, P., Delbaen F., Eber J., & Heath D. (1999), "Coherent Measures of Risk," *Mathematical Finance*, 9, 203–228.

26. Acerbi, C. (2002) "Spectral Measures of Risk: a Coherent Representation of Subjective Risk Aversion," *Journal of Banking and Finance*, 26, 1505–1518.

27. Actually, ξ can also take negative values (Pareto type II distribution), but this case is not relevant for risk management purposes.

28. McNeil, (1999) "Extreme Value Theory for Risk Managers" discussion paper, ETH Zentrum, Zürich.

■ Chapter 6

1. With this definition, leverage is always greater than one, which illustrates its magnifying impact. An alternative, less convenient, measure of leverage is the ratio of debt over equity—that is, $\frac{D}{E} = \lambda - 1$ in our notation.

2. For simplicity, we do not compound interests and take the horizon T as the time unit for computing interest rates.

3. The coefficient d is a measure of the duration of claims.

4. In Chapter 9, we discuss the dangers of this "normal" approximation.

5. In this section, we rule out default risk. Therefore, these cash flows are certain. The only risk comes from interest rate fluctuation.

■ Chapter 7

1. In general, government bonds are also more liquid.

2. *See* Chapter 8 for a precise definition of risk aversion.

3. The notional value of a CDS is the maximum possible loss incurred by the protection seller. The aggregate notional on all CDSs grossly overestimates the real risk exposure for two reasons: net exposures are much smaller than gross exposures, and recovery rates are not zero. Still, \$45 trillion is an astronomical number; it roughly corresponds to \$7500 per inhabitant of our planet!

4. Note that the RN probability is computed on the basis of asset prices, which are forward-looking: they depend on investors' expectations about future cash flows. By contrast, the historical probability, as its name indicates, is backward-looking.

5. This is explained in detail in many mathematical finance textbooks—for example, Bjork (2004), Duffie (1992), or Musiela-Rutkowski (2000).

6. Cited by B. Malkiel in "The Efficient Market Hypothesis and its critics," CCEPS working paper 91, 2003, Princeton University.

7. We only consider the (increase in) shareholder value created by the new assets and neglect the assets already in place.

8. This is because our simplified model has no capital expenditures. However Result 7.1 (the Modigliani Miller Theorem) is also valid if new investments are taken into account.

9. This is a first approximation: If the impacts of winning the World Cup are different in different countries then the diversified portfolio will contain different numbers of shares of the two companies.

10. Strictly speaking, this is only true for risk transfer operations. Loss-control activities that reduce the probability or cost of accidents do have a value even in the world of perfect markets.

■ Chapter 8

1. There is no discounting because the time lag between paying the lottery ticket and receiving the prize is negligible.

2. This result can be obtained by differentiating (with respect to x) the classical formula:

$$1 + x + x^2 + \cdots x^n + \cdots = \frac{1}{1-x}.$$

We obtain:

$$1 + 2x + \cdots nx^{n-1} + \cdots = \frac{1}{(1-x)^2}.$$

When $x = \frac{1}{2}$, this gives:

$$1 + 1 + \frac{1}{2} + \cdots \frac{n}{2^{n-1}} + \cdots = \frac{1}{(1-1/2)^2} = 4.$$

Multiplying by $\frac{1}{2}\ln 2$ and using the fact that $\frac{n\ln 2}{2^n} = \frac{1}{2^n}\ln 2^n$, we obtain the desired result.

3. In Chapter 9 we study the consequences of the "normality" assumption on different aspects of risk management.

4. This feature was already present in the bottomry contracts used in the Renaissance for financing risky trading expeditions.

5. Because all payments are made at the same date (futures contracts), risk neutral probabilities q_1, q_2 are just equal to future prices P_1, P_2 of insurance contracts (there is no discounting).

■ Chapter 9

1. We have already seen a particular case of this property when the individual has an exponential utility function with risk tolerance coefficient t: $u(x) = t(1 - \exp - \frac{x}{t})$. In this case, we have an explicit formula for the certainty equivalent of $\tilde{x}$:

$$\mathcal{E}u(\tilde{x}) = u\left(\mu - \frac{\sigma^2}{2t}\right), \text{ and thus } CE(\tilde{x}) = \mu - \frac{\sigma^2}{2t}.$$

However, the above property is very general, as it holds for arbitrary utility functions.

2. For simplicity, the investor's initial wealth is normalized to 1.

3. Investing in a Treasury Bond with a maturity that differs from the investor's horizon is risky, because interest rates fluctuate over time. As we have seen in Section 6.4, this exposes investors to reinvestment risk (if the horizon is smaller than the maturity of the bond) or capital risk (in the opposite case).

4. Note that when $\rho = -0.5$, the total investment in the risky asset is $2 \times 0.8 = 1.6$. Because this investment is bigger than one, this strategy implies some leverage: the investor invests more than his wealth in the risky asset. He has to borrow 60 cents for each dollar that he invests out of his own funds.

5. It can be shown that this region is delimited by a branch of hyperbola. Take the example of two stocks with expected returns r_1, r_2, standard deviations σ_1, σ_2, and correlation ρ. Consider a portfolio with θ units of stock 1 and $1 - \theta$ units of stock 2. Its expected return is $r = \theta r_1 + (1 - \theta) r_2$, whereas its variance is $\sigma^2 = \theta^2 \sigma_1^2 + 2\theta(1 - \theta)\rho\sigma_1\sigma_2 + (1 - \theta)^2\sigma_2^2$. Replacing θ by $\frac{r - r_1}{r_2 - r_1}$, we can express σ^2 as a quadratic expression of r, of the form $(ar + b)^2$. The equation $\sigma^2 = (ar + b)^2$ represents an hyperbola in the (r, σ) plane.

6. This assumes $\theta \geq 0$. The portfolio associated to any $\theta < 0$ is dominated by the one associated with $|\theta|$.

7. The distribution of the return $\tilde{R}$ is thus a mixture of Normals. Its density is a convex combination of two Normal densities with different variances; unfortunately, it is not Normal.

8. This analysis is based on the article of R. Stulz, FT June 27, 2000.

9. This is without loss of generality: if V is singular, one of the assets has the same return as a portfolio composed with the other assets. Thus, this asset is redundant and can be eliminated. This process can be repeated until the var–covar matrix of returns on (remaining) assets is non-singular.

■ Chapter 10

1. In practice, there are often conflicts of interest between managers and shareholders. These conflicts are the source of financial frictions, that can be reduced by appropriate risk management decisions. However, managers and shareholders may also have conflicting views on risk management (Chapter 13).

2. Although this "fundamental" value is impossible to estimate precisely, it seems clear that stock markets are not always efficient: stock prices often differ from (fundamental) shareholder value. This may result from speculative bubbles (which lead to overvaluation

of shares) or alternatively from the failure of financial markets to incorporate some elements of shareholder value, such as long-term investment opportunities.

3. The model can be generalized to a large firm and to several periods.

4. Recall that the risk-free rate is normalized to zero and that the investment returns nothing in case of failure.

■ Chapter 11

1. It can even lead to value destruction by managers (empire building, perquisites*) as postulated by the "Free Cash Flow" theory of Jensen.

2. Managers would often prefer to accumulate as much cash as possible. We develop this point later.

3. Typically $r_0 < r$ if $m_t > 0$ (interest received on cash balances) and $r_0 > r$ if $m_t < 0$ (interest paid on overdrafts).

4. This assumption is made to simplify the analysis. Allowing costly recapitalizations leads to analogous, but more complex, results.

5. By contrast with the Leland model of Chapter 12, expected earnings per unit of time are constant and equal to μ. This is because y_t is i.i.d. (additive random walk), whereas Leland assumes that y_t follows a geometric random walk, hence the option value that is not present here: default is never strategic in the present model.

6. This is, of course, an extreme assumption, but it serves as a simple benchmark to represent the imperfection of financial markets. Most of our analysis remains valid when the firm can (at a cost) issue more debt and equity.

7. This law asserts that if we take the expectation of the conditional expectation of a random variable x (thus if we take iterate expectations) we obtain the (unconditional) expectation of x.

8. The general case can be solved numerically and gives the pattern represented in Figure 11.1.

■ Chapter 12

1. This would modify the shareholder value function.

2. Some insurance contracts can also provide this kind of hedging. For simplicity, however, we associate hedging with financial derivatives.

■ Chapter 13

1. Since this period, leading re-insurance companies have also developed life funds, which is another type of ILS where the trigger is the flow of premium from life and saving products. This vehicle should be considered more as a mean to provide capital to an insurance company than a vehicle to cover a risk.

2. However, it should be noted that some of these captives are inactive.

■ Chapter 14

1. Note that managers may have mixed views on mergers and acquisitions, as these can be an opportunity for growing but also a risk of losing control.

2. We assume that the margin rate ($\frac{9}{27}$) stays the same for the first year.

3. We assume that the price earnings ratio ($PER = \frac{100}{8}$) stays the same.

4. By this, we mean that Med Corp can find cheap coverage on the market.

5. Note that the structure is capped at $3500 million. The risk above this threshold (supersenior tranche) are retained by the company.

6. Finite contracts are presented in Section 13.3.3.

■ INDEX